An Underappreciated Squi

I get my squid from Milford Haven.

Queen are very ordered and they come in together.

Brian is the politest. If they don't know what something is, Freddie will ask.

To be honest squid is a disaster at the studio. No bands like it and they freak out at tentacles. I persevere. It might end up being fried calamari instead.

2-3 medium whole squid
4 shallots, thinly sliced
8 or more cloves garlic
fresh tomatoes, or tinned if you must
white wine
coriander, chopped well
salt/pepper

First fry shallots, then add the garlic in olive oil. Then add the tomatoes. Follow with white wine. To make a rich sauce, add butter.

Cut the squid, include tentacles (best bit). Clear out stomach contents, which freak you out – like the little fish – but you like the glassy cuttlebone.

Put the cut squid in the sauce and gently cook and then leave to rest. You don't want it rubbery, do not overcook!

They are much better left for 2–3 hours.

Before serving, warm up gently, pepper, maybe more salt. Finish with coriander (which I now grow at Rockfield).

Also by Tiffany Murray

Diamond Star Halo
Sugar Hall
Happy Accidents

My Family and Other Rock Stars

Tiffany Murray

FLEET

FLEET

First published in Great Britain in 2024 by Fleet
This paperback edition published in 2025 by Fleet

1 3 5 7 9 10 8 6 4 2

Map illustration by Liane Payne

Some names and other details have been disguised to protect the privacy of the people concerned.

A CIP catalogue record for this book is available from the British Library.

ISBN 978-0-349-72755-4

Typeset in Sabon by M Rules
Printed and bound in Great Britain by Clays Ltd, Elcograf S.p.A.

Papers used by Fleet are from well-managed forests and other responsible sources.

MIX
Paper | Supporting responsible forestry
FSC® C104740

Fleet
An imprint of
Little, Brown Book Group
Carmelite House
50 Victoria Embankment
London EC4Y 0DZ

The authorised representative
in the EEA is
Hachette Ireland
8 Castlecourt Centre
Dublin 15, D15 XTP3, Ireland
(email: info@hbgi.ie)

An Hachette UK Company
www.hachette.co.uk

www.littlebrown.co.uk

To my family, Joan and Laurence, and to my childhood family, the Wards of Rockfield Studios, with love

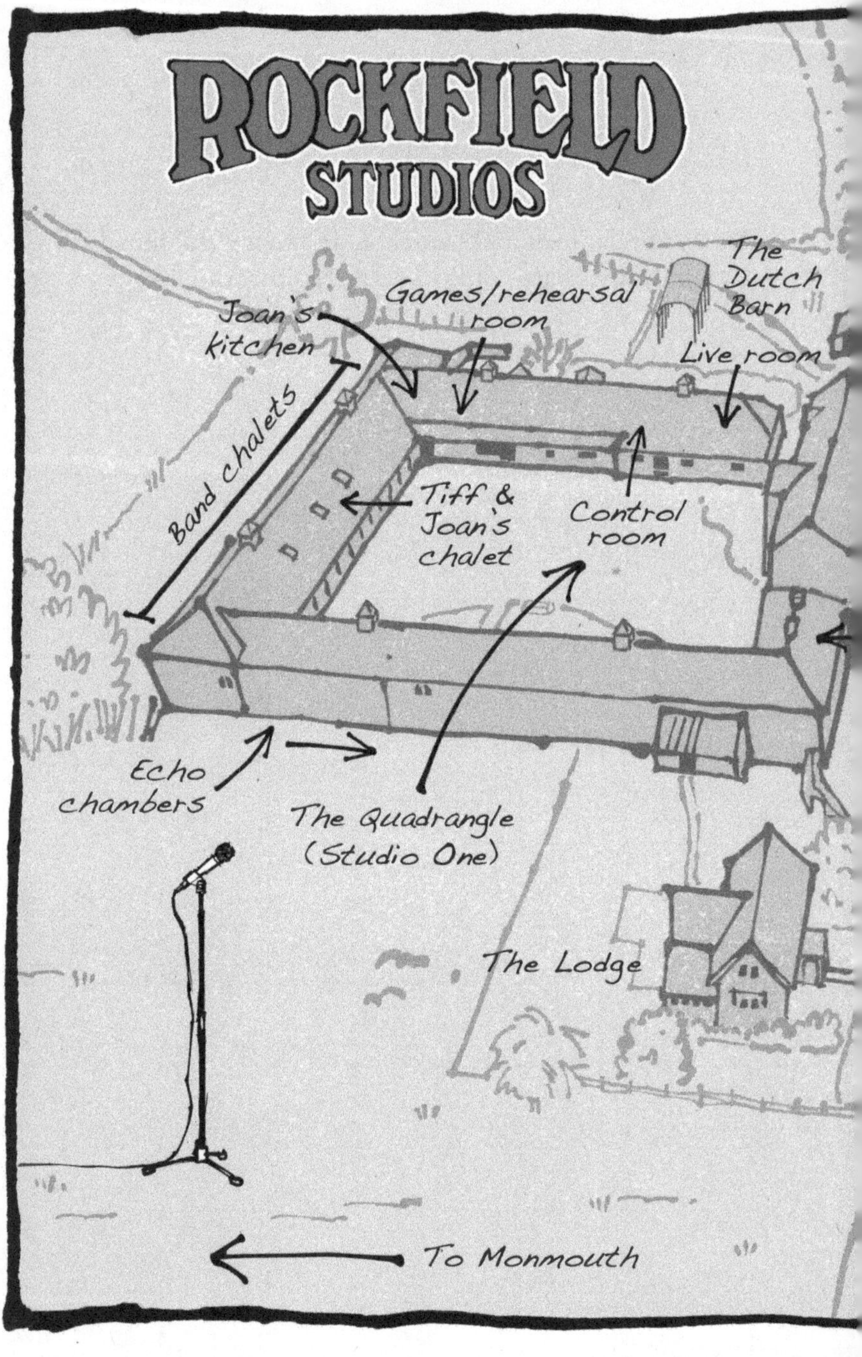

ROCKFIELD STUDIOS
The Dutch Barn
Games/rehearsal room
Joan's kitchen
Live room
Band chalets
Tiff & Joan's chalet
Control room
Echo chambers
The Quadrangle (Studio One)
The Lodge
To Monmouth

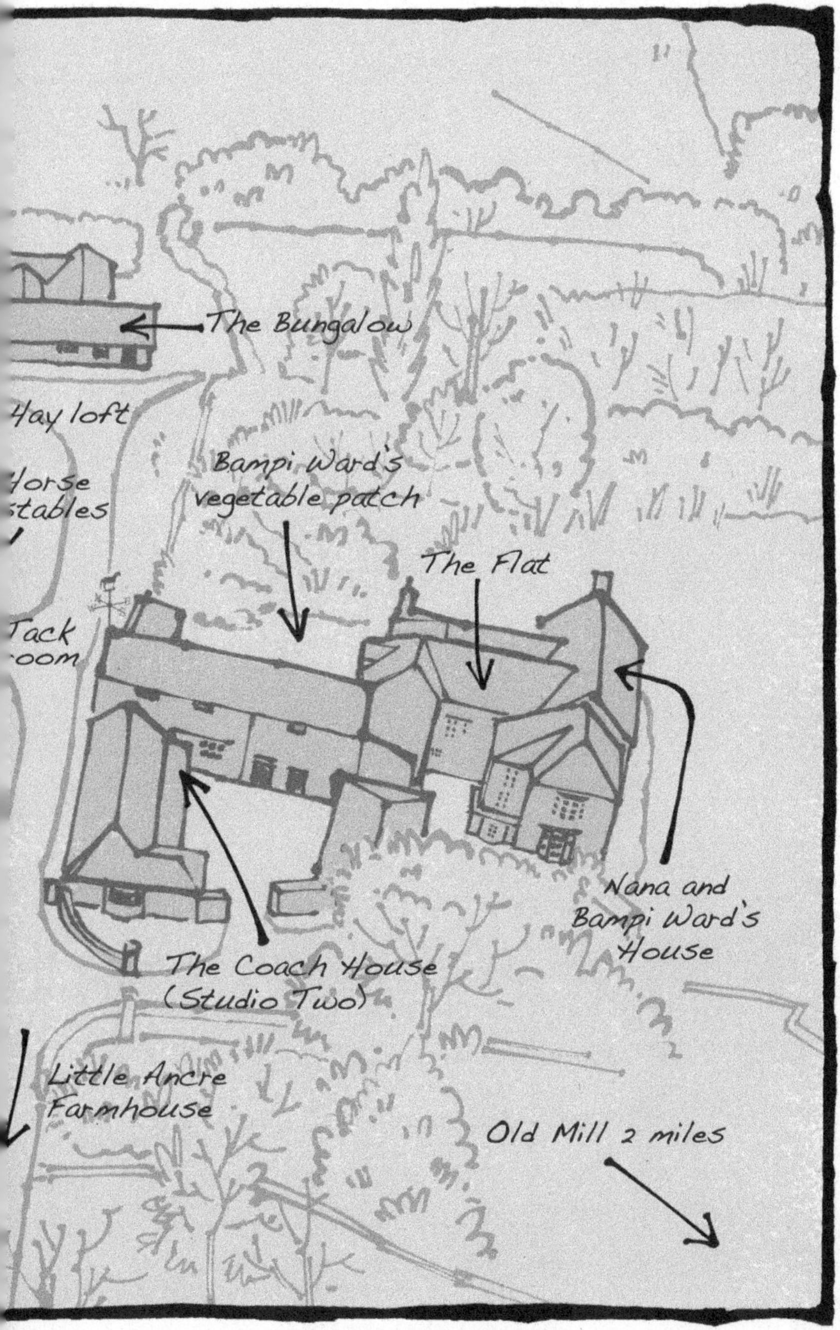
The Bungalow
Hay loft
Horse
stables
Tack
room
Bampi Ward's
vegetable patch
The Flat
Nana and
Bampi Ward's
House
The Coach House
(Studio Two)
Little Ancre
Farmhouse
Old Mill 2 miles

'Life's a Gas'

Marc Bolan and T-Rex

'Everyone Says "Hi"'

David Bowie

Joan's Whole Poached Salmon for Iggy Pop and his friend David Bowie (and Simple Minds if they keep running up from Studio Two)

The first lie is that the salmon is whole. Who doesn't improvise in a kitchen? If you're cooking in the Rockfield oven, it's too small, so I cut the big Wye salmon in half with my Sabatier knife when raw.

The second lie is the 'for'. I doubt they'll eat it, but I'll hit the roof if they have another food fight, especially with my fish. All David seems to ask for is milk.

If the salmon's still in the fridge Sunday night, I'll freeze it and turn it into a terrine later. Or, like today, wrap up the two salmon halves, put them in the back of the Audi, and drive them to your grandmother's Sunday luncheon buffet for Bodenham church. She won't thank me for it, Tiff, but waste not want not, and Jim Osterberg gives to the Church of England.

1 Wye salmon
the frilly top of a fennel
dry white wine
lemon juice, no pips
generous butter
black pepper, little salt

Decoration (you love to do this, Tiff).

cucumber (peel skin for patterns)
lemons thinly sliced

Gut, descale, pat dry salmon inside and out with paper towel. Tuck the fennel inside, with white wine on the bottom, then add generous cubes of butter on the top (and inside to keep it moist) plus lemon juice, sea salt and ground pepper all over. Make sure you roll the tinfoil into a loose parcel, leaving a gap at the top, do not pull tight.

Cook for about 20-30 mins at around 400F, just enough that when you put a long skewer in, it comes out clean.

Never overcook, it falls to bits and tastes of nothing, a disaster fund. It will continue to cook in the tinfoil so unwrap immediately, test. Once opened leave in juices for about 20 minutes then slide onto a plate.

For sauce: first boil up prawn shells, sieve, then add the salmon and butter juice from the foil (sieve this too if you wish), a little wine, maybe more butter, and lemon. Taste. Reduce. Use it to keep salmon moist or put in jug. Taste, taste.

When still warm, skin the salmon but leave the head, put the two halves together on an attractive plate, skinned cucumber down the join, and/or thin lemons, plus my home-made lemon mayonnaise.

Sometimes you put on lemons if I thinly slice them.

No one ever questions, *why is it in two halves, Joan?*

On the whole they freak out at the head, so better to chop this off actually. I do the same to the Saturday buffet suckling pig, which I also have to cut in half to cook.

My Home-made Lemon Mayonnaise (don't ask for Salad Cream)

2	*egg yolks and 1 egg*	*salt and pepper*
	lemon juice	*little Dijon, little sugar*

Put all in the liquidiser bit of my Kenwood Chef. Whizz it. Run olive oil through quietly.

Once upon a time I did it by hand. There are too many bands to cook for now.

Prologue

Slip-sliding into the 1980s

Rockfield Studios

'It's Just a Story'

I open the front door of Rockfield Lodge to Siouxsie Sioux. She's shiny vinyl in the Welsh sun. She's Venus on the concrete step in thigh-high PVC boots. Her crimped black hair is soft-spiked, and I want to run my sticky fingers through it.

She's an artwork, Corrina says.

She's looking for Steve Severin, Brigitte says, and we put on our wellington boots.

We go out to the cow fields and call for him, like we're calling for a lost dog.

This is Rockfield Studios. It is also a farm, and I am here because my mother, Joan, is the cordon bleu chef. Brigitte and Corrina Ward are the two oldest of five Rockfield kids. Being a Rockfield kid means Kingsley or Charles Ward is your dad, because Kingsley and Charles Ward built Rockfield Studios with their bare hands. Neither of them is my dad. I am an extra, but being an extra Rockfield kid still means making tunnels through towers of hard hay bales that can crush, and maybe Hawkwind dragging you into Studio Two to sing a chorus. Growing up an extra Rockfield kid also means swooning over the Teardrop Explodes as you serve them your mum's Barbary duck in gooseberry sauce, then remembering your biology homework.

I am thirteen. Brigitte is eighteen, Corrina is seventeen, and they are goddesses. Together we are girls with vinyl at our fingers and rock stars in the barn. I am please and thank you, cold knees at winter bus stops, and school scraps; they are crimped fringes and powder-white faces, but together we are a walk to the Rolls Hall in Monmouth on a Saturday night to dance to 'The Sound of the Crowd' by the Human League. We are drinkers of half a snakebite and black, of Malibu and pineapple. We're spinners of Ouija boards, holders of horse brushes, bridles, kohl pencils and crimping irons.

I don't think we want to be kids of penthouse and pavement in Sheffield, of Bowie Nights at Billy's in London, of Blitz, of Soho, of Sex at World's End. We don't have cars, and there's no milk train back to these Monmouthshire fields.

We pose in the garden for Polaroid photographs in cut-up jodhpurs that smell of horse, and tweed jackets that stink of long-buried ancestor farmers. We belt our home-made clothes tight, spray our hair stiff and dance to our records in the Lodge's swirling carpet kingdom, while the makers of the records sleep soundly in their beds, further up the Rockfield farm track. The bands are a trot-on out of the Lodge's front door, a giddy-up the hill, a bridle-nudge left into the Quadrangle, and a *whoa, steady, steady, girl*; right there behind the double doors of Studio One.

It's a strange word, 'Quadrangle'. It makes me think of maths. What it means is a rectangle block of stables around a courtyard. Rockfield horses nod in the real stables opposite converted ones where bands sleep, eat, rehearse, record and watch the telly. Everything is connected: the dining room is next to the rehearsal room is next to the control room is next to the live room, and when bands throw open the doors of Studio One, bridles in the tack room jangle to bass guitar. At night, passing foxes pitch in with harmonies. Lead singers sneak into ridge-and-furrow fields to find their melodies. Sheep fart to the bass drum, and our mums clean trifle from the control room motherboard after food fights.

My mum's kitchen is nestled here, in the corner of the block closest to the studio, up three steps and through a dining room where I serve David Bowie poached salmon he won't eat (I can't look him in the eyes, either one of them, and some nights I dream of his left, other nights I dream of his right). Here, I hoover around Pete Murphy from Bauhaus. I stay up with Bad Manners to watch *A Clockwork Orange* on VHS, and my mum tells me off.

But my favourite place at Rockfield is back down the rough track to the Lodge, and the small living room there, its walls decorated with leather straps of horse brasses. I'll be with Brigitte and Corrina and their record player in the alcove next to the gas fire. Here vinyl slides easy from the sleeve. We slot it onto the silver spike without thinking and hold hands as the stylus drops and bumps and hisses. We wait. Then we're screaming to 'Hong Kong Garden', to 'Hanging on the Telephone'. We do the hold-hands, knee-up, shoulder-to-shoulder dance to 'I Travel' by Simple Minds while they're across the track in Studio Two. We pogo to 'New Rose', we twirl to 'Flowers of Romance'. We pose against flock wall-paper to 'Fade to Grey', 'Gentlemen Take Polaroids', and 'Are "Friends" Electric?'. We grind to 'Young Americans' (although we are Welsh, or part-Welsh, or border, or over *theeeeeeeer* in Monmouthshire).

In the Lodge's kitchen our different parents sing 'Oh Boy!' and 'Blue Suede Shoes' on acoustic guitars because that is theirs, but this is our music now.

Sometimes the bands run down to the Lodge like they're the children, and when our mums are out we don't know what to say, if we can say anything at all. Musicians knock on the door because they're lost, or hungry, or bored, or tired, or lonely, or stoned, or can't sleep for ten days straight, or looking for a football, a bag of balloons for a water fight, a Frisbee; or they're homesick, or American, or Dutch, or scared of cows, or scared of horses, or sheep; or sad, or looking for a pub, a limousine, a helicopter, a reason for why they are stranded in these Welsh fields forced to dream up songs.

When we let them in, it's Alice walking through the looking glass.

'Would you like a sandwich?'

'No thanks.'

'Would you like a cup of tea?'

'No thanks.'

'Do you want to go horse riding?'

'Not now.'

'We can make you beans on toast?'

'No.'

'Tiff, will you make Julian some squash?' Brigitte asks.

I do as I'm told because I am so much younger than these two almost-sisters, the Lodge isn't my house so I must behave. This isn't my family, but I pray to the great gods of Rockfield that it will be. *Dear Queen and Black Sabbath on high, dear Rush, Iggy Pop, and dearest Lord, holy of holies, David Bowie. Dear Ace, Brinsley Schwarz, Graham Parker and the Rumour, Dr Feelgood, Dave Edmunds, Nick Lowe, Robert Plant, Ian Gillan, Hawkwind, Motörhead, Judas Priest, Budgie, Van der Graaf Generator, Echo and the Bunnymen, Simple Minds, Adam and the Ants, and our founding Fathers, Kingsley and Charles Ward. Dear Julian Cope from the Teardrop Explodes who's parked his* M*A*S*H *jeep outside the Lodge gate and is sitting on the living-room floor in his army clothes right now, pushing that VHS into the machine to watch his band on* Top of the Pops ... *For ever and ever* *amen, please make me a Rockfield Ward, not a Murray.*

I mix the bright orange Quosh with tap water as if Julian Cope is a friend come to play. I look out at the fields and try to think when it all started. It wasn't here at Rockfield Studios. It was in a vicarage in Herefordshire. There were no almost-sisters there; no swirling-carpet kingdom of a turntable and our hands holding to dance. At the Vicarage there was no Rockfield prayer, but there was a downstairs gothic hall where the bands rehearsed. There was a church next door with a golden cock weathervane, and a graveyard where yew trees sucked at the blood and bones of the dead until their berries burst red. There was a magpie in a small cage at the edge of the farmer's field, and there was Mum's boyfriend, Jackson, who kept half-bottles of Haig whisky in our wellington boots. There was a Great Dane, Cleo, who lived in a white caravan that she ate from the inside out.

Part 1

This Is How I Remember It

The Vicarage

The First Half of the 1970s

The Vicarage became like a factory for making gear and making sounds, it was the classic ‘place in the country’ where bands could ‘get their heads together’ . . . Hugh started building his infamous organ. I dreamed up this incredible electronic saxophone system for live work and had this customised packing-case made to house all my ‘Jaxon’ equipment in one place when touring. I christened it the ‘Vangogh’.

David Jackson, Van der Graaf Generator

Set List

'Killer Queen', Queen
'Vicious', Lou Reed
'Where do the Children Play?', Cat Stevens
'Kooks', David Bowie
'Tiny Dancer', Elton John
'My Sweet Lord', George Harrison
'Land of Hope and Glory', Edward Elgar & Arthur C. Benson
'Don't You Worry 'bout a Thing', Stevie Wonder
'In the Ghetto', Elvis Presley
'You're So Vain', Carly Simon
'Me and You and a Dog Named Boo', Lobo
'Without You', Harry Nilsson
'Nighttown Boy', Horslips
'Long Haired Lover from Liverpool', Little Jimmy Osmond
'The Puppy Song', David Cassidy
'Wasn't it Nice?/ Black Boy', Trax
'Amazing Grace' by Pipes and Drums and the Military Band of the Royal Scots Dragoons

Pike Quenelles

At the Vicarage people knew I was a cook. Men knocked at my door in the middle of the night dangling a brace of pheasant, rabbit, hare, a bucket of eels (no thank you), a salmon, a pike. I didn't ask questions and I'd get the pike free. 'Bloody muddy ugly bugger' the men called it and I thought, *What shall I do with this bloody, ugly, muddy bugger?* Freddie liked my Coronation chicken, my ribs, my chilli con carne, and I think he liked the concept of quenelles, but he ate like a bird. Speaking of birds, do you remember my big Victorian bell jars filled with little emerald, iridescent hummingbirds on branches? What are they called? Taxidermied, that's it. Anyway, Freddie was fascinated by them. He'd lie on the deep-blue bergère sofa in the drawing room and write, those bell jars around him. Cleo our Great Dane would lie on the rug beneath him. The only times I saw him stay still was at the piano or writing with Cleo. I wish I'd taken a picture.

Pike isn't a delicacy as it is in France and quenelles are not for the impatient, but I felt in control making them. Cooking was my performance. Quenelles are also great to freeze. Do you remember my big chest freezer, Tiff? You'd climb in it. You'd close the top and shout, 'I'm hiding, Mum, I'm hiding!' I mean I knew where you were, but still, you could have frozen to death. I'd lift you out, grab a bag frozen gooseberries.

I don't know why it was bands. Quite honestly, we needed an income, and I had the idea because of the big atrium hall.

3 lb	*of pike*
	milk
4	*shallots*
	loads of parsley
2	*bay leaves*
	loads of salt and pepper
	half a pack butter
2	*eggs*
2	*tablespoons flour, sifted*
	at least 4 tablespoons of single cream

Don't seriously ask me about amounts. I don't weigh. I do it by spoonfuls and taste.

Into casserole dish on the hob, place gutted whole fish, equal amount of milk and water, loads of parsley, bay leaves, salt and pepper.

Cook gently until fish is falling off the bones, cool, then sieve liquid and keep. Remove all the bones and skin, you will only end up with about 2 lb in weight.

I say 'taste, taste, taste' but with pike it's 'bones, bones, bones'.

Reduce remaining liquid for stock, and then sieve again.

Melt a good bit of butter in a pan, add flour, keep stirring, then add the stock bit by bit. Add the cream, salt and pepper. Taste it.

Let it go solid and cool and add fish meat (check again for bones). I then mix it all together in my Kenwood. Make sure it's cold, beat two eggs, then add them. This is to firm it, not to make scrambled egg. I use my big spoon with a point at the end to shape into quenelles. Lay out on floured tray.

Put in fridge overnight, or for at least two hours.

Make a roux in a pan, add cream, nutmeg and a tiny bit of Gruyère. Taste for salt and pepper. I sometimes added lemon if too rich. Put quenelles in big casserole dish, they can't touch. Pour over the sauce. Remember they are already cooked so only need about 20 minutes at 360F.

It takes an age, but I loved it.

It can stink in the making.

Some bands came with a cook, but I couldn't help it, I cooked, too.

1.

'Killer Queen'

Before Rockfield, before Brigitte and Corrina and Quosh with Julian Cope, I am five and three-quarters and I live with my mother in a vicarage in Herefordshire, at the mouth of Wales. We came back to Herefordshire because my grandad was going to die. It's been two years, and he hasn't yet.

Because she's a chef Mum wears pink plasters on cut fingers and the gloss of butter on her burns. We don't live alone in the Vicarage. I have my Great Dane, Cleo. Mum has her boyfriend, Jackson, and sometimes bands live with us.

The bands have strange names. Strange to me, at least: Black Sabbath. Horslips. Trax. I suppose the name 'Queen' isn't that strange. I watch Freddie Mercury pick up our no-name cats, one by one. He tries to pet them. *Careful*, Mum says, *they're feral.*

The bands stack Vox or Marshall amps in our fireplace. They tape black cables down onto the bright Victorian tiles. They come to us because of our hall. *Acoustics*, Mum says.

We have a hall so big if you shout your voice------

echoes

e x p a n d s

explodes

The acoustics wake the bluebottle husks on the rafters, shaking them awake to a buzz.

As Mum cooks, I sit on the stairs and watch the bands. They prance in velvet, in denim, in leather, on the zigzag patterns of the hall floor below. They swagger past me, up and down the carved pine staircase in daps, zip-up platform boots, in no shoes at all. They march along the landing like crazed Pied Pipers with penny whistles, flutes, maracas, guitars, cow bells and castanets. The men, because they are always men, say 'onetwoonetwotestingonetwo' into silver ice-cream cones on silver poles that whine sharper than the bats in the barn. These men curl themselves into thin bundles like our cats do: on windowsills, sofas, hard kitchen chairs, and they write their songs on scraps of paper and fag packets. Mum cooks for these men, but not all of them eat.

I have learned new words:

Marshall
Vox
Roadie
Mic stand
Stratocaster
Feedback
Gear
Jack Daniel's
Plectrum
TestingTestingOneTwoOneTwo

These men play the same beginnings to the same songs again and again and again, and it's the loudest thing I've ever heard.

Waa-waaa-waaaaah!

My ears itch to the whine of electric guitar. I like it.

Doof-dah-dah, doof-dah-dah.

Drum kits rattle my growing bones. The dairy cows in the farmer's fields cry out. The postmistress is deaf. Mum keeps the parish council letters of complaint under the fruit bowl.

Onetwoonetwotestingonetwo.

Children are invisible here.

It began when she opened a big *Times* newspaper at the breakfast table. I climbed on her lap and put my finger under the words of her advert to sound them out, but Mum has no patience.

'Tiff, it says, "*VICARAGE Rehearsal Space for bands, no heavy rock*".'

'What's "heavy rock"?'

'Loud guitar, darling. I doubt Jackson would like it.'

Jackson wears glasses with black frames like Michael Caine. He laughs with Mum but not with me. She says, 'Some people are just not children-people, Tiff. But you have me and your animals.' Jackson is from Kent, we've been at the Vicarage for two summers with him, but I am still a cat around Jackson: I keep myself to myself. He does, too. Jackson has an office I am not allowed into, and big, framed pictures of ships that sail up the stairs. His two records sit on his drinks cabinet in the dining room: 'Land of Hope and Glory' by Edward Elgar & Arthur C. Benson, and 'Amazing Grace' by Pipes and Drums and the Military Band of the Royal Scots Dragoons. Mum prefers Lou Reed's *Transformer.*

She says the advert is in *The Times* because *we'll lose the house if we don't rent it out, and that would be a disaster fund.* A lot of things are a disaster fund to Mum. She's tried everything: gourmet B&B weekends for couples from

Birmingham, summers of German students in deni
and a little Parisian boy who came to us every hol
didn't want to leave. None of this worked out *mone*

Moneywise is a problem word.

When Hazel comes up from the village to help with the beds and the kitchen, I hear Mum say, 'Oh, just leave them,' when Hazel finds Jackson's whisky bottles between the airing-cupboard sheets, as well as in the porch wellies.

When she moved us across the herringbone yard into the red-brick stable, the radio played 'Tie a Yellow Ribbon Round the Ole Oak Tree'. She told me to call the stable 'the pottery' to make it sound less rat-ish and horse shit-ish. I watched her clear crates, straw and pigeon crap out with two men from the pub (the same men who poach salmon from the Wye, which she then poaches with fennel). Soon there were sheets of Perspex to cover the gaps in windowless windows and doorless doors, and I played with Cleo in the dusty cleared-out rooms. Mum said, 'Over there,' and the poacher-men put up a makeshift kitchen on milk crates by a Belfast sink; I had a mattress downstairs and Mum and Jackson had the space in the pottery loft as their bedroom. She said it would 'only be a matter of weeks' and I'd be back to my Jimmy Osmond and David Cassidy posters on my proper wall in the Vicarage, but I'd already gone off Jimmy. Mum told me the outside loo worked, 'but please, Tiff, don't call it the bloody "toilet"'. She said we can top and tail at the sink with a flannel, 'like Grandad does because he can't climb the stairs at the farm'. She smiled. 'It's almost summer and there is a hosepipe we can use, and I'm sure the bands wouldn't mind us taking a bath now and again, would they?'

I wanted my bedroom back.

'Tiff, you scared the living daylights out of that guitarist this morning. You can't just walk into your old bedroom holding that pet chicken of yours and stand at the foot of his bed like some bloody child-ghost. Please. Poor man nearly had a heart attack.'

'But I wanted to show him Road Runner.'

'He does *not* want to see your chicken.'

'But it's not his bed, it's *mine*.'

'I know, darling, but you have to understand, you can't sleep in there now.'

'Why?'

She sighs. 'Because the bands live in the house. We live in the pottery.'

'But it's *my* bed.'

'Well, he's not bloody Goldilocks, is he? And isn't living in the pottery an adventure?' She's trying to be bright about it.

'You mean like Rupert Bear goes on an adventure?'

'Christ, I don't know, Tiff.' Mum looks tired. 'Think of it as a den with, what are their names? Ratface, Weasely and Mrs Tinkywinkle?'

I shake my head; these are not the right names *at all*.

'Or Rumpelstiltskin – you love him.'

I do, he's got stripy legs on my Ladybird book. Mum reads him to me at bedtime.

'It will be like camping, Tiff.'

I may be five and three-quarters, but I know my mother hates camping.

She has rules for me now:

1. Please, try to keep your cats, litters of kittens, Cleo the Great Dane, Nanny the goat, the hamster, and that cocky sodding Bantam cock Road Runner, my peacocks, the wounded birds and rodents you gather up (yes, the dead ones, too) out of the main house, Tiff.
2. Again, under no circumstances should you pick up the lost causes you find in the grass and stick them in my oven. They will not 'wake up'.
3. Please stop peeing on the lawn, there are guests now, and for the love of God, darling, stop driving Jackson up the wall.

A call came from a manager or a record label far away and Mum told me this new band, Queen, was from London where once upon a time she had all her good times in a flat behind Harrods, because it was the '60s and everything was Biba-and-Julie-Christie-better then, particularly round the back of Harrods. She said this band sounded royal and jolly and it would be fun. When she picked me up from school the day the band arrived, she told me they'd come with a white baby grand piano strapped to a lorry and wasn't that exciting?

One of them sleeps in my bed. He can stare out of my window at the church tower and the golden cock weathervane, at my Jimmy Osmond poster, too. The others are in the spare rooms, the attic and Mum and Jackson's four-poster bed, watching the sun rise through apple orchards. I bet it's Queen's fingers poking into her jars of face cream, opening the tissue of her Roger & Gallet soaps, and squeezing out all the bright green Badedas I am only allowed two drops of. I wonder if they'll find my hamster, Hammy, who I lost again under the stairs?

*

I can't sleep. It's that funny *not-quite-night* time in the countryside, long after the dog fox has barked himself out and the vixen has screamed herself into pup. It's almost morning, but the birds and the farmer aren't up yet. I want to pee, but this means rats because our loo is outside. I listen to the hit of fat rat bums on the other side of the Perspex. The pottery smells of fish because Mum made her quenelles in here.

A light comes on in the Vicarage kitchen across the herringbone yard. I get up to spy. He's at the sink in a dressing gown covered in bright flowers. He's making tea or coffee or wine or whatever adults do in the dark of the morning. Mum is sometimes thirty minutes standing up at her turquoise and silver Vitamaster machine, because the vibrating strap will 'slim' her hips. In the kitchen light, the Vicarage – our house – is tall and red and Victorian gothic and it has bricks like surprised eyebrows above the window frames. The church next door is in the same red brick; and did you know if you scratch the bark of a yew with a kitchen knife it bleeds red?

I wanted to listen to him play his piano and sing. Because he was in the kitchen, I knew I could sneak into the front hall without being seen, so I jumped into my dungarees and in the half-dark I ran barefoot across the yard, through the door in the red brick wall, past the pond and over the bite of sharp gravel at the front of the house. I waved at the farmer's magpie in his steel cage at the far end of the lawn and tried not to think of toothy rats or the graveyard over the hawthorn hedge. I jumped into our black and white timber porch: safe. The front door, older than a monk in a monastery, was hard to open but unlatched.

Now I'm sitting halfway up the stairs *inside* the Vicarage. Two no-name cats have followed me in, tortoiseshell and black. They're walking on the keys of the white piano, which is part-crammed beneath the staircase, *plink-plonk*.

I'm out of breath because I'm scared. It's dark and this doesn't feel like my house; it smells different, there's less dog, more man. Vox amps hum and wink red eyes at me from the mouth of our fireplace. Bedroom doors are open on the landing. I can hear men breathing, snoring.

I decide to be excited not scared because it is *my* bedroom at the end of the landing, and I could run up there now, pinch a sleeping man's foot and yell, 'Get out, you bugger!' like the farmer does when he finds Cleo, my Great Dane, in his field.

I weigh up Mum's rules. I know I shouldn't creep into the house this early, but it's his fault, the singer in the dressing gown with bright flowers. He's Fred and Freddie and his front teeth press out of his lips in a way I can't stop looking at. He smells lovely, like sweet wood and oranges, and he's quiet, apart from when he sings or laughs, and when he sings or laughs, he throws his head back like a thin heron gobbling a fish. In the daytime Freddie walks our wide garden with a notebook and pen, then he curls up like a no-name cat on the blue velvet sofa in the drawing room Jackson says I'm not allowed in. Freddie writes while stuffed hummingbirds sparkle green inside bell jars on the scatter tables around him.

Most of the time, though, he is here under the stairs playing his white piano.

Smoke curls up. His cigarette is in the ashtray on the piano's top and he's gently lifting cats from the black and white keys. *Plink-plonk*. Table lights are on and the hall looks pretty. Freddie sits and starts to play. The piano sounds he is making are slow and sad.

Dum-dum-dum-dum, dah-dah-

Dum-dum-dum-dum, dah-dah-

It's sounds more like Jackson's music, his 'Land of Hope and Glory', than Mum's bam-bam-bam, 'Satellite of Love'. I press my toes into the stair rug but the moment before I get too sad, the piano is suddenly bright and silly. Freddie is singing something about Moët and Chandon. Mum keeps a bottle in her fridge. He pauses and then sings about going to sleep, and I can't resist.

I have a rug over my legs when I wake, but Freddie is gone. A cat is throwing up in the long dining room, while something half-eaten drags itself into the hall.

Jellies

The vicar before us planted everything from figs to Jerusalem artichokes that made us fart. He must have loved red gooseberry, redcurrant and raspberry because there were bushes everywhere. You and Cleo spent hours picking and nibbling the fruit then you'd moan about your stomach.

Out of season I'd defrost the top and tailed gooseberries, boil them up with sugar and good Muscat (not crap) and make gooseberry jelly for savoury dishes (gooseberries have loads of pectin).

You'd make real raspberry and redcurrant sweet jelly with me. Of course, you had to keep opening the fridge, sticking your dirty fingers in and asking, 'Is it ready yet, Mummy?' Drove me mad. But I couldn't stop you. I used your grandmother's jelly moulds and served it with cream. It was like a birthday party for the bands.

Leave the gelatine to soak in warm water (about 6 leaves or 3 tsps of granules, never boil).

Heat water and caster sugar gently in pan.

Add raspberries (about 4 cups to 2 cups of sugar), bring to boil then right down and simmer for about 5 minutes, don't mash.

Sieve into measuring jug. Add the gelatine and stir. Add to oiled jelly mould. Overnight in fridge to set.

It could be hit or miss. Rigid or liquid, but it was a fun thing to do together.

I'd also add whole redcurrants, but more sugar. You'd stick your fingers in.

Sometimes you'd ask for Rowntree's jelly, and I'd have to stop you eating the whole block raw from the package.

2.

'Where Do the Children Play?'

Mum said, 'You're not a particularly imaginative child, are you?' when I called my acorn-coloured hamster 'Hammy' and my Nanny goat, 'Nanny'.

'For God's sake, "Nanny" is what you insist on calling your grandmother.'

She's wrong about the imagination: I have lots. My bantam hen with a black comb is 'Elvis'; my uncatchable cockerel is 'Road Runner' but he follows me everywhere. At bedtime Mum asks, 'Is that chicken in your bed, Tiff?'

'No.'

She points at the red floppy comb sticking out from my blankets. 'I can see him.' Road Runner clucks and purrs. Mum laughs.

At the Vicarage I can lie on the grass, cover my face in feral kittens and giggle at the tickle of their dried-up umbilical cords. Afternoons go like this. I can find all sorts of animals, ignore Mum's rules, and lay the half-eaten softly in the bottom door of her log-burning Aga (with daisies). But there are things I'm *absolutely* not allowed to do here.

Like touching the cold metal of Jackson's Purdey guns and twelve bores in his unlocked gun room.

Like telling my primary school I have rock stars in my house. Yesterday I marched my class home at breaktime, 'Along the main Hereford Road, Tiffany!'

I don't know any other way.

My class ran up our drive to spy on Queen. We saw Freddie in the breakfast room, but he wasn't singing, he was eating an egg. We hid behind the drum kit to wait for Roger, and his cymbals made a shimmering sound. The headmaster called and when Mum found us, she freaked, then drove carloads of us back to school in Jackson's Jag. The phone has been ringing with parent complaints ever since.

Yes, most of all, I can't bother the bands.

*

If I press my hands flat on the porch door the beat thuds into my wrist bones. Queen are warming up. *Boom, dah-dah. Boom, dah-dah.*

The Vicarage porch is like a big doll's house with black timber and white walls. Bright nylon fishing nets and crab-less plastic buckets make me think of a caravan in Pembrokeshire and Mum battling the pages of *The Times* on a windy beach. I step past Jackson's whisky-wellies and press my ear to the front door.

Boom, dah-dah. Boom, dah-dah.

Drums. That's the blond man, Roger, and he's pretty as my Tiny Tears.

Woawww-woaw-woaw-wooooaaaaaaww-eeeeeeeeeee.

Lead guitar. That's Brian. He speaks softly but plays his guitar so loud the glass in the windows shakes. Brian is tall and thin as a silver birch. I want to hug his long legs, but I stop myself. Mum says Brian is terribly kind and polite.

'Ohhhbaleedahdahdahshooobadoodah!' Freddie is singing words so quickly I can't keep up with the story. Maybe it's a Rumpelstiltskin riddle? I take my chance and push my bodyweight, which isn't much, into the heavy door. It creaks open.

Sunlight from the tall window halfway up the stairs makes Queen look holy in our hall. Freddie is at the piano, head bent. He's wearing slippers and white trousers with a white shirt. Pretty blond Roger is talking behind his drum tower near the fireplace. Tall Brian has his back to me. I check for my mother then drop to my knees and slide across the zigzag pattern tiles. I'm belly down, a snake, my body bumping against taped cables. Safe behind a Vox amp, I peek out and I see what I'm looking for.

The wide trouser leg of the bass player, John, is brushing against her paw, but Cleo doesn't twitch. Queen start a song; Freddie sings and I let the sounds he's making pour into me. It's a journey and I don't know where it will end. Cleo doesn't wake up. Mum says Cleo is immune to noise or quite possibly deaf. Oswald, the old man who scythes the grass from the graves next door says I could put a saddle on Cleo, but I don't want to. Cleo is the love of my life. Everything about her is astonishing: her head is bigger than my top half, her Great Dane feet smell and taste of Rich Tea biscuits, and when she sleeps, I can open her fleshy mouth and stick my arm in.

A drumbeat thuds into my hipbones. The guitar plays high, *weee-ooo-weee-oww.* Freddie stops singing, he is saying, *no, no listen*, and he stands up. He's showing them, marching up and down as he sings. He uses his arms like we do in gymnastics, spread *wide like Jesus!* Silver bangles shimmer on his wrists. His chin points at the rafters like Road Runner when he cock-a-doodle-doos. Freddie is crowing too. It's funny how his singing voice is huge when his talking voice isn't. His lips are wet, glossy. He turns and marches again, sometimes jumping on the different-coloured tiles like it's hopscotch. I think he might step on me, so I slide until I'm back at the staircase. I climb up and press my face through one of the carved shapes in the stair panel. Freddie sits back at the piano beneath me.

When Cleo gets up and stretches with a slow bow, the band stop to watch. When she shakes, head to tail, which takes a while, Freddie laughs, and when she trots up the stairs to me, the band look up. I blush but I don't move. They go back to playing, and I try to follow the story in Freddie's singing words but it's hard. My ears ring. I watch dust bounce to drumbeats.

Mum is standing at the newel post, the strings of her striped apron trailing the tiles; she is pointing to a spot in front of her. This means 'come here'. Cleo runs down to Mum's command, but I linger. Mum doesn't take her eyes off me; her teeth are set, her head tilted; this means, 'Come here now, *child.*' The band keep playing. *Doof-dah-dah, doof-dah-dah. Wooaaaahhhh.*

Mum prefers to tell me off *in private*, so she walks me out of the porch onto the gravel at the front of the house. Then it's a sharp left – *Yes sah, Sergeant Major!* – as bells ring from the church behind us. Her peacocks squawk from the larch: the far green hills are Wales. Cleo trots out in front, past the pond and through the door in the red-brick wall: she's off to the herringbone yard and her caravan.

'I've told you, Tiff.'

'But I was looking for Cleo.'

'No buts.'

Later, when life has calmed her a little, she will say: *You had such a thing about being on those stairs, halfway up. You loved the music, but you didn't understand that these men weren't friends to play with. You just didn't get it.*

Mum marches me until we're in the brick-walled yard where Cleo is now tearing strips of cladding from her caravan, like I tear skin off a Sunday chicken.

Cleo poos caravan.

Freddie's girlfriend Mary is standing on the steps with a glass of white wine; she smiles when she sees my mother. They sometimes laugh together and talk about London and Biba, and Mum shows Mary her dresses and coats.

I slip into the Vicarage kitchen. A steel mincer is clipped to the edge of the sideboard; Mum's white and blue Kenwood mixer stands next to it. Her sacred black Sabatier knife is out on an oblong chopping board. These are Mum's holy relics: this is her altar.

The sounds of Queen seep under the gaps of the closed doors from the hall, through the corridor, past Jackson's gun-room, the pantry, the breakfast room, to us. Cleo trots in and spreads out in front of the brown Aga; Mum says Jackson is good at feeding it with wood in the morning.

She's already picked Swiss chard from the garden that came with the Vicarage. Now she's grinding meat in the steel mincer, and it makes the noise of Bugs Bunny sawing Elmer Fudd in half, *eee-eee, eee-eee.* She has a glass of white wine, and a cigar in her mouth. Mum smokes Café Crème which don't smell of coffee or cream. Mum says, 'Blanc de Blanc' and, if times are good for a minute, 'Moet & Chandon'. *Café Crème Blanc de Blanc de Blanc Queen Queen Moet Moet Moet.* In a picture above the sink a cartoon girl skips on a rope, above the words, 'Here I am Little Jumping Joan. When nobody's with me, I'm always alone.'

Mum puts her whole back into the grinding of meat; the sideboard and her tower of *Cordon Bleu Cookery Course* magazines tremble. She puts out her cigar, washes her hands, and starts soaking clear sheets of gelatine. Once, Mum filled a see-through jelly with salmon and pike, and no one knew what to say about that.

She's busy cooking so I climb onto a stool and open the fridge. I take out a plate of her tomato and golden syrup spare ribs. I like chewing bones because Cleo does. Mum says, 'You eat adult food, not child food.' I'm not sure what the difference is.

When Freddie walks into the kitchen I notice the music has stopped. He talks quietly to Mary on the outside step. I watch and chew sweet, cold tomato meat.

'What are you making, Joan?' Freddie asks. She tells him the jellies, but he doesn't look interested. I hope there will be no fish jelly.

'That's very kind, Joan. Thank you,' and he smiles, and the cream phone around the corner in the breakfast room rings. Mum picks it up and walks back with the long spiral cord trailing: she stirs gelatine and talks. 'Yar?' she sucks a finger, shakes her head. 'Tell him I'll be there as soon as I can, no . . .'

I don't know what the voice on the other end is saying.

'. . . no, do not let him out of your sight. Do you understand me?' She walks back into the breakfast room. I hear her dialling another number. I suck a rib bone. Cleo pushes my shoulder with her heavy nose.

Mum is taking her apron off, 'Stay here, Tiff. I won't be long.' Her car keys jangle.

'Where are you going?' I whine.

'Off to see a man about a dog.'

I know this riddle: she isn't.

'Hazel is coming to look after you, and you won't be alone, Tiff, don't freak.' She points at Freddie and Mary.

'*Muuuum—*'

'All right, come with me. I'm picking up Jackson.'

I stop moaning immediately and go back to my rib.

She takes her Biba coat, says something to Mary on the back step, then I hear the clownish splutter of the purple Beach Buggy Jackson bought for her. It was green but she changed it to purple. Jackson put in a Porsche engine, and it regularly breaks down on Herefordshire lanes. Mum grew up on a farm, she thinks the Beach Buggy is stupid.

I think it began like this:

1. Jackson leaves most mornings with a briefcase because he has meetings.
2. Jackson doesn't always go to an office. Jackson goes to places called the Bunch of Grapes and England's Gate.
3. Until Mum gets a phone call and must pick him up.
4. This means not even parcels of beef joints from Nanny (the human one) dripping blood and sent via Royal Mail can help. This is why Mum invited bands into our house. She says they keep the wolf from the door. I've never seen the wolf, but I want to.
5. When Mum's friend Clodagh rings from London to cry about men, Mum tells her Jackson's bad days are outweighing the good and as much as she loves him maybe this is it.

Cleo does a long stretch-fart in front of the Aga; it takes some time. I hold out my plate for her to lick and Freddie is watching me, or maybe he's watching Cleo.

'Shall we go for a walk?' he says, but I know it's not to me. I have already shown him all my places. He only looked interested when I pointed out the litter of no-name kittens in the shed. And when one of Mum's peacocks spread its tail and screeched, he said, 'What a noise! Magnificent.' He loves Cleo: he hugs her when I'm not looking. I saw him in his white suit when she was standing up on the white metal garden furniture and Brian was taking a photograph; Freddie hugged Cleo across her wide chest like he meant it. The thing you don't know about Cleo is her bigness makes the world a surprising place. You must understand the weight of her head, the give of her jowls, the expanse of her drool and the way the long bones of her wagging tail leave bruises. She *is* magnificent.

'Yes, and the size of her bloody shits are, too,' Mum says.

Paella in the Pan

Cooking paella makes me happy.

The first time I served it to a band, I put the paella dish on the table and they asked why the rice was yellow. They left the prawns in shells and the squid tentacles, so I learned I had to shell the prawns. Why should a band know what to do with a prawn? I bought my first paella pan at fifteen. I was camping with my cousins near San Sebastian in Spain. I soon booked into a hotel. The pan went everywhere with me. I still have it.

10	*chicken thighs, keep skin on for taste*
1	*large Spanish onion*
8	*cloves of garlic? Probably more knowing me*
	paella rice, 3/4 of a bag
	chicken stock, white wine
	*saffron strands, a healthy pinch.**
	lots of raw prawns, peeled (leave 12 with shells for show, do you need me to teach you how to peel a prawn?)
2	*small squid, cut into rings and tentacles*
	salt and pepper
	chopped parsley

*I'd drive up to London to this tiny hole-in-the-wall Spanish shop in Soho. A wonderful sour smell of cured meats and cheeses hit me as I walked down the street. They had wooden crates of spices and sea salt. I'd help myself and hit my head on dangling blood sausages and chorizo.

Sauté the chicken slowly, browning lightly. Remove from the pan, including any juice.

Add onions. Fry but do not burn – you want translucent gold. Add garlic. Add the rice (don't wash), first coating it with the oil by turning it. Add the stock.

Simmer and keep adding stock and the dry white wine. Soak saffron in water. Then add good pinch (must be saffron; no substitute and not the powder).

When the rice is still chewy, add the small squid rings, then the cooked chicken and juices.

Do not turn rice over once this process has been done. Don't worry about it sticking, with olive oil this is the sticky golden bit. Keep it topped up with stock as needed and then add the peeled prawns. They take mins to cook.

Add salt and pepper and taste.

In the meantime, cook the remaining prawns in shells with olive oil and garlic. (Takes minutes, as soon as they turn pink). Make sure the rice is cooked. Place prawns around the paella. Add lots of chopped parsley to all. It will look beautiful. At least if some bands saw chicken, they would eat that.

3.

'Kooks'

Mum cooked paella; now she's laughing with her friend Liz Griffiths on the outside kitchen step.

I'm with the Griffiths kids spying through the crack of the kitchen door into the breakfast room, because that's where Queen are eating lunch, and we want our share. 'We' are the *Bash Street Kids*, but really, it's me scrunched up in the middle of the Griffiths kids. Mum calls them this and it makes sense: there are four but sometimes they feel like one, like Queen is a four but they are a one.

I love the Griffiths kids.

Abby is the youngest and smallest, so she is at my shoulder, then Ivan is just above the crown of my head. Ivan and Abby have beautiful dark hair and blue eyes and I stare at them. Their golden sister Briony and golden-er brother Jason are also beautiful but older. I feel hot, shivery and happy in this huddle that smells of Bazooka Joe bubble gum, coconut NICE biscuits, grass, damp and milk.

We're not allowed in until Queen have pushed their cutlery together, wiped their mouths with napkins and said, 'thankyouverymuchJoan', like good children. They are eating slowly, like grown-ups can.

'Have they finished yet?' Ivan says.

I wriggle in deeper hoping Ivan's black hair is catching. I'm Ivan's age and I think he's my boyfriend which means he must give me his Spangles. The Griffiths kids live with their Mum, Liz, in a big house twenty minutes away, but they only have *one* musician staying with them. Theirs is Mike Oldfield and he has very blue eyes, even bluer than Ivan's and Abby's. I don't care about that, but I do care about being a Griffiths kid. I must make do with being smothered in this handsome ball of siblings.

I hear chair legs on floorboards. 'They're getting up,' Ivan says.

But it's only Freddie fidgeting, he does that. Queen know they can't get down from the table until they finish what's on their plates.

'Kids, wait,' Mum says, and she goes back to laughing with Liz. Today it is Moët & Chandon because the manager or the record company paid and *sod it*, Mum said, *it's a treat*. We sniff the golden rice aroma, the saffron, the crispy chicken. We might be drooling as we listen out for the crash of drums, the raindrop plink-plonk of the piano, which means Queen have gone back to rehearsing and we can eat what's left: but there's nothing yet. Cleo has less patience than us. She pushes between our bodies, and because she's stronger than all of us together the door flies open. We squeal with laughter. Freddie is standing by the table: Queen have finished. Cleo barks, wags her whip-hard tail at him and he is saying something to her. He smiles and laughs a short laugh and follows Brian, Roger and John out of the room and into the corridor.

Mum says we are gannets and she and Liz laugh, again. It's

a good day; Jackson isn't here. Mum tells me to wait my turn because guests always come first.

Remember, Tiff, if you stick your hand in a paella pan the deeper you dig the hotter the golden rice will be, and plasters don't work for burns. You must quick as a flash put your fingers under cold water. That's the only thing that will make it better.

Jason pulls out the cutlery drawer, but there is already a chewy tentacle between my teeth. We know how to peel the prawns; our mothers cook for rock stars. The peacocks shriek from the apple trees as Roger's drums start up in the hall. Cleo howls and we howl too, and we're not five children and a dog, we're a band, a pack, a tribe that just might tear through this vicarage, bite the ankles of polite musicians, bark and slobber into the microphones, mark our territory on the Vox amps, chew up drumsticks, guitar necks, and chase Queen up the stairs.

That night, on my mattress in the pottery, I make Cleo lie on top of me; she's heavier than any single Griffiths kid. Maybe she's the same weight as them all together.

I've overheard Mum tell her stories, how I was the last of her many babies but I was the one to live.

There we are and that's life and what can you do about that, we all have these tales of woe, don't we? It's in the past, and the past is the past when nuns shoved dead babies in hospital cupboards and down rubbish chutes; when Catholic priests yelled about condemning my baby to limbo because who thinks of a baptism while I'm gushing blood in a hospital bed? The past is the past and you must never live there. That's what I say.

Mum says it's why she'll never go near a nun or a priest

again. *It's a good thing, too. I mean I was getting rather Catholic*, she laughs.

People usually say, 'You are a hoot, Joan,' and, 'Joan, you're the life and soul!' But when Mum laughs about the things that have happened to her, the people she tells don't always laugh with her.

Joan falls for Elizabeth David

I don't know why you keep asking me these bloody questions. I hate talking about myself. No one is interested. It's boring. I was a chef, so what? Everyone cooks like this now. Of course, *then* you had to drive up to London just to get pitta bread or coriander.

I discovered Elizabeth David in the '50s. I don't know who gave me her books, certainly not my mother, but when I was still a child I became completely absorbed in reading (and not wholly understanding) her *Mediterranean Food* and her *French Country Cooking*. Because of her and a benevolent grandfather, I went to the Cordon Bleu school in London. Then one spring day in the '60s I walked into her shop in Pimlico. There was this spicy smell of cigarettes – *Gitanes*, I thought – and I heard this wonderful, low, ginny voice saying, 'What are *you* looking for?' I knew straight away that it was Elizabeth David and I pretended to know lots about her kitchenware. I wanted to tell her she saved me from over-boiled vegetables and milk puddings. I wanted to tell her she was the reason I drove to the south of France, then Italy, at eighteen in a 2CV, and ate everything, including raw mussels from Naples Bay (which unfortunately gave me hepatitis). But she saw right through me, and I could tell she thought I was completely dim. It didn't matter. I had met my idol. And she did say, 'If you want to come back in give me a call.' I worshipped her and I still do.

Perhaps it's not surprising I was drawn to food. I grew up on a farm with a kitchen filled with women cooking and preparing. We had a paraffin cooker that gave out a stink, and an Aga that ran on anthracite. They were probably both killing us. My mother suffered from headaches and took to her bed, particularly at Christmas, so I cooked my first Christmas Lunch at twelve years old on the anthracite Aga, and I loved it. My father and much older brother told me I'd underdone the sprouts and carrots, but I knew my vegetables were right. I was bloody-minded even at that age.

When she didn't take to her bed, my mother was an excellent farmhouse cook. Roasts, casseroles, heavy baked puddings, and yes, pity those poor vegetables boiled to death, sacrificed for good gravy. She had a pantry for the roasts. My father would scrape the mould off, and he was never ill. We made our own cheese, and when the pig man came, I was told to ride my horse across Herefordshire to my aunt's Gloucestershire farm. I'd ride all day with a saddlebag of beef sandwiches, lemonade and a Kunzle cake or a Victoria sponge in a tin for my aunt. I stopped in fields, asked at farmhouses for water for my horse. The next day I'd ride back with pretty much the same packed lunch, and when I walked into the kitchen at home it would be filled with women from the village making faggots, brawn, pork scratchings, while the halved pigs hung in salt in the cowshed. Soon the pigs would be above the breakfast table, dripping from the wooden beams into our porridge. I remember being appalled by this when I came home from London in the '60s but I didn't think of it as a child. It was a farm.

Am I boring you? No one asks me about my life. I live in the now. You wouldn't know about the 1950s but when I was sixteen my mother gave me a perm, a twin set and pearls, and I had to go to balls with Young Farmers who weren't young at all. Ghastly. Cooking gave me as much freedom as the '60s did. It was my escape and my first job, apart from that time I worked for a private detective, and I had to carry a big recorder in my handbag. I found myself in a wardrobe in the Dorchester, or was it the Grosvenor? I was meant to be spying on the Duchess of Argyle and I didn't like that at all.

4.

'Smokestack Lightning'

It was as simple as: I went to school in the morning and when I came home Queen were gone. I looked in the airing cupboard, but I only found a whisky bottle between a folded sheet.

The hummingbirds in the bell jars are quiet. Vox amps don't wink red eyes at me from our fireplace. The white piano under the stairs has disappeared; the orange and spicy wood smell of Freddie has blown away. Mum said it was Givenchy. We moved back into the Vicarage and I ran up to my room, and stamped on my floorboards like Rumpelstiltskin, shouting, 'Mine, mine, mine!' as Cleo barked. I'm back with my David Cassidy and Jimmy Osmond posters and Mum has put a padlock on my bedroom door because I'm sleepwalking again. She's found me in cupboards, and in the graveyard. She caught me considering the jump from the landing bannisters down to the hard zigzag hall tiles below.

She's with Hazel, cleaning the kitchen for the next band. Jackson's at the Bunch of Grapes or England's Gate, and I'm up in the attic playing my records with Cleo. I have three, in white paper sleeves:

'In the Ghetto' by Elvis Presley
'You're So Vain' by Carly Simon
'Me and You and a Dog Named Boo' by Someone I Can Never Remember

I don't know where these singles came from.

There's a round window up here, like the round window on *Play School*. Mum's white fantailed doves strut and purr from the guttering. I see the church tower next door, and the golden cockerel weathervane turns in the wind as the church bell clangs. The yew trees in the graveyard aren't any less bloodthirsty in daylight.

The attic is my playroom, but a full ashtray of cigarette butts now sits on a low table. The men who slept here on single beds were the men who ran up and down the two flights of stairs in flared blue jeans and tight T-shirts, coiled cables in their hands. They tuned Brian's guitars, set up Freddie's microphones and rolled his piano about.

It's easier when bands are here, Mum says. We are all on edge, like her doves on the guttering.

I pick up 'In the Ghetto'. The orange label says 'RCA' and 'Victor'. The date is @1969 and I wonder if it was a Monday, Tuesday, Wednesday, Thursday, Friday, Saturday or Sunday when Elvis sang 'In the Ghetto' into his microphone? I wonder if it was snowing and cold and windy for Elvis, like it is in the song? I slide the single underneath the others so it's the first to play, and I slot all three records on the silver spike of Mum's Dansette. I wait for the crunch of its little gears. 'In the Ghetto' drops, the arm jerks up and across, and hovers over the black single like a teasing cat's paw. There's a thump, a crackle, and I lie back on Cleo's barrel chest: the gloopy thud of her heart beats into my back. I reach up for the big flap of her ear and hold it, soft, in my fingers.

The running pluck of an acoustic guitar comes first.

Doooom-dadumdaddumdadum-doooom—

Strings play, Elvis rumbles his sad story. Backing singers echo his words and Mum's fantailed doves purr along, too.

'---co-co-ooooooooh!'

The sound of Elvis makes me want to rub myself along the carpet, hard, like Cleo does when she has worms. I turn over, my face in Cleo's fur, and I press my hips into the floor. The ladies sing higher, then higher: *In the ghettoooooo-OOOOOOH!*

Elvis sings, and I have a sensation like I need to pee.

Whenever I play this song Mum says, '*Uh-uh-uh-hu-uh-hu*,' and curls her top lip. 'Where in the world did you get that single, Tiff?'

I don't know the answer to that. Mum's records are:

Lou Reed, *Transformer* (I can't help staring at the sharp hipbones of the long lady in black tights on the back)
David Bowie, *Hunky Dory*
Cat Stevens, *Tea for the Tillerman*
Elton John, *Goodbye Yellow Brick Road*
Steve Wonder, *Innervisions*
George Harrison, *All Things Must Pass*
The Rolling Stones, *Out of Our Heads*
J. S. Bach, 'Sheep May Safely Graze', because she once played that on the Hereford Cathedral organ

These records are downstairs, some covers as colourful as my books, *Struwwelpeter* and *In the Night Kitchen,* or the stories I make up with my Fuzzy Felt Farm.

*

There has always been music in the homes I've shared with Mum: 'Where Do You Go To (My Lovely)?' in the flat round the back of Harrods where I chewed prawns and spat out their shells. 'My Sweet Lord' in Scotland, in the white caravan that's now Cleo's home. 'Without You' in my grandparents' spare room. But Mum hides her most precious records because of Jackson's guns and my sticky fingers. I have seen and heard them, though. They sound like a bad throat *and* a train, and they make me stamp my feet right back to the olden days. Their labels say *Atlantic*, *Chess*, *Sun* and *Aladdin*. Mum says the thick ones with blue and red labels are 78s: *Colombia*, *Capitol*, *Bluebird* and *His Master's Voice* with a happy Jack Russell. These need a record player with a handle you wind, and she has one in this attic.

'He sent them in a crate packed with straw, all the way from Texas,' Mum told me. 'I was twelve years old, it was Christmas, and I was home from boarding school. When I picked through the straw, I couldn't believe the names. "Lead Belly"! I mean, have you ever heard a name like that, Tiff?'

I hadn't.

'And "Howlin' Wolf". Can you imagine?'

I wanted to.

'On a Herefordshire farm I fell in love with the blues. Do you know what the blues is, Tiff?'

I did not.

It was a Texan cattle farmer who sent her the records. He would come and stay on my grandparents' farm because Grandad's red and white Hereford cattle were famous. The wide and tall Texan man liked to fill his ships with them and sail them to America, mooing all the way.

'Poor things,' Mum said, 'but one night, as we sat in that awful bloody "lounge" of your grandmother's, listening to the boring old radiogram, the man asked me, "What music do you like, honey?" and I knew I liked playing my older brother's Louis Armstrong and Billie Holiday records and I knew I hated *South Pacific* because it was the only record my mother had, so I said, "The blues!", not knowing quite what I was saying. Oh, the look on Mother's face!'

I like to think of this part of Mum's story: they are sitting in Nanny's lounge (a word Mum forbids along with 'toilet', 'serviette' and 'Nanny'). They are sitting in Nanny's lounge, possibly with serviettes, thinking of toilets, and the Texan man's legs are so long they reach right across the good rug, and his cowboy boots poke up. He stubs a fat cigar in Grandad's Hereford bull ashtray and cries, 'Yee-haaaa' before he throws a lasso above his head to rope the ceiling light like it's a steer. My grandmother clears her throat and says, 'Not inside, dear.'

'... and Tiff, the crate arrived soon after that. Your grandmother wouldn't allow it in the house, so I asked Stan, who helped on the farm, to open it with a crowbar in the cowshed. My brother was in Canada, and I took his wind-up gramophone, sat on the cold concrete and played my first blues record, "Good Morning, Blues". I had a very peculiar feeling there in the cow stalls. I had to lie down and later your grandmother had fits about the muck on my dress. Lead Belly. *Lead Belly, Tiff.* Wild! I played that record again and again. I mean, just listen to the names ... Muddy Waters, Peg Leg Howell, Big Bill Broonzy, Willie Mae Thornton, Bessie Smith, Ma Rainey, Robert Johnson, and that gorgeous big growling man Howlin' Wolf. It was better than South bloody Pacific. There were over thirty records in the straw; he said he'd collected them just for me. He then sent me my own record player, and I'd sit on the concrete floor, cows shitting around me, and dream of the Mississippi because of "Mississippi River Blues". Of course, I had to look it up on a map. I still dream of the Mississippi river. I want to ride it before I die. I did see Howlin' Wolf in London. He was astounding. I still think that sound does something to you. Unsettles not only your bones, but your membranes, your cells, your veins, capillaries, and very possibly your brain, Tiffany.

'And when I was pregnant with you, after the gynaecologist sewed me up so I wouldn't lose you, I rented a bungalow in Bosham and listened to the blues all day. Of course, I had that Pyrenean Mountain Dog, Faceache. You won't remember Faceache, but he bit you when you were still in my stomach. I was seven months pregnant, and it was a panic at the local hospital. I had more stitches, on the outside this time, but you lived. Poor Faceache ... first your grandmother drove from Herefordshire to Sussex to take him back to the farm. I'll always remember this tiny four-foot-nine woman in patent leather high heels, dragging this massive Pyrenean Mountain Dog with my blood on his muzzle into the back of her car. *Poor Faceache*, he went to the postman, then he attacked the postman. He was insane.'

Mum's stories go like this: a silver ball in a pinball machine.

In the Vicarage attic, Cleo's heart beats into me, still gloopy. Elvis has finished his 'In the Ghetto' and Carly Simon has dropped on top of him to sing 'You're So Vain'. It's about a man at a party. Mum says the song is about a man being a twat.

I don't hear the car door slam, but I do hear Nanny's voice from the gravel driveway. 'Joan? Are you home? It's your mother.'

Nanny likes to announce herself.

I know it's a *disaster fund* that I call my grandmother 'Nanny' rather than Grandmama or GamGam or Nar Nar, but Nanny is Nanny, goat or not. When we lived in the caravan in Scotland and I tugged the cord of a boiling kettle and scalded my legs to the emergency room, Nanny posted joints of Hereford beef instead of get-well-soon cards. Nanny really is four foot nine and she does wear black suede or patent leather high heels in her farmyard. Nanny's hair is golden, hard with Elnett, and she is, according to the village, a very beautiful, petite woman. I love staying for weeks with Nanny at the farm and I come back *utterly spoiled.* She doesn't have dogs or cats, but I imagine her pulling a mad, white Pyrenean Mountain Dog into the back of her small car, my mother's and possibly my blood on its muzzle. Whenever Nanny invites me to kiss her on the cheek, she says, 'Mind my make-up.' I hover and get a cough of Coty powder.

'Joan?' she cries from the gravel. 'Have those strange men gone?'

I run to the attic landing as 'Me and You and a Dog Named Boo' drops onto Carly Simon. I pause because it's the happiest story-song, a gasp of hot summer air, a dog, and a car driving as the good dog's ears flap-flap-flap. There are no children in ghettos or men at parties being twats.

Cleo shakes, stretches, farts.

'Joan?' Nanny cries from the gravel. 'Don't let that big dog jump up. Please.'

Sticky Spare Pork Ribs

This is a wonderfully easy dish but make sure your ribs are brown. For the ribs, ask your butcher to cut them up. Don't buy enormous ones, you want ribs that are satisfying but can be held. I used a lot of golden syrup in the '70s.

I'd serve them with watercress and orange salad, my rice or a new potato salad with home-made mayonnaise and chives. I still dream about going down the Mississippi on one of those old steamers. Maybe one day I will.

It's true those old blues records ruled my childhood. I was sent to boarding school at six and later they were my only happy reason to come home. I lie, I loved my horse and my dog, but when Pugh the neighbouring farmer complained, my father had Bonzo shot, and one Christmas my parents told me they gave my horse away. I tried not to make a fuss. The records? I have no idea where they are now.

large jar of passata, but to be honest I made my own

12 *cloves of garlic (less if you wish, but why?)*

sometimes I'd also put in thinly sliced shallots

small bunch of coriander

round about 24 belly pork ribs ***WITHOUT*** *the skin.*

about half a tin of golden syrup, but cover the ribs

Mix the passata/home-made tomato sauce with some garlic and coriander in a blender.

Lay out ribs in a pan, or two pans. Not too close otherwise they don't brown. Pour on the golden syrup – straight from the tin if you like. Turn the ribs. Now pour on the passata mix and extra whole garlic. Turn the ribs again. Don't be afraid of getting your hands dirty and really work the sticky sauce into the meat. They must be covered.

Rest them for 5-10 minutes.

Cook in fan-assisted pre-heated oven at 350F for at least one and a half hours. Cover top in foil for first 30 mins, then remove. Up to 370F at end to get brown; baste like you would a roast. You can turn the ribs so they don't burn.

Taste the sauce for seasoning: too bland? Add pinch of sea salt and pepper. If they are getting too black cover very lightly with tinfoil. The garlic should melt and the sauce should be pretty thick.

5.

Paranoid in the Graveyard

We are sleeping in the Vicarage because Black Sabbath are from somewhere near Birmingham and they don't need all the rooms. Some roadies drive home each night. Only the band stay over and not all the time. If they see me, they sometimes say 'all right, bab?' In my proper bedroom I kiss my David Cassidy poster, sort of smile at freckled Jimmy Osmond and make beds in two cardboard boxes for the bantams, Road Runner and Elvis. I open my *Tale of Samuel Whiskers* to peek at him being turned into a roly-poly pudding, then I jump on my bed and shout. No one will hear me no matter what I do because the band downstairs are the loudest I have ever heard. Their guitar makes my eardrums and bones shudder. The singer screams high, but in tune. I think the glass in our windows will shatter.

It's the middle of the night but the graveyard has woken me up. I'm brave enough to get out of my bed and stand at the window. There's a bright full moon and I see the church tower and the golden cock weathervane. They're glowing. The graves are black teeth. There's moon shadow, too, and a figure is dancing around the graves.

It's screaming, 'Aaaaaaaahhhhhhh!' and, 'Eeeeeehhhhhhh!'

I blink. It could be Rumpelstiltskin.

A torch beam flashes, and the lurching hawthorn hedge, the crooked branches of the witchy yews light up. I don't know why I don't scream; maybe it's because the figure hasn't got any clothes on.

The man who scythes the grave grass, Oswald, was the one who told me that as well as all the blood business, yew trees ward off bad spirits. Their spell isn't working tonight.

'Haaaaaaaaaa! Eeeeeeeeeeeee!' the bad spirit cries in the moonlight, then it falls over. 'Ahhhhhhh, bluudy hell!'

The spirit in the shape of a man with no clothes on speaks English.

I watch it flail on its back like an upended crab. Maybe it's not a bad spirit at all but the Green Man who's coming to suck my blood while I'm still alive as sure as the yew trees will suck me dry when I'm dead.

This time I do scream.

I hear Cleo's deep belly bark from the hall below, then the

scramble of her running up the stairs. She's my very own Scooby Doo, but brave.

'Whhhhhooooooooo!' the Green Man/bad spirit calls.

A fist bangs at my door. 'Tiffany, what the HELL is going on?' Mum's trying to unlock the padlock that stops me sleepwalking.

'MUUUUUM!'

'Wooooooooo!' the voice from the graveyard moans.

My door opens and Cleo leaps onto my bed, barking. Mum runs in to pull me away from the window; she's probably frightened it's open, that I'm sleep-jumping out of this house. I'm too scared to speak so I point, and she sees what I have seen: the spirit-man with no clothes on who speaks English dancing around the graves.

She relaxes. 'Chrissakes,' she says.

My hamster, Hammy (newly found), spins – *eee-eeee-eeee* – in his wheel.

I burst into tears. Cleo howls from my bed.

Mum *freaked*. She banged on doors, 'sort your bloody charge out,' she told the men. I crept out of my bedroom and onto the landing as she marched out of the open front door to the porch, the sergeant major of our vicarage again. 'Go and get him *now*.'

I sat down on the Vicarage landing, stuck my whole head through a shape in the wooden balustrade, and I waited.

My head might be stuck it's been so long. From outside I hear 'catch him!' shouts and laughter. The church gate creaks. A scuffle on the gravel is coming closer, then the mess of men are in the hall below me, out of breath.

'Just keep him under control, for Chrissake!' Mum is

saying. I can smell him as well as see him: soil, whisky, man-sweat and something that tastes of metal. He's laughing and he hasn't found any clothes. He doesn't look made of wood like the Green Man, but like the yews, he might have been drinking the blood and bones of the dead. Mum barks, 'Be quiet, you silly sod, the farmer will be out soon.'

He skips over guitars, jumps onto amps. He dodges behind the drum kit as the men run after him.

This spirit man looks happy in a birthday party way. He grins and laughs and jiggles. I don't think he wants to go to bed.

'Oz, Oz, Ozzy, come on mate.'

Cleo is chasing him around the hall. He squeals like Grandad's pigs at her cold nose as she puts it up his bum. Mum is standing on a chair at the foot of the staircase. She's waiting. As he skips past her, she throws one of my grand-mother's Welsh rugs over his head. He's suddenly quiet: a canary in a cage. The men grab him.

'Put him to bed,' Mum tells them, 'he must be freezing.' There are more than the usual number of plasters on her fingers. The blanket falls but the men have him now, arms looped around his: he follows.

'And he does *not* throw up, do you understand me?' Mum has *AN ABSOLUTE THING* about sick.

Her shoulders drop. Mum is post freak-out. She sees my face staring down from the landing and tells me to take Cleo and go to her bedroom.

I wait for the men to lead him up the stairs to his room first. It takes some time. Mum glares up from the hall, arms folded.

'If he jumps,' she says, 'I will kill him.'

'She can't sleep between us, Joan,' Jackson says.

'She's petrified.'

I can't stop crying. Mum sighs but hugs me. 'Dear me, what a fuss.' Their four-poster bed smells of beeswax and although it's big enough for Cleo too, she is not allowed. Red dawn blasts through the tall windows over Mum's dressing table. I stare at the hanging straps of her Vitamaster machine.

Jackson fidgets. His black glasses are on his side table. His face looks naked without them, but the rest of him is wearing ironed navy pyjamas.

Mum is decisive, 'Look, I'm telling them to leave in the morning. I cannot cope with this crap—'

Cleo whines from the floor.

'Be quiet, dog,' she says, and at last the whole house is silent.

I am asleep against my mother before I can fight it.

I wear my coat to test the ice on the pond. I worry about the orange fish in winter. I could walk out past the bulrush to stand and wave at the orange blobs moving cold and slow as dinosaurs beneath the ice, but I worry about that, too. Mum says I would worry sheep, just like her old dog Bonzo, the collie Grandpa had shot.

Cleo pushes her nose against the ice. Bubbles appear and she jumps back onto the bank with a bark. Today the air is heavy with the stink of cow shit because although it isn't spreading time, it is for us. The farmer has been spreading our boundary with shit every morning since the spirit in the shape of a man with no clothes on danced naked around the graves in the churchyard. Word got out. Graves were tidied with new turf, bouquets replaced. The lady who stabs flower stems into green blocks at the altar said she needed a chaperone. The vicar summoned Mum to another parish council meeting. The postmistress shut for the day. The farmer was out for revenge: the naked dancing man had worried his milk cows.

A green van with gold writing turns up our drive. I hold onto a thick reed by the frozen pond and try to sound out the letters, but they swirl. The van parks up. The driver opens the back and carries out the biggest toy owl I've ever seen. Cleo bounds up to him and the delivery man freezes, the owl towering in his arms. Cleo barks. Mum and the band manager come out of our black and white porch.

I recognise the writing on the van now. It says, 'Harrods'.

'What's all this?' Mum asks.

The Harrods man hands her the owl.

'What in God's name—?'

The Harrods man is now carrying two green hippos, one under each arm. I kick through the bulrush. Mum marches to the open back door of the van. I must get to her before she sends it away.

'What the hell are all these toys?'

The driver hands her a piece of paper, but she bats him off. He picks out two more green hippos, smaller this time.

'Will you stop—' Mum stands in his way.

Black Sabbath's manager appears. He is trying to calm her, shaking his head. 'I'm telling you, Joan, I didn't order these. It must have been Ozzy.'

She folds her arms like she doesn't believe this for a minute. 'No, this is ridiculous. There are more toys here than my daughter gets in . . . her whole bloody life.'

The delivery man is pulling something heavy out of the green van. I spot a head and a mane: it's a rocking horse. I squeal, bolt across the grass, then duck down behind the white metal garden furniture. If Mum sees me now the toys will go. The Harrods driver sets the rocking horse down on the gravel, just as the man who danced around the graves walks out of the porch, with clothes on.

'Ozzy, I want a word with you,' Mum says, and he mutters

something I can't hear. 'Furious doesn't cover it. She was too scared to go to school yesterday.'

He mumbles, looking at the ground, kicking the gravel like the boys do when the headmaster tells them off. The muck spreader is back at the boundary. Shit flies and splatters against the larch.

'I know you're sorry, but the farmer will be muck spreading my garden for weeks.' Mum gestures at the flying shit. 'And these toys—'

She doesn't finish the sentence, and the Harrods man doesn't stop emptying his van. I see a dog puppet with a yellow shock of hair and a purple octopus big enough to sit on. Ozzy watches too. He looks a bit frightened, or confused, and I don't know if it's the octopus or my mum. He says 'sorry' again and backs away.

That afternoon Mum puts the toys in a bit of the attic I'm not allowed in, because *there is no way on God's green earth you're having them all at once. It will, spoil you entirely, Tiffany.* She lets me keep the rocking horse because it's too heavy to move. A day later she tells me to choose one toy – she can't bear my whining a second longer. I can't decide so she hands me the dog-faced puppet with its frizz of yellow hair.

'There, your very own rock 'n' roll dog, Tiff. That should keep you happy. But you have to learn to make decisions, darling. Why don't you call it "Ozzy"?'

I don't. I don't name him at all, but I do put my hand into the cavity of his back and down his green sleeve to his yellow paw. I hold the stick that pokes out of him, and I make his dog-muzzle move up and down and it's magic. His pink felt tongue lolls as he speaks or sings to me, and his yellow hair is soft as chick feathers. I chase Cleo around the garden with him until she howls. In the summer Nanny takes pictures of us in front of her roses.

Poor Cook Summer Lemonade

Poor Cook was my bible for a while.

This recipe sounds a bit Famous Five, but some bands loved it, particularly with vodka or gin. Ha, ha. Don't forget they were boys not that long ago. You loved it, too, Tiff, then complained about stomach ache when you drank it all.

7	*Lemons*	*1*	*pint boiling water*
1lb	*sugar*	*½*	*oz citric acid*

Thinly pare the lemons (no white).

Pour on the boiling water.

Add sugar and juice of lemons.

Steep overnight and strain, stir in the citric acid.

Keeps for a week in a screw-top bottle.

6.

Dancehall Sweethearts

When the phone rings Mum answers, 'Yar?'

She follows this up with real words: 'A little folk band?' Her fingers play with the holes in the plastic dial. 'Did you say Ireland?' She nods into the phone. 'Yar, yup, yaryar.'

She's writing things down on the back of her cheque book. 'Could you say that again?' She listens. 'HORSE LIPS? And not too much noise? Yaryar. Yup Yar.'

Mum says although the Vicarage came with plums, figs, gooseberries, raspberries and an asparagus bed, too much of that will make you sit on the loo (not the toilet) all day: we need an income again. Mum says when the electricity goes off it isn't always the blackouts. Jackson packs his briefcase; he's off to the Bunch of Grapes.

Because we must move back into the pottery with the rats, I run to the fridge for Mum's sharp lemonade and fill myself up. Today I must terrorise.

Cleo taught me this. She may be a girl, but she'll start in her white caravan with a bobbing curtsey and a spot. Then she'll trot out to the herringbone yard, give a half-bent lady-squirt and it's out through the door in the wall and on to the shore of the pond. She gushes there, right onto the fleshy waterlily pads. It's the churchyard wall next.

'You could put a saddle her!' Oswald cries.

'Don't want to thankyouverymuch!'

Cleo trots to car wheels, hard for a girl but she manages with a half-squat, half-cocked aim and the tyres of Mum's purple Beach Buggy are sprayed. Soon it's the lawn, where she takes her time because she must be running out of pee by now. It's a little dip and a dab on the peeling white croquet hoops and a special slop on Jackson's bright red tractor-lawnmower.

Cleo is terrorising. Mum explained it to me.

'She's marking her territory, Tiff, terrorising the countryside with her pee.'

'What does that do?'

'It tells other animals to sod off.'

It's not the animals I want to sod off, it's the men. The bands keep coming. Now, instead of doing one long pee on the lawn, I pee purposefully: like Cleo, I save it up and let it go in short bursts. I'm starting behind the holly tree, but to keep the bands away I have to terrorise all my places, and I have hundreds, thousands, millions, trillions, gazillions of them. Today I'll be back and forth to the fridge to drink a whole jug of lemonade until my pee stings.

His name is Jimmy and Jim, and Jimmy is *grand, grand, grand*. I tend to fall asleep on him but today he is marching up and down the gallery above the hall, playing a silver flute. I follow behind, step by step. It's 'What's the Time Mr Wolf?' but Jimmy doesn't know he's Mr Wolf. I freeze to a statue when he turns. He laughs and I squeal with delight. The little folk band from Ireland are here, the house smells of boeuf bourguignon, and Horslips like me.

Mum keeps asking the band, 'Are you sure she's not bothering you?'

'No, Joan, she's grand. Grand.'

She told them their music 'doesn't sound like folk to me, the dog's howling,' and they laughed. Horslips are loud. The farmer's slurry spreader is back. The postmistress told Mum the farmer has truly taken against us now. Mum said, 'That's not news, Betty.'

Horslips have penny whistles, flutes, a cowbell, a drum that looks like a big tambourine, and they play a violin called a fiddle that sounds like lead guitar. They also have regular drums, guitars and keyboards, and all together the sound makes our rafters shake with centuries-old dust. Their songs tell me stories of blind men and mad men and dancing when 'the evening turns to gold'. When Horslips hold or wear or sit behind their instruments, I can walk up the stairs and dangle my legs through the shapes in the balustrade because they don't mind me watching at all. I stare down at the crowns of heads and say their names out loud: 'Jimmy. Barry. Eamon. Johnny. Fritz. Charles. Man Horrid.'

Man Horrid wears a sweatshirt that says 'Man Horrid'. That's how you know. He ironed on the transfers himself. He's also 'Paul' and he came with the band to cook. He made a drinkable fruitcake. Horslips prefer Mum's food.

'Onetwo, onetwo,' the band say at the mics. They tune guitars and fiddles and run about with cables. When they start the song, it makes me jump up and hop-dance. They stomp on the pretty hall tiles in black platform zip-up boots, and they sing about being lonely nighttown boys.

'Try it again, Jim,' Barry says. Barry has a bass guitar in the shape and the green of a shamrock. Two of the band wear chokers at their throats and I can see the bones below their Adam's apples. They told me this album is about a blind Irish harper from centuries ago, a man called Turlough, and I try to follow the story, but it's hard when the songs stop and start, stop and start. I like it when they sing a whole song to me about Mad Pat.

These men call me 'Tiff'. I am not invisible. I've stopped peeing in the garden.

Very Good Things about Horslips:

1. Their talking voices say *caaaam* not *carrrrrrm* and, *grand, grand, grand.*
2. Mum says they are nice, kind, family men, she loves having them in the house and at least she knows where I am now: with Horslips.
3. They sing stories about the best years of their life spent 'in barrowlands and borderlands'.
4. Their producer, Fritz, has a black and white, one ear up, one ear down, limping dog called Boggle, who cocks his leg and pisses on Mum's big bag of onions. She hates the dog. I'm fascinated by him. His head's too big for his body, bits of him don't work, his black and brown splodges aren't making a proper pattern on the white of his fur, but he is still a dog.
5. Sometimes Horslips pull me around the garden on my toy truck, the Vicarage's kittens in the back trailer.

It's very early and the band are sleeping when the police arrive. Mum is preparing spare ribs in the kitchen; I'm nipping parsley from her pots with my fingernails.

She cuts the rind from the meat, then works the sauce in with her hands. 'You're obsessed with garnish, Tiff,' she says, 'but very good at it.' She's right, I dress her plates with patterns of cut-up cucumbers and frills of parsley and watercress.

The kitchen is steamy, Mum's fingers have the familiar plasters, but she's happy: the band love her food, and Jackson's here so little I often forget about him. I climb on an upturned milk crate to reach the taps and wash my hands because a cook must always have clean hands.

A bang at the front door makes Mum swear: 'Fuckssakefucksakefucksake, what now?' She wipes her meat, tomato, garlic and golden syrup hands on her striped apron. Cleo barks and runs with us through the breakfast room, the corridor, past Jackson's gunroom and across the hall with the instruments, to the porch. I shout, 'Coming!' and Mum shushes me.

She opens the front door to two policemen *in* the porch. One takes off his funny egg-cup hat. There's a crackle to the air.

Mum goes white. 'Where's Jackson?'

Cleo shoots out and the shorter policeman jumps back to the gravel because she's gone straight for where his willy is: this is normal and how dogs say hello.

'Ma'am, please control your dog.'

'Where's Jackson?' Mum repeats.

I try to pull Cleo back, but she's strong.

'These vehicles.' The taller policeman gestures at the band's Mercedes and a big black truck with huge wheels. 'Are they yours, ma'am?'

'What?'

Cleo barks.

The tall policeman points again to the black truck. It

came off the ferry carrying the band's amps, drum kit, maybe the long-necked shamrock bass guitar. 'They have Irish number plates, ma'am.'

'What has that got to do . . . where *is* Jackson—?'

'Please answer the question.'

She blinks and the crackle in the air is different now: my mother is angry. I think if I put my finger up between her and the policemen, the crackle would burn my skin like a lit gas burner.

'Is this why you're here?' she says and steps forward. They step back. Cleo whines, then goes to Mum and licks her raw-pig apron. Mum pulls me back by the arm, and behind her.

'Ma'am, are these vehicles yours?'

'Do not call me "ma'am", it's Joan, and they belong to my guests.'

'And who are your guests?'

'None of your business.'

'We've had complaints.'

'I'm sure you have.'

'We wish to talk to the owners of the cars—'

'You can't. They're sleeping.'

'Ma'am, we'll have to insist—'

'Insist all you like. And it's *Joan*.'

The smaller policeman is looking at Mum's hands, maybe because they are red and sticky with tomato puree.

'The men in your house have been seen in the village. At the pub.'

She laughs. 'Is that a crime?' And she takes out a thin tin of Café Crème cigars, and a box of England's Glory matches from her apron front pocket. She lights her cigar, silent, as the policemen stare. She puffs smoke because Mum can't inhale. Cleo goes nose-first back to the shorter policeman's crotch. He tries to bat her away.

'Control your dog, ma'am.'

'It's her territory.'

Cleo circles them, wagging her bone-hard tail at their legs. They wince and weave. She thinks it's a game and jumps up to the tall policeman's shoulders.

'Ma'am! You must control your—'

'Cleo,' Mum puffs, 'down.'

Cleo does exactly as she is told. The policeman brushes a hefty smear of Great Dane drool from his jacket.

'Good girl,' Mum says.

A car squeals on the Hereford Road, its radio playing 'Devil Gate Drive'. My white goat, Nanny, is pegged to the lawn and she bleats.

Mum throws her cigar to the gravel. 'Who complained?'

'I can't divulge that.' The taller policeman moves forward. He is coming in.

'No,' is all Mum says, but she seems to widen across the threshold. Cleo joins her, licking her pig-meat apron again.

'Ma'am?'

'Stay here. I am going to call the SAS base. I presume that's the problem?'

The taller policeman looks flustered.

'The men in my house have *nothing* to do with all of that crap.' She gestures with a red-sticky hand. 'Tiff, make sure these *kind* gentlemen,' she says this through her teeth, 'make sure they *stay*—'

Cleo sits.

'—they know they can't come in without permission.' Mum glares at them. 'Don't you?'

The policemen are angry, but I'm used to angry men. Behind them at the edge of the lawn Mum's peacocks screech and turn, dragging their show-off tails. I reach up and grip the thick iron hoop of the porch-door handle. With all my might I close it a little.

The police car has turned back down the drive and now it's speeding out of the village. Mum doesn't move from the lip of our terrace until the car is out of sight. She tells me it's lucky she knows the right officers at the SAS base just down the road. She says she is sick and tired of this stupid little arsecreeper country and stupid men with small petty minds, and her spare ribs will be burnt now, and I'm not to say a thing to the band because they are nice family men.

'Do you understand me, Tiff?'

'Yes, Mum.'

I have learned new words since Horslips came to live with us:

Penny whistle
Turlough
Jig
Grand, grand, grand
Shamrock bass
Caaaaaam
SAS
Arsecreeper

Now when Hazel comes to help, she'll stand at the sink and count the police cars that drive past. 'There's another one, Joan. He's come by twice today.' Hazel and Mum laugh.

One day I open the door to a policeman on my own.

Before he can say a word, I tell him: 'My mother doesn't let policemen in her house. You can go away.' Then I remember to be polite: 'Thank you very much.' I push the hall door shut.

Smoked Trout Mousse

I loved doing dips for Horslips, so they could eat when they wanted. I'd make fresh taramasalata, chicken liver pâté, avocado dip. Horslips ate like horses, ha, ha. I wanted them to have something to pick on.

For 8–10 people:

- *7 smoked trout*
- *7 fl oz of single cream or cream cheese*
- *juice of ½ a lemon (but taste before and add lemon gradually as you taste)*
- *2–3 teaspoons of creamed horseradish (depending on preference)*
- *salt and pepper*
- *I'd probably add garlic and parsley, knowing me*

Put all ingredients into the mixer, check for seasoning, this should speak for itself.

If it is too liquid, I use gelatine, or cream cheese. It can be messy.

You and Cleo would lick the bowl.

7.

'We Bring the Summer with Us'

Last night someone had a fight with our holly bush and slept in a puddle. Today Mum has dragged our small telly out into the porch to show football matches from the World Cup in Germany that sound tinny. The sun is shining on the apple orchards, I'm in my dungarees, and Horslips are running about the lawn with croquet mallets, laughing and hitting the balls into the wrong places. The black and white splodged dog, Boggle, is chasing croquet balls and trying to fit them into his mouth. Cleo watches from the gravel, her skin twitching. I had to lock the chickens away because Boggle would eat them. Nanny the goat can stand her ground with headbutts, but the peacocks wail down at him from the larch. I did try to show Boggle my pee places, but he limped off, tail up and showing his pink hole.

I dodge the telly and Barry's shamrock bass guitar as I skip through the porch back into the hall, and run to the kitchen. Mum is cooking paella and the kitchen smells of the sea. I bounce about and gather up garnish. Jackson isn't here. I don't ask when he'll be back.

Mum's browned the chicken and now she's chopping squid,

throwing small purplish tentacles into the paella pan. She pauses.

'One thing, Tiff, would you stop climbing all over those poor men? You're like Velcro.'

I ignore her because Horslips say, 'She's grand, leave her, Joan, she's grand,' whenever I sleep in a denim lap, limpet myself to a cheesecloth shirt or ask to be swung by my ankles on the lawn.

'It's very clingy.' She chucks squid eyes in the dog bowl. Cleo eats them.

I know from Mum that children who won't say boo to a goose, who can't blow the snot candles from their own noses are clingy. I blow my own nose, so I am *not* clingy. Mum may not climb on their laps, but I know she likes Horslips as much as I do. In the evenings, when they stop playing 'King of the Fairies' to visit in her kitchen and ask, 'So what are you making, Joan?', she'll throw a hand in the air with a flourish and say, *Oh I don't know, smoked trout mousse boeuf en croute monkfish with tomato spare ribs taramasalata chilli con carne moussaka chicken in tarragon suckling pig!* Mum is showing off. She says there's nothing wrong with showing off if you're good at something, but if you're not, it's *a bore.* All this English-wilting-daisy-don't-draw-attention-seen-and-not-heard crap really pisses her off. People are eating her food and she is thankful. Sometimes that's all she needs, she tells me. She even manages a smile when Boggle's owner, Fritz, comes in for seconds and thirds. Fritz loves Mum's food, but she doesn't like him because he wears *ghastly Jesus sandals*, and she can see his feet.

I'm carrying a bowl of smoked trout mousse with a wedge of lemon and watercress garnish. I must not be clumsy. Mum is carrying the paella pan, arms wide like a queen, yellow rice steaming and long pink prawn hairs curling out at the pan's edges. I pray she doesn't trip on the guitar cables or the World Cup telly or the green shamrock bass in the porch. On the lawn Horslips are thocking different-coloured croquet balls into different places, there aren't any rules. Boggle runs up the slope to the smell of food and Mum barks, 'Get out from under me, dog!' Boggle does what he's told.

There are more football matches on the small telly through the weeks, and Mum pretends she loves and understands the games. Horslips sing about a blind man who's made of straw, shuffling 'down the night' and 'visiting little girls who never do things right'. The song makes me think of the Scissorman from *Struwwelpeter.* Some summer nights I sleep with Cleo in her caravan. Mum has time to clear away the boots and the fishing nets in the porch.

I still don't know where Jackson is. I don't ask. Mum continues to say 'arsecreeper'.

8.

'King of the Fairies'

I'm sitting on a kitchen chair with one hand in the paw of my crazy-haired rock 'n' roll dog puppet. Jim, the Horslip who plays the flute and the penny whistle and the keyboard, is sniffing the air as Mum lifts a brown Barbary duck from the hot pan, one big fork in the bum and the other in the neck. She sets it on a willow-patterned plate and talks about 'meat resting'.

'I'm surprised the smell hasn't brought in that man with those awful sandals,' she says.

Jim laughs. 'You know that's Fritz, Joan.'

Mum nips off the hairy ends of her red gooseberries. I don't know why she's pretending to forget Fritz's name; she is excellent with names.

'Well, tell him dinner is Barbary duck in gooseberry sauce.'

I hear the rumble of the spreader from the garden boundary, slip off my stool and skip into the breakfast room. With my arm still in the puppet I press my nose against the glass of the tall window. Brown splats whizz up into the air against blue sky to land on our drive, our grass, a croquet hoop.

Sometimes Horslips are as loud as Black Sabbath, but it *is* a wonder the farmer has so much shit. Mum is a farmer's daughter, so she doesn't really care about cow shit. She laughs and says, 'It's good for the garden.'

It's evening though it's light and that means blackbirds shrieking, a gin and tonic for Mum and whisky for Jackson because he's back. In the hall, he's telling Horslips that the ships in the pictures up the stairs are all his: the band nod politely. I walk outside because it's still bright blue. Boggle is down by the fuchsia bushes, cocking his leg. He has to hop to keep his balance. Cleo is locked in her caravan. Mum told me she is 'in season', which means Boggle pants.

'What are you up to, Tiff?'

I jump and squeak. I see Jesus sandals: it's Fritz sitting outside on the white metal furniture. Fritz doesn't say *caaaam* like Horslips, he says *baath* not *barth*, and *booogadeeboooogadeeboo*. He does have ugly feet.

'Where's the big dog?' he asks.

'That's Cleo.' I brush my trousers down.

'She's yours?'

'Yes.' I frown because that's a lie – Cleo is Jackson's dog.

'Well, that's my dog, Boggle.'

I frown harder. 'I *know that*.'

'I bet you didn't know Boggle rides the buses in London, on his own, to meet me after work.'

'Well, Cleo can eat a whole caravan, and she's "in season".'

Fritz laughs and his top two teeth poke out of his lips, not nearly as much as Freddie, but they still poke. 'I saved Boggle from a condemned building. He was stuck in there; they had the dynamite in place, they were about to push the switch, but I ran in and stopped them.'

'Poor Boggle,' I say. I wonder if the dynamite is where he got the limp? He does look as ragged as Wile E. Coyote. I wonder if my mother would have preferred the dynamite to go off?

'Bog!' Fritz cries and Boggle hops up from the lawn. 'Watch this,' Fritz tells me.

He holds a thick stick up high in the air and Boggle, with only three good legs, jumps for it. He misses. He jumps again. He misses. I think the showing off bit is over when Boggle runs off, but he stops at a distance, turns; then he's sprinting back to us, gearing up for a running jump which he does, but up Fritz's leg and his body, his arm, until Boggle has the stick in his mouth. He dangles. Fritz doesn't let go.

'Watch!' Fritz takes the stick in both hands and starts to twirl in a circle, slow at first and then faster, faster; and there's Boggle, the thin, black and white and brown splotched dog, biting onto the stick, his back legs pointing straight out mid-air like he is Super Dog. Boggle is flying.

This must be why his teeth are worn down to nubs and his back leg is bent.

I'm jealous and I pray for a giant to come to our house and do this with Cleo. Maybe I'll be brave enough to ask Fritz to do this with me.

9.

Side A: 'Wasn't it Nice?'/ Side B: 'Black Boy'

When Horslips leave for a place called Rockfield, even Mum is sad and she doesn't get sad. I find a tortoiseshell plectrum and a silver penny whistle and I keep them under my bed. I pick Boggle's white hairs from the rugs with my fingers. It's strange that I miss him the most.

Jackson's gunroom is unlocked because he is back all the time now: there's a new twelve-bore hole in our ceiling. The peacocks are quiet, but Mum and Jackson row. Mum says that without whisky, Jackson is a kind and funny man.

She takes me out a lot. 'Get out from under his feet.'

We go to her friends Guy and Ian, and Guy says, 'You'll love this, Tiff,' over the lunch he's cooked, and I do because I love all food unless it's a raw tomato. I make daisy chains on their lawn as they talk about Jackson. 'Come and stay with us, Joan,' Guy says. I'd love to live with Guy and Ian. I wonder if they'll let me bring Cleo?

Mum takes me to the Green Dragon in Hereford. She revs her Beach Buggy's Porsche engine in the Vicarage driveway while I pull Cleo by the collar.

'They don't allow Great Danes, leave her, Tiff.'

I have seafood pancake and Mum has a glass of house white and a pink, gold-tipped Sobranie. I count the ticks of the grandfather clock in the damp-smelling lounge-restaurant. A waitress in a white crown files her nails at the till. Mum asks for ice for her drink and the waitress gives her one cube. The radio plays 'Seasons in the Sun'.

I feel sick with creamy prawns as we drive round and round Hereford. We pass Chadds, and Chave and Jackson the Chemist. Mum tells me stories of how bored she was in this town as a girl when the shops were called Augusta Edwards, and Ferris in High Town. It's why she ran away to London and had her adventures there, *but don't think of the past, Tiff, never live in the past.*

We bounce along narrow Herefordshire lanes in the purple Beach Buggy until it gets to dusk, which takes for ever because it's summer. The air is sweet with the tickle of hops. Couch-grass fires glow in gardens; bough-heavy apple trees bend in roadside orchards.

*

The next band come and it's a relief. Jackson goes back to England's Gate with his empty briefcase. Mum says this new band are boys from London. They arrive in a white Bentley with an open top, and their hair is bright orange. I think they look as bright and sparkling as the hummingbirds in the bell jars in our sitting room.

'It's orange from a bottle,' Mum says. I think of Lucozade.

Trax play different music to the other bands. It still shakes the glass in the windows but there are no penny whistles or fiddles, screaming vocals, lead guitar solos or waterfall pianos. This music thuds and trumpets and twangs with a *wang-a-wang-a-wang.* Mum calls it 'funk' and it makes me happy in a birthday party way. They sing, 'Wasn't it Nice?' and I jump-dance. Their song 'Black Boy' is slower, but it does *wang-a-wang-a-wang* all the way through, and it has trumpets. Mum drives Trax around our lanes in the Beach Buggy with the plastic top off, *to really piss the farmer off.*

Trax are rehearsing in the dining room today, not the hall. The door is open but I've been standing on the threshold for ages. The *wang-a-wang* gets me somewhere in the stomach. The trumpet starts up and I can't stop a bubbling giggle.

'Come on in then, girl.' One of Trax is in front of me. They haven't told me their names yet but I remember that London sound. *Cam on in then, gel.* I step in and blush so much I get scratchy.

He adjusts the mic down to my level. I stare up at his bright orange hair and they all say, 'Sing us a song!'

My neck flushes with panic.

'Sing anything.' *Anyfing.* He's from London. *Laaaandaaaan.*

He lifts me until my mouth touches the microphone's cold metal mesh. 'Know a nursery rhyme?' he asks.

The drummer hits a cymbal and I take a breath, 'Mary had a Little Lamb his fleece was white as snow and everywhere that Mary went that lamb was sure to go—'

Trax laugh and shake their bright orange heads. My voice is loud and alien in the amps and I hate it. The drummer hits the cymbal again, the Trax who's picked me up puts me down, the trumpet starts up and they are *du-doom, du-doom, wang-a-wang-a-wang* back to the funk. I am forgotten. I run out but I dance in the hall.

Trax go pony trekking for the day in Wales. It's not far. A few days later a photographer from London appears with tripods and flashes and timers, and I follow the band as they grin in the aisles of the apple orchards. They ask if the apples are ready to eat.

'Of course, they aren't,' I tell them, but I keep the secret that there's still time to write your name on the apple skin, to watch it grow into a scar.

Nanny is in the pottery kitchen, and she won't sit down. To be truthful there isn't anywhere to sit. 'You were seen, Joan,' she says.

Mum is cutting onions. I don't think she needs to cook onions, but she must do something with her hands when my grandmother is here. Nanny steps back in her black courts, her powder-blue eyes are sensitive.

'You were seen in Hereford, Joan, in a white Rolls Royce, with *those* men, *that* dog and *your* daughter.'

'It's a Bentley, Mother.' She chops the onions fast,

chopchopchopchop. 'What do you mean, *those* men, Mother? They're barely boys.'

'Don't be difficult, Joan. To be seen, in Hereford, and with that poor child.' Nanny points at me and sniffs. 'Joan, it's worse than when you canvassed for that Wilson man.'

Yesterday was like living in the song, 'Me and You and a Dog Named Boo'. Trax drove the big white car with the top down all the way into town. Red Herefordshire mud splashed the white doors. Cleo barked next to me in the back seat, her tongue lolling and her ears flapping, and me holding on to her for dear life because the back seat was big and new and slippy.

Trax sang all the way into town and all the way home and Mum and I sang with them. Malcom the trumpet player has the highest voice, and I joined in with him. In high town Cleo barked at pedestrians when we stopped at the traffic junction where a tall brick building had a sign in capitals, Franklin Barnes. Women in summer macs, buttons done up tight as string around a Sunday beef joint, stared. Mum did a Queen-wave (the lady not the band). When men in flat caps gasped, roll-ups stuck to their thin bottom lips, I sang out, 'Me and You and Dog Named Boo!' but no one heard me over Cleo barking and the car radio playing 'Remember You're a Womble'.

We drove on. By the time we reached Broad Street we were all singing 'Remember You're a Womble'. We turned towards the Green Dragon where my grandad's friends from market day came out to stare; we passed the huge grey dinosaur of the Cathedral and the green, and it didn't rain once, not a spot. We could smell the bitter spice of the hops, and it was the best day in the world living in a song.

*

In the pottery kitchen Nanny folds her hands and clears her throat. It's a nervous thing, *ca-ca-ca-ca-ca*. Mum's words still ring. She said, *What's so unusual about Tiffany and me, a giant dog, Trax with their bright dyed-orange hair all squeezed into a white open-topped Bentley on a sunny afternoon on market day in bloody Hereford?*

I mean what's so unusual about that, Mother?

Nanny looks around the dusty makeshift kitchen, at the milk crate sideboards, the old groaning fridge. 'I should be taking poor little Tiffany Jane away from this terrible place.' Only Nanny uses my middle name.

Mum holds up her Sabatier knife because she often uses it as a talking tool. 'Over my dead body, Mother.'

I hear the breath come in and out of Nanny's handsome nose, mottled with Coty powder. 'And where, pray, is Jackson in all this, Joan?'

Mum puts the knife down and sighs. 'Mother, I have absolutely no idea.'

'You can't go on like this.' My grandmother sniffs and leans over to give me clear instructions on how to kiss her on both cheeks but mind her make-up.

When she puts me to bed that night, Mum says when she lived in London in the early '60s, she still saw those awful signs in windows: 'The ghastly ones, the ones that said, "No Irish, No Blacks, No Dogs." That is why we're doomed, darling.'

The house echoes: Trax have finished rehearsing and they've gone home to London. The *wang-a-wang-a-wang*, the *toot toot parp*, the bright orange hair has left and the joy has left my stomach too. Jackson is back. I don't like this house without Horslips or Queen or Trax, though I'm fine about Black Sabbath. After I lock up the chickens, I sit in the copse with my torch and shine it on the hen house, on the trees. Some nights Mum sits with me until she gets bored, which isn't long. I count the noises I am left with: tawny owl, dog fox, blood-sucking creaking yew, church bells, night-time muck spreader, purring chickens, cars on the main road driving away from here, Cleo barking from the skinned caravan, and a distant phone trill from the red box in the village.

Mum restarts her B&B weekends and I stay with Nanny. When I come home, Road Runner, Elvis and Nanny the goat have gone to stay with the Griffiths kids. When more gun-holes appear in the ceiling, Mum hides the key to the gunroom. I hear her on the phone to Clodagh. 'I can't cope,' she says.

At night Jackson plays 'Land of Hope and Glory' and I'm sure it's louder than Black Sabbath rehearsed. In the day I play my records in the attic: Elvis on top of Carly on top of whoever sings 'Me and You and a Dog Named Boo'. When Jackson is out Mum plays 'Vicious' by Lou Reed.

One night Mum's quartered ducks are ready on plates by the Aga. She's clearing starters from her faithful B&B guests in the dining room. She has a full house. When she goes back into the kitchen, Jackson and a man she has never seen before are standing over her plated ducks. They have taken exactly one bite out of each breast. They have come from the village pub, and they are drunk.

She waits for Monday: she waves her guests off, still apologising that the duck was off, and how she hoped the rump steaks were a fair substitute. Jackson is asleep. That night we are leaving for Clodagh's in the stupid Beach Buggy, and I am crying for Cleo.

From the front seat Mum speaks over the rattle of the plastic top. 'I couldn't take her, darling, she's *his* dog.'

Emergency Recipe

Take:

one   *Sabatier knife*
one   *child*
one   *purple Beach Buggy with a*
stupid Porsche engine

10.

'Band on the Run'

I'm in the sea.

Italian kids swear at me from the shoreline, 'Fuucker!'

The sun-brown girl in the bikini with the pot-belly (Mum says worms) leans over and scoops up another handful of wet sand. Her little brothers scuttle round her like crabs and cheer. She chucks the sand at me. 'Fuucker!' she yells, and the gold blob plops in the water. Waves heave me up and take me out.

Beneath the surface my hands and feet are eels in spasm because I'm trying to keep my head above water. My breath comes fast as I tilt my chin up, salt in my mouth, my eyes.

'Fuucker!' The voice sounds further away.

Mum is on the beach, but she thinks the Sardinian kids are playing with me. The pot-bellied girl is very good at holding my hand and kissing me when Mum buys them Coca-Colas, then she and her little brothers take me to the other end of the beach and rub me in sand. Then I'll have to watch them run in and out of the sea and roll their bodies in it, until they're covered top to toe, sand in their mouths and ears, up their nostrils. The pot-bellied girl will laugh and dance in her sandy bikini, shouting, 'Fuucker! Fuucker!' at me. Mum will then buy them more Coca-Colas and I will have to sit with them at the beach bar with *their* sand in *my* cracks and holes, and the pot-bellied girl will kiss me on the cheek with a big showy smack and she'll sing, '*Ba Ba Baciami Piccina*', but she will also put her finger to her sandy lips and whisper, '*Fuu-ckahhhhhh*,' into my ear.

I hate Sardinia.

Doggy paddle has got me this far out. I didn't get beyond it at St Michael's Primary when they bussed us to Hereford for widths with armbands. I tread water, and let the swell have me. My breath comes short and fast as I stare up at the burning mountains that circle our beach. The mountains have been on fire all month. No one seems that worried about it. The air is scorch but also nougat because up there, funfairs *tingalingaling* like a distant ice-cream van. At night in our little hotel room, we listen to the burning hills sing and flicker, as Mum puts cold flannels on my sunburnt shoulders (she's searched *high and low* for Ambre Solaire on this *sodding* island).

In the sea a wave takes me forward. I go under and hold my breath: 1-2-3-4-5-6-7-8-9-10!

Tink-tink-tink says the underwater sea.

'Fuuuuckaaaah!'

I kick back to the surface.

'Fuuuuckah!'

The pot-bellied girl can go all day.

I spit out seawater and turn to the horizon with tired doggy-paddle arms. I think of Cleo and something other than salt gets me in the throat. If I run after dogs here, Mum yells, 'Rabies!'

'Fuuuuckaahhh!'

Is the pot-bellied girl in the bikini getting tired or further away?

I hate sand so much I'd rather drown. That's why they throw it at me, to see how far out I'll go. Mum hates sand, too. She sits on a chair at the shoreline. She says it's ludicrous to hate sand if you've run away to an island beach but, *aren't we all ludicrous, darling?*

I don't ask her about Cleo any more. She will only repeat, 'I couldn't take her, she's *his* dog.'

Sun scalds the crown of my head: I take a breath and sink to cool it. The *tink-tink-tink* of under the sea speaks to me again. *The Water-Babies* is my favourite book now and I'm working up to taking a full lungful of seawater to swim away to another life like Tom the chimney sweep did.

I don't know why we came to Sardinia.

We didn't stay long at Clodagh's because Jackson turned up on a motorbike. We moved to my grandparents' farm but that didn't last long, either. Jackson kept calling. One day Mum said, 'We're going to London for the day, Mother. The Natural History Museum,' and Stan who helps on the farm drove us to Hereford train station with his comforting smell of Woodbines and Brylcreem. We went on to Dover, with no luggage, *only cash and passports, Tiff.* After days of trains and a ferry, we were here in Sardinia and Mum said, 'No postcards, no telephone, it's just you and me, kid.'

She bought me new clothes and a pair of sandals, and after a week in a flat with a brick-wall view, she found a deal on a hotel room with a loo down the hall but a bath in the room.

'Why have you decided to hate spaghetti, Tiff?' she asks me in the evenings. She eats *freshfishfreshfishdarling* at the beach bar. She sucks up the orange meat of glossy, black-spiked sea urchins; she gobbles cheese with maggots in because it's a delicacy here and it would be rude not to. 'It's called *casu martzu*, it's delicious!' she says, and a maggot wriggles at the corner of her mouth, until her tongue pops out to get it. Sometimes we go out at night if someone invites us, and I fall asleep face-first in my spaghetti.

'Why *have* you decided to hate spaghetti, Tiff?'

I've decided to hate everything here: I sulk in whatever shade I can find, which isn't much because it's so hot the hills are on fire.

I am a *spoilt brat*.

*

Under the sea, something touches my leg. I gurgle in saltwater, my throat burns, and I kick up to the surface. The sun is too bright and my lungs hurt.

'Fu-----k-----aahhh!'

The girl's call is distant, like a bored, dim seabird.

I bob. Salt dries instantly on my face, my cheeks tighten. The mountains are orange-bright with fire. I watch the smoke, but I'm drifting out. My arms, my feet are heavy stones. I go under again.

'Tiff------ffff-----any!'

I hardly hear my name in the *tink-tink, plink-plink, plonk-plonk* world beneath the waves. But there is another sound: a churn of water like Nanny's mangle makes in the cowshed. That voice comes again: 'Tiff------ffff-----any!' There's a big splash, more churning and a mechanical squeak. I want it to be a whale I can live in, but when something grabs me across the chest, I kick out. I'm so tired my kicks aren't much, and anyway they are hands that hold me, not fins or teeth or *baleen* (I learned that in a book). My head breaks the surface, and a hand pushes my chin up, sharp. I breathe in hot air.

'Tiff! For Chrisssake, swim!'

It's Mum's voice, but these aren't her hands. I look above me and see the upside down face of the waiter from the beach restaurant. Mum is floating above us on a yellow pedalo. She waves her arms in her white cheesecloth top. 'Help her. Oufa!'

I think 'Oufa' is Mum's made-up Italian word.

A wave comes. I spit out water. Mum pedals into the next wave, and she's lost to me for a moment. The hands that hold me keep firm. Then Mum is there, so close she reaches down, grabs my wrist, and pulls while the waiter pushes up my bottom half. '*Allora!*' he says.

My body squeaks onto the hard plastic pedalo.

Mum holds me as the man takes the wheel. '*Never, ever* go out of your depth again, Tiffany,' she says.

In the hotel room, she's at her dressing table in white knickers, brushing her hair that's all blonde now. When she looks at herself her lips puff open like she's a fish.

'They're not calling you a "fucker", silly.'

'But—'

'Darling, they are calling you a *seal*. "Foca" sounds like "fucker" and it's Italian for seal.'

'But—'

'You're not stupid, you know what Italian is.'

'But *why*?'

'It's another language, Tiff!'

'No, I mean why am I a seal?'

She pouts in the mirror, sprays a cloud of Yves Saint Laurent around her: Mum wears perfume, no make-up. 'Your swimming style is very ... splashy, then you disappear under the water and when you come back up you just bob there with your face staring up at the sky. It's very odd.'

'I'm not a seal.'

'Well, we all have our crosses to bear, darling.'

'I'm not a seal!'

She turns around. 'Well, it's better than being a "fucker" isn't it?' My mother squirts more Yves Saint Laurent. Then she's up, walking about our small room.

I cough. 'They throw sand in my hair, Mum.'

She grimaces but says, 'Sand isn't going to hurt you.'

I cross my arms on my brown chest, my chin jerks down, bottom lip out.

'Please don't sulk, Tiff.'

I kick my bare heels against the wooden bedframe. It hurts.

'Don't make a fuss, darling. We're going out.'

'Don't want to.'

'You can't stay here on your own.'

'Not coming.'

'Yes, you are.'

'I'm not a seal!'

'Beggars can't be choosers.' She holds up a dress to the mirror.

'*Imnotaseal.*'

'Don't swim like one, then.'

'*Imnotaseal, Mum*!'

'Well have it your way, then, you're a fucker!'

I feel the brush of a dress on my raw shoulders as she pops one over my head.

'Come on, we're going on an adventure. End of story.'

I want to pee, but I don't like going down the dark corridor on my own and finding other people in the shared loo, so I hold it in.

As we walk through the hot streets of Bosa, Mum smiles and I do too. I've forgotten all about seals and sand, apart from the grains I can feel in my knickers. I don't know where we are going but above us the hills on fire spike flames. If you put your hand out, you'll feel soft rain, but it's not rain, it's ash.

I wish I knew the Italian for 'are we there yet?'

Fire at the side of the road licks the wheels and I move closer to Mum on the hot back seat: my skin sticks to the plastic. The two men in the front of the car are taking us up to the fair at the top of the mountain. They don't speak much English and Mum is saying, 'Oufa!' a lot. The radio is on, and it's a jingly-jangly up-and-down boom-tatty-boom Italian song. It's still light. I see birds of prey in the sky above the smoke. I don't know these men. One is dark-haired, the other almost blond. Mum said they are boys, and they came to talk to her at the beach bar and the blond one asked in a bit of English if we wanted to see the fair in the mountains. Mum said yes.

If it wasn't so hot, if there weren't so many flames around the car and if it wasn't taking so long, I'd be more excited. I've had to pee on a smoking verge, worried my sandals would melt but glad I had pee to put the fire out. Mum reaches for my hand: we are both sticky. I watch little flames dance and fall asleep against her.

I was right, the air up here does taste of nougat because that is what they're selling on stalls, white blocks of it piled high and I want to get it stuck in my teeth, but we are following the men. They tell us we are safe in this town even if the mountains are on fire. It's dark now, but the street and the food stalls are lit with strings of fairy lights. A group of men are singing, and it sounds strange, like a vibration, like the ill man in the Bunch of Grapes in Hereford who had to put a microphone up to his throat to talk to me. I smell rosemary, fennel and wine: a suckling pig is skewered over hot coals, prizes dangle from strings in the fairy lights. *Tingalingaling*, says the fair.

The two men try to touch Mum as she walks. She pats them away. People stop to stare at us. Some of them point. Mum grabs my hand.

Mum bought me nougat and it's sticky, melting between my fingers. We are sitting listening to men sing their vibration songs under the fairy lights. They play guitars but don't sound like the bands at the Vicarage: these men pluck their strings like it's the saddest thing they've ever done. The two men who drove give us salty ham and sausage: they tell us, *mangia mangia*. They give Mum a clear and short drink she spits out. The men start to argue, loud and with their arms. I hunker down in a plastic chair. When I turn to Mum, her eyes look dark and she's frowning. The ham is salty. There's no wind, and I'm hotter than I am on the beach. This island is on fire, but nobody seems to mind. Maybe that's what the sad old men are singing about. My mouth is so dry. I'm still excited about the fair, but somehow, even under these fairy lights, I'm afraid. Mum takes my hand again and holds it.

I have a bed in a room that smells of old woman and meat. There's a picture of the Virgin Mary in a blue dress on the wall and she is crying. The stone floor is sticky, so I keep my sandals on even though I'm on the bed. It's too hot to move but I can hear voices on the other side of the door, and the door is locked from the outside.

I want my mother.

There's a glass of cloudy water on the bedside table but I don't drink it. The last time I saw Mum she looked funny, but not haha. I can hear her voice somewhere in the house telling me that everything is fine, *go to sleep, Tiff,* and I know she's lying. I have done a dreadful thing. I couldn't help it. There is no loo in here and no one would listen. I have peed myself.

I hear the men outside the door. I know it's the blondish one because he speaks in little spurts of English and he's shouting that my mother should be happy. The other man shouts in Italian. I don't think they're boys at all.

This room smells of old woman because it's their mother's room: I don't know why it smells of meat. The men are brothers and when we first walked into this house, because I wanted to pee, their mother fed me pasta which was the best I'd ever tasted, and she gave me that cloudy glass of water. Then she shouted at her sons and ran out of the house. She hasn't come back. The dark one locked me in this room.

I'm so thirsty I reach for the glass and drink the water.

It isn't the gunshots that wake me but the car, and I know the difference. The car keeps revving and screeching and reversing and driving past the house: again, and again. When the gunshots come glass shatters. Mum screams. One man is yelling from outside, maybe from the car? The other man is yelling from somewhere in this house and he is screaming in the same place Mum yells the words, 'Get down, Tiff, get under something!'

The car and the gun stopped. Mum spoke to me through the thin wall, telling me to stay under the bed. I stare at the wooden slats. It's like waking up after sleepwalking and you don't know which way is up and which is down, and you want your mum to find you. *It's OK, Tiff. It will be OK. Just stay down. Go to sleep*, she says. I lick the sticky nougat and ham sweat from my lips. The old woman hasn't come back. I worry about her finding me under her bed and if she'll know I didn't take my shoes off when I was on it.

It's morning and I am in the back of a car. It's a different car to yesterday but the blond one is driving it. I haven't seen his dark-haired brother since last night. The car jolts on the bad road. There is too much sleep and salt and maybe ash in my eyes for them to open properly. Mum is in the passenger seat. I am the thirstiest I have ever been in my life, but I am also embarrassed because I must smell of my own pee. I use my fingers to pull my eyes open and I think of the feral kittens at the Vicarage and their gummy half-opened lids. The verges are not on fire today, but they are smoking. Mum is very upright in the front seat; she doesn't say a word. The man keeps hold of her hand and puts it on the front of his jeans as he drives.

It is past lunchtime when we get into town and I recognise the shops, the restaurants, the alleyways to the beach. I want to jump out. The man is taking a long time to park. I don't think he is a good driver. I have my hand on the back door handle, but I don't run. I watch my mother's shoulders as they rise and fall. I can hear her measured breathing through her nose that is exactly my grandmother's nose, I realise. The man doesn't say anything; he has both hands on the wheel now. He shuts off the engine. There is a moment of still. I hear kids playing on the beach; the sand-throwers, the fucker-callers, and I would do anything to have them chase me now. I hear glasses and cutlery clinking from the beach restaurant; fishermen laughing.

Mum suddenly jerks back, grabs my hand, and pulls me with such force across the gear stick that it hits me. I kick out at the man, but he doesn't do anything back. Mum pushes the door on her side and drags me out of the car. She picks me up and runs, carrying me like I'm a toddler but I'm too big and she can't do it for long. I straighten up the moment my feet hit the street and we both run, together.

She's shouting as she runs but it's not a scared shout it's an angry one. People come out of shops to stare. We run along the beachfront past our hotel, and I don't ask Mum why. She pulls me into the beach bar, catches her breath, and I see the pot-bellied girl; she smiles at me, and I am so happy to see her I smile back.

Mum looks out. 'His car's gone,' she says, and her voice is croaky. She backtracks to the hotel. We run up the stairs. She fumbles in her bag for her keys, then pushes me in. Mum stands with her back against the door and she locks it. 'Fucker,' she says, and I know she doesn't mean 'seal'.

After she runs a bath, we sit in it together and she flannels my eyes open properly. It is hot and my stupid shoulders are still sunburnt. She doesn't say much apart from, 'I'm sorry, Tiff. I was an idiot to go up there,' and, 'let's have a sleep then go to the beach.'

There's a huge wind; the fires are moving down the mountain. By evening we've been evacuated to the beach. They told us to leave everything and go straight to the water. It's almost cold in the sand, but we huddle together: the people from the restaurant, the holidaymakers, the whole town.

The electricity goes out. People gasp in the darkness. The beach is packed; it murmurs with hot bodies. The pot-bellied girl from the restaurant sits at my back, plaiting my hair. Her thighs hold me in place. She sings, clear and pretty and high. The waiter who pulled me from the sea is also singing sweetly, next to Mum. I wiggle my toes deeper. Mum talks in broken Italian to a couple from Rome. They laugh a little as smoke itches our eyes.

The pot-bellied girl pulls my hair too tight. My feet push harder into the sand, and it's colder the deeper I go. Maybe we could dig down to Australia. The girl stops singing. We can all hear the fire now, how it cracks and whistles with its own song. I listen hard for the push of the tide, and I wonder how long I could tread water out there in the sea. I'm glad I'm a seal now. I wonder if Mum knows where that yellow pedalo is.

'We'll be OK, Tiff,' she says, and laughs more with the couple from Rome. The people from the beach restaurant bring us towels for the night. Someone shines a torch and I see the smoke. People cough. In the light we watch ash settle on the sand.

*

The fires have almost gone, and Mum is reading *The Times*. It's from a week ago but she was so happy to get it. She is back to *freshfishfreshfish* at the beach restaurant and days in her chair on the sand. She tells me she won't let any stupid boys ruin *her* sun, *her* holiday, and as long as I am all right, that is all that matters. I don't think about the mountains, I'm back to worrying about the pot-bellied girl, her brothers and the sand.

I stay in the shade of the parasol, but suddenly I see long pages of *The Times* separating and flying across the beach in the breeze. Mum is staring out at the sea. She is crying. I don't want to go to her because Mum crying is unusual. She kicks her sunchair into the sand.

'For fucksake!' she shouts, and I don't know why until later when we are sitting at a hot restaurant, she is drinking wine, I am pretending to be asleep and a couple on the next table ask her what the matter is. She tells them that her friend Clodagh has killed herself.

'The obituary said, "died tragically",' she tells them, 'but I know what that means. She always threatened to, and now she finally fucking has. And she didn't have to: she didn't have to at all.'

The couple don't reply.

'We have to go home,' she says to no one in particular.

I think of words I've learned in Sardinia:

Foca
Oufa!

That's all I can remember.

Joan, Many Years Later

'Can I ask you about Sardinia, Mum?'

'Of course'

'Are you sure?'

'I don't see why not.'

'We were kidnapped.'

'Oh, that. Yes.'

'They had guns, Mum.'

'Oh, everybody had a gun in the mountains.'

'They locked us in separate rooms, didn't they?'

'Yes. That's when I realised, *we've been kidnapped.* Then they had their wicked way with me. And I had to play their game because I was scared stiff they'd hurt you. But they didn't touch a hair on your head. That was all that mattered. The mother fed you! Then she pissed off into the street yelling, but no one came to help us.'

'What about you, Mum?'

'As long as you were all right, I was fine. I was a naïve idiot getting in that car. When I told our friends Ian and Guy, Ian went crazy. He knew Sardinia and said I was a fool going into bandit country with strange men. Everyone was getting kidnapped, and worse, remember the Getty kid?'

'Not really.'

'Anyway, it was such a shame because up until then I'd felt so free. Possibly for the first time in my life. I would read on the beach, try to communicate with people. Everyone was so incredibly kind to us, and they adored you, although you were going through a stage and had decided you hated spaghetti and sand and that was that. Then I got into that car. But I didn't bloody leave the island, either. Sod them. The next morning, I was out on the beach, and you were playing in the sea with your friends. I told a couple on the beach about it – about being kidnapped at least – and they said, "What do you expect?" They were right.'

'I'm not sure I should write about this, Mum . . .'

'Oh, you'd worry sheep, Tiffany.'

'How long did we stay in Sardinia afterwards?'

'Until the money ran dry, and then, Clodagh. What a way to find out, in the obituaries. And you remember what happened when we reached Dover?'

'What?'

'After days on ferries and buses and trains, we were arrested. Your grandmother had reported me to Interpol. Said I had kidnapped you. The bloody irony. They took us to a side room, then they wanted to separate us. You were terrified.

You thought you'd done something terribly wrong. I held onto you and said, "over my dead body." They gave in. I was so angry. And that night we were back at the mausoleum of my parents' farm. You were utterly spoilt by your grandmother, of course, but I had to leave you with her.'

'Why?'

'I had to work, Tiff. There was only me to support us. We didn't even have a place to live. I was off to Rockfield Studios, but first it was cooking for Horslips, in a place called Tipperary.'

11.

'Where Did You Sleep Last Night?'

A vixen barks from the farmyard. It's dark and I'm properly cold for the first time in weeks. I'm standing on the parquet floor of my grandparents' living room, Sardinian sand in my Clarks shoes. Mum is in the kitchen with our suitcase, arguing with Nanny who says, 'Keep your voice down, Joan.'

Tick-tock, tick-tock, tick-tock says Nanny's mantel clock, while the beeswax from the black furniture and the cow shit from the yard tickle my nose.

I hear the *thud ... thud ... thud* of the rubber end of Grandad's walking stick as he loops the ground-floor corridor. Grandad is a quiet man, he doesn't shout, he shakes and hobbles because of heart attacks and polio which turned one leg thin, and his toes had to come off.

Three weeks is almost a month, and almost a month goes very slowly on a farm without your mother. She's in Ireland. I go to a new school with a red uniform and Nanny feeds me Special K, wheatgerm and hot milk in the morning. She combs knots from my hair, and buys me new shiny red shoes with a band across the front she calls Mary-Janes.

Yesterday I tuned the Bush Radio until I heard the song 'O-o-o It's Magic' by Pilot, but Grandad said, 'Please can I have *The Archers*?' because Grandad is polite. I did find a record player in the polished drinks-cabinet in the room Nanny calls 'the lounge', but no records. There's a piano in there and if Nanny unlocks it, I am allowed to sit and hit out ugly sounds with one finger. Silver frames on the piano top hold photographs of the Beavans of Glascomb, Radnorshire, where Nanny is from; my great-granny Annie Beavan looks just like Mum.

There aren't any new words at my grandparents' farm, I know them all. There are sounds and rhythms, though.

Cah-cah-caaaaaaaah, say the crows.

Ahhh-ahhh, ahhh-ahhh, the gulls in the ploughed furrows laugh.

Cows stand in the fields, milky sacs of calves half-hanging out of them: they say 'uhhhhhh-uhhhhhh-uhhhhhh' but louder and not like Elvis Presley's 'uh-uh, uh-uh' at all.

I love Nanny. I sleep in her eiderdown-ed bed, warmed by airing-cupboard blankets and hot-water bottles. I eat her boiled potatoes and thick chicken gravy. Together we nibble blocks of Rowntree's jelly from the packet in the cold living room, and when she makes blancmange, she doesn't tell me off if I stick my finger in and skim off the orange-cream top. Nanny puts ladybird slides in my hair and presses my nose between her finger and thumb: 'That's better,' she says, but looks disappointed when my nostrils don't stay thin. In the afternoons Nanny talks to the vicar on the phone. She organises salmon luncheons for the church, while Grandad reads the *Western Mail* in his pickup in the yard, one polio leg and his walking stick poking out of the open door. I now wear dresses from Chadds in Hereford, tight across my chest and belly and so short they show my legs: I miss my dungarees. I use up my Save the Whales bubble bath. On my own in the living room I watch *Fingerbobs, Pipkins* and *Rainbow.* In the evenings it's *Morecambe and Wise* and *Planet of the Apes* with Grandad. I miss my mother. I am, as she says, *bored out of my tiny mind.*

Grandad's milk cows split-splat-split out a rhythm with their shit on the floor of the milking stalls. They moan – *uhhh, uhhhh, uhhh* – as machines gobble and *shuuuck-shuuuck-shuuuuuuuck* at their swollen udders. The cows cry for the calves, but the calves have gone.

I can't play with the animals here.

In the backyard barn doors slam in a wind that whistles a tune through the zinc bars of the feeding stalls: it sounds like a giant harmonica. This wind races to the long shed where Mum's things are stored. It flicks the switch of her Kenwood mixer, and the metal blades roar into an empty bowl.

Rrrrraaaaaaaaahhhhhh!

The wind takes its time making her empty wine glasses tinkle-tinkle-clink, while the browned pages of her Elizabeth David's *French Country Cooking* flutter.

When Mum comes back from Ireland, she collects the Kenwood mixer, but I stay with Nanny. 'Let me find my feet,' Mum tells me, and I look down at her high-heeled boots.

It's November and I'm staying at my new red school for the term.

*

There's a tiny door in the corner of one of Nanny's bedrooms (Nanny has every room up here because Grandad can't make the stairs). If you push through this door you come to a narrow but magic room with towers of Chadds of Hereford packages; some are wedding presents Nanny didn't bother to open a million years ago. There are piles of *Woman's Weekly* and *Farmers Weekly* and *Reader's Digest*s, and old black and white photographs of farmers' dances with Nanny perched on the arms of men and elegant sofas. On the back of these photographs, difficult-to-read writing says, 'The handsomest woman in the county' and, 'A fine Horsewoman'.

You must move sideways through the aisles of boxes and packages, and if you switch on the overhead light, you'll see my uncle Brian's tin drum. There's a big dent in the side because one day he twirled it above his head by the strap, faster and faster, and threw it into Mum's face. It bashed out her upper baby teeth and any thoughts of second teeth, too. She said they teased her at boarding school for 'no teeth' until she got a set of new pearly whites on wire. My grandmother also has false teeth; she had her real ones out for her wedding. I bite down: I'm holding onto mine for all I'm worth.

Mum's old blues records are in this secret room. They're stacked in a pile in brown card covers. Some are thicker 78s, with *Musicraft, Paramount, Bluebird, Colombia* and *Capitol* on the pretty labels. Others are a normal size. I think of the Texan man who gave Mum these records and filled a ship with my grandfather's cows and bulls.

I choose two: Howlin' Wolf, 'Smokestack Lightning' and Lead Belly, 'Where Did You Sleep Last Night?'

I pull the Lead Belly out: it is thick, heavy and I put it up to my ear because I don't think that record player in the lounge cabinet will work. All I can hear in this farmhouse is the whispers of the 'To Do' lists that litter Nanny's stair carpet, the bubble of her boiled potatoes in the kitchen beneath me, the scrape-shuffle-scrape-shuffle of Grandad's one polio leg as he gets up to switch on his Bush radio, and it tells us, '… German Bight … two to three and rising'.

I smell chicken gravy.

I look up, and the eyes of my Aunt June's glossy-faced doll click. June died when she was three. Pneumonia. When Nanny takes me to the churchyard, I sneak one or two of June's purple quartz pebbles from her grave, and into my pocket.

This farmhouse is full of ghosts.

Coq O' Vin Tipperary style

Arrive at rehearsal house in Tipperary to a small bare fridge, a small electric cooker and a hungry band. Take the only jalopy car they have and drive along small lanes I don't know in the dark. Worry about the hungry band and no shops. Find a small pub. Go inside. The barman stares because I am wearing a short skirt and what you call my 'rabbit coat'. The barman offers me a half a Guinness. I decline because I must not only find food but buy it and cook it.

'Ah, you'll like my Guinness,' he says but I don't like Guinness. Out of politeness I sip. 'You're English,' he says, and I can't argue. There are no other women in the bar. I ask to use the pub phone. My father answers and I have to talk to your grandmother to get to you. I hate being away from you, but you can't be here, and I must find my feet with something.

The phone call depresses me. I wait an hour. Drink more Guinness. I'm surprised how long it takes to pour. It's like a Béarnaise – you need patience. I'm also surprised by how much I like it now and how kind these men are.

I take off the rabbit coat. Test the room. Wait another hour.

The bar is full now and the men here have been dreadfully kind. I have two unplucked, full-headed, clawed chickens in greaseproof paper, a slab of farm bacon, a bag of onions, carrots, potatoes and a bottle of cheap white. I am also pissed as a fart. I haven't laughed this much for a long time. I love the black stuff now and I promise to cook beef in it for everyone here. The barman drives me back to the rehearsal house without me giving directions because everyone at the pub knew as soon as I stepped in that I was 'with the Horslips up there'. I have absolutely no idea where 'up there' is and certainly not now I have drunk my body weight in Guinness. I know the record company are paying me to feed these men because these men like my food. I am unsure if I have the shopping under control, but I clutch the feathery chickens in the front seat and ask the barman if he has any herbs, particularly thyme, and he laughs, and I think he promises a delivery of beef tomorrow. I owe him because I only have English money. Again, this shouldn't concern me as I am unsure if I will be alive tomorrow: Guinness is stronger than I thought.

Rest for ten minutes in the passenger seat.

When we get to the dark house, I say goodbye to the barman but it's hard to get the words out. He promises to drop my car back tomorrow. The band are making their noise in the main room, and I slam the limp chickens on the kitchen table, chop off their heads and drink a glass of water.

I set to plucking; it's something I enjoy. I am drunk but I am a farmer's daughter. Thank God I brought my Sabatier knife, garlic, oh, and I did bring herbs and the rock salt.

Peel and wash potatoes, find a pot in the damp cupboards.

Horslips' producer, Fritz Fryer, comes in and insists on calling it 'Coq O' Vin'. He has to explain the joke to me.

Horslips Coq O' Vin

2 *Tipperary farmhouse chickens (more like capons with nice yellow flesh; pluck, dress, remember the gizzards, cut into 8 pieces)*

bag of onions (silverskin onions best but take what you are given)

farm bacon (the best bacon I've seen in years)

bag of carrots (which I shouldn't really put in a coq au vin or a coq o' vin but I am pissed)

garlic

bottle of white wine (of course it should be a red Burgundy but there isn't any)

bag of potatoes. They do not belong in coq au vin.

Cut up thick, fatty bacon in small pieces, cook. Add onions until translucent. Remove, leaving fat.

In another bowl, flour chicken (really well) with added s/p. Fry in bacon fat, get a good colour on it, transfer everything to a casserole.

Onion/bacon/chicken add wine, and carrots if you must.

Drink more water. Make coffee. There is only awful instant.

Maybe I do the potatoes separately.

The saving grace is 30 mins before the end, I remove some of the juice from the 'coq o' vin' in a saucepan, boil it up and add port. Taste … taste. It's too sweet. I flame it with brandy (sorry boys, your brandy). That makes all the difference, there's depth to the sauce.

I taught myself these tricks cooking on a charter yacht in Malta. '67 I think?

Maybe it is a disaster fund. I am still rather pissed.

It isn't a disaster fund. The band love it.

The next morning when it's hard to open my eyes, or walk, or breathe, the publican arrives with a great side of beef that won't fit in the small kitchen oven. I set about hacking it up at the kitchen table. I make a promise to call you, Tiff, from the pub phone later, and to save the bones for the irritating hopping, black and white dog, Boggle.

When I leave Ireland, I go straight to Rockfield Studios in Wales. Kingsley Ward rang me up and said they wanted a cordon bleu chef, bands from the Vicarage who went on to record at Rockfield raved about my food. I drive to the studios to sit at the farmhouse table with both brothers, Kingsley and Charles, and their mother. I didn't realise it was an interview.

At her farmhouse kitchen table Mother Ward says, 'She'll do, boys.'

I tell them, *Yes, OK, but I work for myself.*

You are spoilt by your grandmother for a little longer. You weren't far away, Tiff, and I had every Saturday night off with you. I did think, *Can I even bring a child to a recording studio?*

Part 2

This Is How It Was

Living at Rockfield Studios

1974–1976

We recorded the first Headstone album at Rockfield Studios, which is really nice. It's beautiful there, the whole environment is really ideal. They've got a lot of little things – like a Cordon Bleu chef laid on, and Charles and Kingsley Ward are fantastic. They have a small 16-track studio which is ideal for small line-ups, it has a really good, funky sound. I think 24 tracks can complicate things unnecessarily – after all, a lot of the Beatles' stuff was done on eight-track.

Mark Ashton from Headstone,
International Musician and Recording World

Set List

'How Long', Ace
Subtle as a Flying Mallet, Dave Edmunds
Futurama, Be-Bop Deluxe
'After the Gold Rush', Prelude
Warrior on the Edge of Time, Hawkwind
On Parole, Motörhead
The Unfortunate Cup of Tea, Horslips
Down by the Jetty, Dr Feelgood
Sad Wings of Destiny, Judas Priest
Nadir's Big Chance, Peter Hammill
'Bohemian Rhapsody', Queen
Cordon Bleu, Solution
Global Village Trucking Company, Global Village Trucking Company
Play Loud, Hustler
Godbluff, Van der Graaf Generator
Bandolier, Budgie
'Three Steps to Heaven', Showaddywaddy
'We Can Take You There', Hobo
'Wide Eyed and Legless', Andy Fairweather Low
The Fish, Barry Melton
Back to the Night, Joan Armatrading
'(What's so Funny 'Bout) Peace, Love, and Understanding?', Brinsley Schwarz
Open Door, Kieran White
Shake Some Action, Flamin' Groovies

12.

Hawkwind and The Trolley, Rockfield Studios, 1975

Rockfield, March to April 1975
HAWKWIND trucks Friday 11am. Band to follow. Dave Brock producing, Dave Charles engineer. Budgie in, Pat Moran to engineer. Fix ballcock in chalet 3. Be Bop Deluxe (Bill Nelson) in with producer Roy Thomas Baker. Pete Akin producing himself. Half Breed producing themselves, Dave Charles engineer. First and second early spuds in. Charles to complete acoustic wall boards. Four cows calving.

Rockfield Studios is a kingdom. There's 'The Quadrangle', with chalets, stables, echo chambers and Studio One; above it is the bungalow and the barn. Halfway down the track from the bungalow is Bampi and Nana Ward's big house attached to the Coach House Studio (or Studio Two). Opposite Studio Two is the Lodge, pretty and pointy as a gingerbread house. Little Ancre is the white farmhouse over the main road, and sharp up the opposite hill. The Old Mill, where bands rehearse and Ozzy and Black Sabbath go fishing, shoot guns and play darts, is about two miles down the road. It's a lot. There's also the duck pond, and fields all the way to Monmouth.

There are two kings of Rockfield: Kingsley Ward and Charles Ward. Kingsley drives a Rolls Royce on the farm tracks; Charles has a shock of yellow hair like Struwwelpeter, but they both sing Elvis songs. The queens of Rockfield are Ann and Sandra. They have five children and two dogs between them. Rockfield Studios is the best thing in the whole world since my Sardinia-burned shoulders stopped peeling under Nanny's Welsh woollen blankets.

I came to Rockfield too late. I missed David Cassidy. On the David Cassidy day, the Rockfield kids – Amanda, Young

Charles, Lisa, Corrina and Brigitte – didn't go to school. Instead, they showed him the horses. They told their teachers David drove from Heathrow and his car broke down on their drive, so they *had* to give him a nice show. In the photograph David is wearing a sunhat and patchwork jeans; his shirt is open to his golden necklace and he's leaning on Peter Pan the white horse. Peter Pan is leaning away – maybe he doesn't like 'How Can I Be Sure?', or 'Daydreamer'. Lisa is on top of Peter Pan and so close to David Cassidy she could reach forward and touch his hair. I've never been jealous of a photograph, but I want to jump into this one. I asked Charles Ward, one of the kings of Rockfield, if David Cassidy would come back, or if Donny Osmond, or David Essex or the Bay City Rollers, or even Jimmy Osmond would visit. He laughed and walked off, his hair bouncing in the wind.

I have been here long enough to know the best place to play 'The Trolley' is in front of the top bungalow. It's not raining today but if we pitch down the Rockfield track we can still splash through puddles and scream.

We must get the timing right on our red-wheeled trolley. If we jump on too soon, we'll grind it to a gravel-stop. Leave it too late, and the trolley will bounce empty and fast down the hill to crash against the wall of Studio Two, beneath the black horse weathervane. There might be a little bend in the steering bar after that.

The other thing with the trolley is me. We must all fit on, and the Rockfield kids were a five, but now I live here, it's a tight six.

'Come on, Tiff,' Lisa says. Lisa is eight, a year older than me, and she's the wisest of us all.

I'm not sure about the name for our thrill ride: 'The Trolley'. Even the bands here give things proper names. Studio One's tape machine is 'Doris', so we should have a name for *our* beloved plaything. *Speedy Gonzales*, I think, but I don't say anything. Not yet. I'm new. When we first arrived, Mum told me, 'Take it easy, Tiff, don't be your usual bossy self with the Rockfield kids.' She shivered in a thin kaftan in the wet morning of the Quadrangle courtyard, because that is where we live now, with the bands. She was peering into car windows, checking for keys in ignitions to drive me to my new school, Overmonnow Primary, because the Beach Buggy's wheels were finally killed in the trenches of the Rockfield track. She picked a manager's Range Rover. 'He won't mind, darling.'

We line the trolley up in front of Hawkwind's bungalow. I think it's Hawkwind, but maybe it's Budgie or Be-Bop Deluxe or Half Breed. There are so many places to sleep at Rockfield. Mum speaks the bands' names in the Quadrangle kitchen as she cooks, but I like to mix them up:

Be-Bop Deluxe Budgie
Half Breed Hawkwind

Lisa has the steering bar in her grip because, once we push off, the trolley has a life of its own. She says, 'You get on first, 'Manda. Then Tiff, then Young Charles, then me. Corrina and Brigitte last.' It's right we jump on by age and size. Amanda's skinny six followed by my seven is lighter than Corrina's cool eleven and Brigitte's elegant twelve. I'm lucky Brigitte and Corrina even play with me.

'Hold on properly, 'Manda,' Lisa says because Amanda is her little sister. 'One ...'

We join in, 'TWO ...'

We're measuring the direction with one eye open, one eye closed. We are experts even if our bruises don't agree. We take a deep collective breath.

'THREEEEEEEEEEE!'

We push and the trolley wheels turn. Potholes catch, we strain, but with the force of six, we're moving. We run, wellies dragging. Amanda bounces on the flat bed of the trolley, light as my favourite pudding, Angel Delight.

'Pothole!' I shout, and we swerve. We're a single brain, a manoeuvring shark heading down the Rockfield track, faster, faster.

'Tiff and Young Charles jump!' Lisa shouts, and I hit my leg on the metal side, but I can't rub it away. Young Charles jumps with me – he's seven, too – then Lisa's on, and she steers the big iron bar at the front. I help her and hold onto it. We're wet jumpers and the spray of muddy puddles as we scream past the Quadrangle turn. My teeth rattle, and if Corrina and Brigitte aren't quick, they'll miss the ride. We laugh at the thuds because potholes are the best part if you don't go *arse over tit* as Mum calls it. Corrina leaps on. Brigitte really needs to, but she keeps pushing us and running, maybe because she's the oldest. We're past the black horse weathervane and, at last, she jumps. We jerk the steering bar to turn sharp left by Studio Two, because we don't want to rattle down to the main road where the cars speed to Monmouth, but the trolley's too fast and the wheels screech and the steering clunks and we skid as we turn, and we tip and crash into the wall.

The trolley has thrown us off. We thump
on
top
of
each
other
in welly-rubber and wet wool.

Hawkwind are sitting on the five-bar gate in the drizzle. They look down at the pile of us and Lemmy says, 'You doing that again?'

Later, roadies come out and take our trolley away.

'It's for the gear,' one of them says, and they load Marshall amps and giant black hat boxes for drums onto our trolley's chipboard top. I know we'll steal her back by teatime.

There are so many new words here:

Studer
24-track tape
Doris
Playback
Local fader
Bass sustain
Motherboard
Pedal legato
Spiral Galaxy 28948

Gymkhana
Live room
The Trolley
Grandmaster
Control room
Threshing machine

I *am* beginning to understand: Rockfield is a farm with rock 'n' roll and my mother is the cordon bleu chef. In the Quadrangle kitchen she plays 'That Ain't the Way to Behave' by Dr Feelgood, and 'How Long' by Ace, because she fed these songs. In our chalet (which she calls a converted stable) she keeps live shellfish in the bath, and they spit at me when I'm on the loo. Charles and Kingsley Ward sit at motherboards in control rooms to make magic songs in their wellies, because they also milk cows and make golden bales of hay from fields of grass with an old tractor. Charles and Kingsley talk so fast it's a new language: I stare up at them, fascinated, but I can't keep up. There are horses and cows and sheep and The Trolley at Rockfield, and although managers and record labels call the two studios 'the Quadrangle' and 'the Coach House', we say, 'Studio One' and 'Studio Two'. Bampi Ward is building wigwam canes for his runner beans and Nana Ward bakes cakes for us with butter cream. Nick Lowe and Dave Edmunds walk the tracks as big trucks filled with instruments and amps turn in the yard, and even though the Old Mill is a drive away, when the wind blows, I'm sure I can hear Black Sabbath rehearse.

Nanny refuses to visit.

At Rockfield my night sounds are back, but they are *so* much louder: the *doof-dah-dah, doof-dah-dah* of drums, the high whine of electric guitar; and now there's the *whhhhheeeee-*

whhhhheeee-wheeeeeee splicing rewind of a machine called Doris. I do miss lying next to my grandmother in her quiet bed, warmed by hot-water bottles, but I think I love Rockfield.

Mum and I are safe here; even if Hawkwind throw open the double doors of the studio in the middle of the night and wake me with 'The Wizard Blew His Horn'.

It's my lullaby.

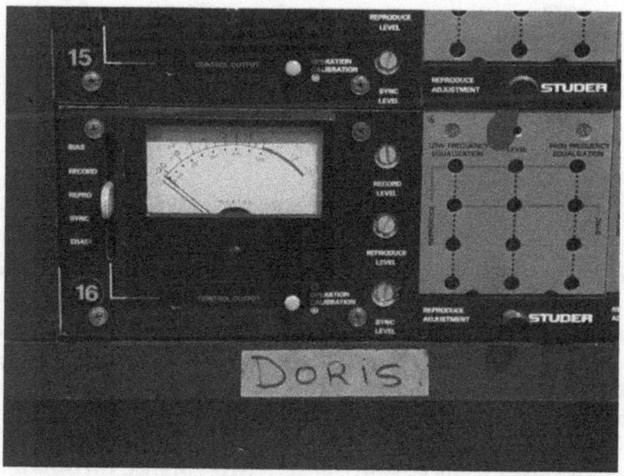

13.

Futurama in Joan's Kitchen, 1975

Joan's Menu

Gourmet Menu

One of Joan's fortes could well be your starter – paté, for which her renown stretches far beyond the confines of Rockfield Studios. Restaurateurs and Delicatessen owners in surrounding counties have hounded her for the secret of her delicious terrines and patés. Or, you could start with lasagne or spaghetti – so much better than many better-class Italian restaurants. Or, (this is a killer with everyone!) sweet and sour spare ribs using a much meatier cut of pork – typical of Joan's way of working, no expense is spared as far as she's concerned! Try the Boeuf en Croute with Madeira sauce, Barbary duck with gooseberry sauce, monkfish and tomato, slow roasted crispy belly pork, or vegetarian options. Joan loves a good Pavlova and bands die for her crêpes Suzette and her lemon meringue pie. Joan makes her own chocolates. No After Eights in the Rockfield dining room!

Cheapo Menu

This could start with a home-made (as is everything!) soup, which is so good that many people have been known to O.D. on it so much, they never made the main course. If you do make that stage, you could be faced with T-bone steak from Hereford's most reputed butcher (and you can't get better beef than that!) or Welsh spring lamb – there again, the world's finest, and accompanied with the best of the freshest vegetables available according to the season. This year, Joan has decided to grow her own veg. Her aubergines would win best at the Royal Welsh Show! Puddings are uncomplicated apple and blackberry crumble with custard, and the odd trifle, just like your mums or your grandmothers make.

Mum says the musicians here are as likely to O.D. on her leek and potato soup as anything else. In the Quadrangle kitchen I stand on my upturned milk crate to wash potatoes and stare out at the fields. I don't know if this is the same upturned milk crate I had at the Vicarage but I don't want to check for Cleo's chew marks; it makes me sad, where everything else at Rockfield makes me happy. I plunge my hands in the dirty water while Mum puts the potatoes in a sandpaper bowl; a big steel claw reaches in, churns and shreds the brown skins away.

The Rockfield kitchen is warm and oblong, and it smells of butter and Mum's Yves Saint Laurent. The tiles on the floor are red, the cupboards are baby-blue, and Mum calls the countertops *Formica*. She's not keen on the small electric oven, but it does have four top burners that glow to spirals. Her Kenwood Chef is here, her Sabatier knife and her meat grinder. It's strange to see these familiar things in this new place; that is until Mum laughs, barks commands over bubbling pans and turns up her cassette player so we all hear Howlin' Wolf. Then it feels like we've been here for ever.

There is one door, and it leads to the dining room where the bands eat. They are only three red tiles away. They can hear us, and we can hear them.

I guard the door when Mum is cooking.

'You can't come in,' I say to bug-eyed lead singers. They look down, confused.

If they ignore me, it's Mum who says, *Could you wait? It won't be long.* Or: *please piss off, I'm working.* Or: *stop picking and wait for your meal.* It depends on the musician, the band, the manager, the producer: it depends on how much the record company is paying her.

'What do we have tonight, Joan?' they'll ask from the threshold.

'Crudities, pea and ham hock soup, boeuf en croute, lemon cheesecake.'

'What's the grub, Joan?'

'Pâté, moussaka, syllabub.'

'What have we got then, Joan?'

'Please get out of my kitchen!'

Mum puts up with a lot in the Rockfield kitchen, and Sandra Ward helps her with this. Sandra is Brigitte and Corrina's mum, and I can't get enough of her. When you make Sandra laugh, you'll see dimples high on her cheeks. She wears black pencil skirts with colourful jumpers, and sometimes long gold earrings that chime. Sandra's hair is dark, her skin shines, and if I fall into her body, she catches me at hip height and she's soft and warm.

'What are you up to, girl?' she laughs and it's a bubbling sound that rises to a trill until the whole room is laughing, too.

Sandra and Mum laugh and share bottles of white and red together. Sandra leans into Mum and giggles, 'Oh, there's no one like you, Joan.' She also calms Mum down if a band is stroppy. 'Don't worry, they'll be gone by Sunday!'

If Rockfield is a kingdom, the kitchen is Mum's queendom, and like any queen she has rules for the bands:

1. Please don't knock at my chalet door in the middle of the night and tell me you want a bacon sandwich. There's proper bread, cheese, Rockfield eggs, butcher sausages and bacon in the kitchen. Help yourself. I have left cocoa out on the stove.
2. No barging into the kitchen and chatting me up when I'm up to my elbows in duck fat. And don't grab the cook's tits from behind. Remember I have a burning Café Crème cigar in my hand, and I know how to use it.
3. Please don't stand over the cooker, stick your fingers in a sauce and say, 'when will it be ready?' Also, you can't say you 'don't like it' if you have never tried 'it'.

4. Attention bands in Studio One and Studio Two, stop the rivalry food fights! Sandra and I are sick of wiping Eton mess and salmon en croute from the studio walls. If you must, do it in the courtyard. Keep it off the motherboards, please!
5. Attention bands and roadies from Studio Two! I cook for you only if your label or manager is paying me. If they're not don't creep up the track in the night and steal food from my fridge. If you want something, ASK. I'm generous.
6. No complaining about piddly things like a matchstick in the Coq au Vin. Yes, I'm looking at you, Wilko Johnson.
7. There WILL be a polite knock at the door. There WILL be a 'hello, Joan'. There WILL be a chink of glasses, and a round of applause when the chef brings out the crêpes Suzette because this is my performance. Thank you.
8. And look, let's be honest, do what you want, I can't stop you.

I see Studio Two roadies follow Mum's new brown MGB GT up the Rockfield track like farm collies, the chains and keys that hang from their belts and jeans jingle-jangling. In the Quadrangle they'll stand at her car boot and insist on helping with the shopping. They carry it in. They'd carry her if she asked because she'll give them a tray of roast potatoes, half a golden syrup ham, in return. 'Cheers, Joan!' they'll say.

At night, though, the roadies give in to temptation. They seek the scent and run up here, snuffling, slobbering, maybe even panting and howling, until they stalk into her night kitchen and steal her adapted Robert Carrier-recipe terrine.

The bands in Studio One can choose from a menu in advance. They sit at the pine table with benches either side. Mum says, *they look like schoolboys* when they bunch up together; but the bands are still men, although some of them are American now. Mum feeds Be-Bop Deluxe, Hustler, Dr Feelgood, Ace, Peter Hamill, Flamin' Groovies, Kieran White, Van der Graaf Generator, and Peter Gabriel when he stayed for a night. I garnish and serve to a room full of man-noise and smoke sweet as chewed Rolos. Sometimes the room sounds of nothing but eating; perhaps they are sick of noise, perhaps they have earache, like me. When they've finished, they say, 'Thank you very much, Joan', or sometimes nothing at all because they're not interested in the food. 'And why should they be?' Mum says, but she slams plates in the sink.

'Tiff, change out of your school clothes, you're getting mucky.'

My school clothes are just my clean clothes, but I run out of the kitchen, around the tight dining-room corner, and down the three steps to the outside door. I'm under the awning of the flagstone walkway that runs along the studio on one side, and 'the chalets' on the other. That's what Sandra calls where we live with the bands, 'the chalets'. Mum said, 'They don't look very Swiss,' and Sandra laughed with an 'Oh, Joan.' The chalets are all in a line. They're 'open-plan', and Mum and I share one upstairs bedroom because I refused to stay on the single bed under the stairs (even when she and Sandra thumb-tacked my Bay City Rollers poster next to a shelf for my books).

'For Chrissakes, child,' Mum said, because she had to ask an engineer and a producer to drag my heavy single bed upstairs.

The Rockfield horses nod from their stables across the yard as Budgie's playback screams from the open double doors of Studio One. Budgie the band are playing football in the courtyard. They're Welsh like Nanny, and we're in Wales. American bands play Frisbee; British ones kick footballs and ask for balloons for waterbombs. Charles and Kingsley Ward and the Rockfield engineers have regular football matches with the bands, but they have to tell the Americans not to pick up the ball. I skip along the flagstones, keeping time to the heavy crunch of Budgie's guitars.

'Goal!' Budgie yell from the yard as their ball hits the slate roof and their playback shouts about 'Breaking all the House Rules'.

Corrina and Brigitte are at my door. It's usually me following them around the Rockfield tracks in my red wellies. I love playing with Lisa and Amanda, and clearing out the chicken shed with Young Charles, but I've attached myself to Brigitte and Corrina; *like some orphaned cat*, Mum says. Last night I slept in their bedroom because Mum's new boyfriend, Kieran, stayed with her. I listened to their records, and gazed at the cover of Corrina's *Diamond Dogs* trying to find the Frankenstein's-monster stitches that make David Bowie a beautiful hound.

'Do you want to come and play, girl?' Corrina asks. She has dark hair like Sandra. Brigitte is fair like her dad.

'I'm helping Mum.'

'Can we help too?'

The sisters love Mum's kitchen. We serve the bands together, and when they're with Mum and Sandra, the noise might be louder than Budgie or Hawkwind's playback. They laugh high and hard and hold onto one another. 'Stop it! I'll pee myself!' Mum says.

'Oh, Joan,' Sandra laughs, and although I don't always understand what's funny, I try to join in.

I'm in new dungarees, I've grown. Mum's tape player is on the kitchen windowsill. She's playing 'Walk on the Wild Side' and we join in with the chorus, *do, do-do, do-do*. Brigitte dances and I want her Suzi Quatro hair flicks. Corrina chops while I go out to lay the long table and stick burgundy paper napkins in the wine glasses. I try to remember the right way round for the knife and fork while I mouth my new words:

Brinsley Schwarz
Van der Graaf Generator
Dolby SR
Self-employed
Self-sufficient
Ludwig
Bridle
Pat Moran
Napoleon Bona-Part One
Napoleon Bona-Part Two
Down by the Jetty
Syllabub
Stirrup
Fairweather-Low

In the kitchen Corrina is talking about a boy she likes. I hear the word 'fancy'. Corrina is my idol because she laughs with a rising trill just like her mum. I run back in; Sandra is smiling but wagging her finger. I see the high dimples on her cheeks.

'Oh, men!' Mum laughs, and they all laugh together, and I try to think what to say about men, but I prefer dogs.

'I fancy Nick Lowe,' I tell them.

They stop what they're doing and look at me. Onions spit from the cooker.

'Don't be ridiculous, Tiff,' Mum says.

'I do.'

'Don't be silly. Go and finish the table.'

Corrina laughs but it's a nice laugh and she winks at me. I'm not sure what 'fancy' means exactly, but I like staring up at Nick Lowe because he's so tall and friendly and he looks like a bird of prey. And I like the song '(What's So Funny 'Bout) Peace, Love, and Understanding?' I go back in the dining room to straighten my untidy cutlery and Kieran is there; Mum's soft-spoken, blond-bearded boyfriend. The blond is almost white above his top lip. He walks into the kitchen without knocking and soon comes out with a plate of food.

I hear, '*Ohhhhhhhhhh, Joooooan*!' from Sandra.

Kieran smiles at me, blushes and leaves.

Something damp is pressing on my lower leg; it scratches past me. It's Boggle's fat and wet stick. Boggle likes to carry a big stick into the kitchen and ram my mother in the back of her knee joint. Sometimes she falls over.

'Get that fucking dog out of here!' she yells.

Boggle is here because Fritz Fryer comes to Rockfield to produce, engineer and mix (I'm learning the words). Kingsley says the best thing Fritz has done in the studio is a song called 'After the Goldrush'. Fritz carries around a hammer and a spanner when he's producing because he can fix things, too. 'It's all hands on deck at Rockfield!' he told me. Fritz is here then he's gone, and I don't see Boggle for weeks.

Our faces are bright red because serving and cooking are over. I love the busy rush of it as Mum says, 'Plate, plate! No, use the oven glove!'

Corrina is at the sink; Brigitte is drying. Mum and Sandra have gone out into the night to get rid of a disaster fund. Mum burnt the boeuf bourguignon; she and Sandra were too busy chatting and laughing. 'A cardinal cooking sin, never leave food unwatched!' Mum said.

This is why tonight was, 'Improvise, Joan, bloody improvise!' The band didn't notice the menu change to sirloin steak and wild mushrooms, and now I'm watching Mum and Sandra under the outside light ladling burnt beef into the bin. A man is talking to them. I sneak closer. 'Don't throw that away, Joan,' he's saying.

Sandra trills her laugh.

Mum steps back. 'Don't be ridiculous. It's burnt.'

The man sticks his hand in the bin, then he's putting his fingers to his mouth. 'That tastes all right to me, Joan.'

'Don't eat it from the bin!'

'But your food's so lovely.'

'Oh, flattery will get you nowhere.'

Sandra's laughing so hard she holds onto the stone wall. The man starts laughing, too. He's a roadie with Judas Priest or whoever is down at Studio Two. He's on the prowl for Mum's leftovers.

'Give us the rest of the stew, will you, Joan?'

She holds onto the pot. 'Absolutely not. I burned it!'

'The boys'll love it.'

I picture Judas Priest eating burnt boeuf bourguignon from the bin, like Top Cat does with a knife and fork and a napkin tucked into his collar.

'Look,' Mum says, 'at least take the bloody pan, but I want it back. Washed.'

'Joan, you're a lifesaver.' He starts scooping up boeuf bourguignon with his hands, back into the pot.

'You'll give them food poisoning. Stop, use this ladle!'

'You're a diamond, Joan.'

Sandra squeals with laughter.

'Look,' Mum tells the roadie, 'next time you want my leftover food, just ask.'

He doesn't look up from his ladling. He's making the most of his chance.

'But if you steal anything from my fridge without asking, you'll have me to deal with.'

'Understood.'

'And you can help us with the bins tomorrow night.'

'Yes, Joan.'

Sandra's giggles echo across the fields. The Rockfield night smells of sweet, burnt meat.

I was falling asleep at the dining-room table, so Mum carried me to bed in our chalet. I can hear her and Sandra laughing out in the courtyard. Maybe they'll go into the studio with the band, or back into the kitchen. I tuck Ozzy's rock 'n' roll dog puppet into my blanket and watch drizzle hit the roof window by Mum's bed. Her Biba and Bus Stop dresses hang from the back of a brown chair: even from there they smell of the kitchen, her perfume, her Café Crèmes.

I listen to the night settle, as much as it can here. Rockfield is home now, even if it isn't mine.

When I lived with Nanny, she taught me to pray; she'd ask me to kneel with her at the pink linen box in her pink bathroom. She pressed her thumbs to her forehead and prayed for her darling, departed baby daughter, June, while I prayed for Cleo. Now I have my own prayer:

Dear Holy Hawkwind and Beep-Bop Deluxe. Dear Peter Hamill, Kieran White, Brinsley Schwarz, Hobo, Solution, Budgie, Judas Priest, Flamin' Groovies, Black Sabbath, Nick Lowe, Ace, Arthur Brown, Van der Graaf Generator, and the Holy of Holies Dave Edmunds, please make me a Ward of Rockfield not a Murray, Amen.

The Rockfield horses neigh. When the doors of Studio One crash open, my lullaby of heavy-metal guitar pours out, and I am asleep in seconds.

Sunday Lunch Like Their Grannies Used to Make

I'd drive to Pritchards in Hereford for a couple of big sirloin joints plus extra fat for the Yorkshires and roast potatoes. In those days joints had good fat on them, so you didn't need to add a lot of oil to the baking pan.

It started with, 'we hate fish, we hate garlic, never had that, it looks funny, don't like it, where are the chips?' Don't get me wrong, I love chips, but Rockfield wouldn't let me have a deep fat fryer. 'Too dangerous' they said, which made me laugh. I mean, they had a lethal old clay pigeon trap and shotguns which Black Sabbath loved. Anyway, by the end of the recording sessions bands would be eating my homemade taramasalata. I suppose I educated them about food, and they educated me about music. I'd often be invited into the studio to listen, not that I ever knew what to say when the bands asked, 'So, what do you think, Joan?'

This was Britain in the mid-1970s: we'd only just discovered prawn cocktail. Some bands knew a lot about food – Queen, Rush, Graham Parker and the Rumour, Solution, Horslips, Ian Gillan – but most of them had little idea. Why should they? They were young boys who'd spent their years since school out on the road, living on takeaways and greasy spoon cafes. They'd know about the British version of Chinese or Indian food. They'd know about a full English, but they wouldn't know about the food I wanted to give them.

I told them boeuf bourguignon was steak and kidney pie without the kidney or the pie. I'd make roast chicken and curries at the beginning of the week. Then I'd push harder: Barbary duck, roast belly pork. I learned the hard way to suit the menu to the band; I mean there's no point in slaving over a bouillabaisse for Motörhead. The thing you forget is how young the bands were. They loved beef and chicken, not so keen on lamb, hated pheasant. Surprisingly, loved guinea fowl.

My bases were Elizabeth David, Robert Carrier, *The Poor Cook* and, yes, Johnnie and Fanny Cradock, then I improvised. I'm not great at following recipes and I had total freedom in the Rockfield kitchen. I loved the bands who wanted to experiment with new food. They taught me, too, particularly the vegetarians, a rare breed in 1975, apart from the folk lot. The producer John Anthony was wonderful and showed me different vegetarian dishes. Returning bands would come into the kitchen and beg for their favourites: 'Please, Joan, could we have the duck again?'

Weekends were a free-for-all. Girlfriends, wives, record company execs, managers, the whole lot came down to our patch of South Wales. I had to think quick, and big. Saturday lunchtime I'd lay out a huge buffet. Glazed baked ham, a whole poached salmon, sticky spare ribs, asparagus and parmesan in season, home-made mayonnaise, loads of salads, and a suckling pig. We'd wrap that in an electric blanket to keep it warm, and a few bands freaked because it looked like a pig. I'd have to take it back to the kitchen, chop its head off and cut the body into sections. They gobbled it up after that. I mean, Rockfield was a farm – maybe some of them learned where meat comes from?

I was the run-around chef. Sandra and I would pack it all in the car and rush from one place to the other. Some nights I'd cook for bands in Studio One, the Old Mill, *and* for bands in Studio Two if they lived up at the white farmhouse, Little Ancre. Do you remember Little Ancre Hill? You'd have to first gear it all the way up and get bashed by tree branches in the dark. How the hell did I have the energy? The milking parlour was up at Little Ancre. Dear Grandpa Ward – Cyril – and Charles and Kingsley trudged up there to milk the herd morning and evening. Sometimes they'd drag a band up to help, and the churns would be at the bottom of the hill for us all.

I'd ask the producers about timing because you can't leave a take if you're in the studio. If they were a band who'd get up at lunchtime and work through the night, I'd do lasagne, chicken curry, chilli con carne, and show them how to warm it up; but most ate it cold. Yes, some bands would wake me up in the middle of the night to make them a sandwich, but they'd only do it once. Sandra was much better. 'Ah, come on, Joan,' she'd say. She was so good with the bands. I had to be careful because I lived in the Quadrangle with them. I had to draw the line somewhere. But I had my fun. Stop asking.

I had *so* much fun with Sandra, and young Dena who I took on later: Dena was a wonderful, calming presence. And we'd *all* go to the pub after clearing up and you would sleep in the back of the car. I felt alive again.

Richard Branson's Manor Studios did ask me to be their chef. I drove over to Oxfordshire, and it was rather posh, less of a farm. But I loved Rockfield, and I couldn't move you from another school. You adored going in every morning with Lisa.

sirloin joints
garlic, about 6 cloves, probably more
dijon mustard (optional)
fresh thyme (optional)

potatoes, lots, peeled and chopped and into cold water to boil
flour
red wine
peas

Stab the joint with garlic, about 6 cloves and salt and pepper. Depending on the band I'd rub with Dijon and fresh thyme. Nothing but the beef in the pan, at 450F in the Rockfield temperamental electric oven for 20/30 minutes to brown the fat.

Baste, then down to 375F for the rest of the time. About 15 minutes per lb. Should be brown crispy fat but fairly pink in the middle.

I fought at the beginning and made it rare. Bands complained so I said, 'There's a frying pan, cook it how you want it.' Then I thought, *Oh God, Joan, come on,* and I kept the joints in for longer until the ends were well done and the middles medium. Compromise.

Rest the meat for 20 mins. I'd cover in silver foil and a tea towel.

While beef cooking, parboil potatoes, about 15 mins salted water, drain, keep back water, and fluff. In those days you always had beef dripping in your pantry so beef fat only on tray in oven at high heat, take out and add potatoes. Shake, salt them. Back in 30/40 minutes but watch and turn. You want them crispy all over.

To make the gravy, use the pan juices (that Herefordian fat), add flour, the boiled potato water, red wine, Dijon mustard. Too much fat? Kitchen paper it off the top.

Serve with peas. They loved peas.

14.

The Unfortunate Cup of Tea

Rockfield, April 1975

FRITZ FRYER to produce and engineer Horslips. Fritz down from London with Boggle Wednesday. Band driving from ferry on Friday with two trucks. (Fritz has asked for orchestra for two days recording, he'll sort it). Kieran White will finish Open Door *with Dave Charles and Donal Lunny. Tell Joan. Sandra change overs. Work on echo chamber. Farrier in. Kingsley London meetings, United Artists. Fertilise grazing fields.*

If Rockfield is a kingdom, sometimes it's hard to find my mother. Is she in the Quadrangle kitchen or down in the stinky darkness of Studio Two listening to new songs with a new band? Has she driven her food, first-gear and fast, up Little Ancre hill? Or is she down at the Old Mill, melting herb butter on Ozzy Osbourne's fillet steak?

It's raining and the middle of the night. I woke because my earache crunches. I've taken Mum's clothes off the brown chair and I'm standing on it, head and shoulders out of the roof window. The Quadrangle is so wide in the daytime I've seen sparrowhawks swoop and echo; but in this dark the white horses, April and Peter Pan, whinny from stables to the sound of an electric fiddle. A new band arrived at Rockfield tonight. I think this place is *The Elves and the Shoemaker* because the work gets done while I sleep. Rusty, the red horse, nods his big head under the outside light. I wave and my muscles are still warm from playing all day with Lisa and Amanda. I watched them ride Orinoco the little bay and April in the lower field. I haven't found the courage to do that yet, so I jump the jumps myself.

Rain rattles gutters; gushes down pipes. I'm getting wet. I think about the song that was made here, 'How Long' and the rain at Rockfield. *Hoow loong …?* The deep mud has turned sheep in the fields into giant red Labradors. I go on tiptoes to watch two men trailing cables across the courtyard as pain in my ear stabs, gluey.

Once they're done with the cables, they talk over a horse trough. The outside light throws their shadows out like a horror film. I know horror films because I watch them at the Lodge with Brigitte and Corrina. I love the thrill of hiding my head under a wool blanket as Christopher Lee hisses through blood-red vampire teeth, or David Warner gets trapped in a haunted mirror.

A flute plays over the running water. The sound echoes around the courtyard: it's so pretty against the rain. For a second the pain in my ear doesn't burn. Mum has no patience with my ear infections; she says nothing will change unless I *desist from* sticking my fingers in my ears after sticking them in dogs and horses and chickens.

The watery flute stops; the men go back to talking.

'Play it like that again, Jim, over the water.'

Rusty the horse whinnies.

'Shit. Start again.'

I cup my hand over my bad ear like the men in the live room do when they sing harmonies. I want to hear the flute again, but the studio doors open, and a blast of playback wakes the night. It sounds like a burping monster, then a guitar and drums start up and I hear the singer telling me about creeping through the night before a chorus sings 'High Volume Love!' The horses kick metal shoes on their stable doors and I wiggle-dance from my chair.

'High Volume Love!'

Thud-thud, kick-kick.

'High Volume Love!'

The two men over the horse trough have gone. My ear

crackles and hums. I hear a penny whistle. I know these voices.

I jump off my chair.

In my nightie and wellies, I catch my breath in the courtyard. I've one hand stuffed up my rock 'n' roll dog puppet. 'My ear hurts,' I tell him, and I pull the cord on the stick that pokes out of his back. His muzzle moves, but I can't think of any words to give him.

I hear the penny whistle again, and the backs of my wellies drag through rocky puddles as I run to it. I try not to think of the Pied Piper.

Children are not allowed in either studio unless we've been dragged in to sing a chorus. There are only two other Rockfield rules:

NO DEEP FAT FRYER
PLEASE DON'T FEED THE HORSES

But my excuse is I have a bad ear, so I reach up and pull the main studio door with all my might until I'm standing on the inside parquet-floor corridor. The door sucks closed behind me: it's pitch black and smells of damp and fags and man. I take a deep, brave breath and feel for the next door handle. I pull and pull until the thick control-room door opens with a slow suck.

Sschhhhhhh-tuck

It's loud in here, and smoke stings my eyes. The band are crowded round the wide and lit-up motherboard; it looks like a cockpit coming into land, dashboard lights flashing; sliding buttons shaped like Black Jacks and Fruit Salads (but don't taste them, I've tried). Fritz Fryer sits at it, in the only leather chair. He's leaning forward, pushing and pulling down motherboard knobs. I spot Doris the big tape recorder, and two round stickers that say, 'Dr Feelgood' and 'Flamin Groovies'. Sounds change, then cut off to a buzz.

The men are talking: *grand*, *grand*, *grand*. I smell wet dog, and sheepskin.

Horslips don't see me yet.

Then they do.

'Tiff!'

As soon as I hear the *caaaam-caaaam-caaaaaam* voices I want to jump up and down with the thrill of them. Instead, I blush, hold up my dog puppet and move his mouth with the string.

'Hello,' my puppet/me says.

It doesn't matter about my red cheeks because Jimmy is picking me up. He sits with me on the black sofa. 'How have you been, Tiff?'

I lean into him, one hand over my bad ear, the other up my puppet. Jimmy smells of tea and smoke, and Jim, Jimmy, is still the grand, grand, grandest man who plays the penny whistle and the flute and the keyboard.

Fritz presses Doris's buttons. She goes, *wibblewibbbleee-wwweeeeeeeeeeeeeee!* Her pitch is high as a cartoon animal running on the spot.

'Jim, bring your flute back into the yard,' Fritz says, and I think how he twirled Boggle on a stick on our Vicarage lawn.

Jim pats my head, tells me to go to sleep. He's going out to the drip of gutters, but there are more Horslips saying, *Settle down there on the sofa, Tiff,* and there's a hand on my head. I clutch my dog-puppet, and my body *caaaam, caaaaam, caaaams*. I lie down.

There are luminous eyes beneath the motherboard, then snarling.

'Quiet now, Bog,' a Horslip says.

The snarl gobbles for oxygen. Boggle is *terrorising*; this is his master's motherboard after all. I growl back from the sofa, then snuggle deeper into a Horslip's side. The Horslip rumbles with a laugh.

When she found me sleeping on the Studio One sofa Mum said, 'There you are! I told you to go down to Sandra's if you're lost.'

But I wasn't lost.

'I wanted Horslips to be a surprise,' she gestured at the band like she'd wrapped them up for Christmas, 'but you found them!'

'Ah, Joan, sit, sit,' they said, and she told them what she had in mind for their meals. Fritz turned around in his motherboard chair to listen.

Now it's morning and the Quadrangle is asleep. I'm on the brown chair again, head out of the roof window, my satchel across my front. Ann Ward will drive me and Lisa to Overmonnow Primary soon because Mum's already on her way to Worcester. She has another job in the early mornings: she drives her MGB GT to set up and cook for a wine bar, then she speeds back here in time to marinate meat, chop, feed me, and then the bands.

I watch rain wave across the stable roof. Peter Pan and Rusty stare out, blank-eyed. Corrina is opening the door of the tack room. She has her Monmouth Comprehensive school uniform on. When I'm in the tack room with her, sometimes we sing 'Bye Bye Baby' by the Bay City Rollers and the stirrups and the bridles sparkle. I want to taste the wax as I rub it into the leather.

Horslips push open the studio doors. I watch the brave ones run out to jump in puddles in their daps, their platform boots, their flares. They look exhausted. Their long hair flattens to their faces, but they laugh like children.

I list my new words and phrases:

Hey, man
Posset
Girth
High Volume Love
Feedback
Noilly Prat
16 Track
Suzette
Echo chamber
The Unfortunate Cup of Tea

Something in my ear has popped: the pain is almost gone but it feels sticky.

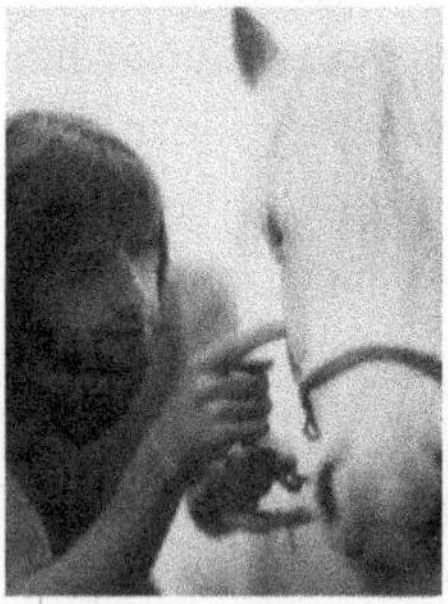

79 AWO

Joan vs the Food Fights

It did piss me off, the rivalry between the bands in Studio One and Two, because it ended in food fights with *my* food in *my* kitchen, *my* dining room, their bedrooms or, God forbid, the studios. I felt sorry for engineers and producers, once they had to take the whole motherboard apart, and a band couldn't record for two days.

One night Sandra begged me to stop a food fight in the control room. I was sick of wiping trifle from the motherboard knobs, so I walked in to read them the riot act. It didn't work – they all threw glasses of water at me! The bastards were lying in wait because they knew I'd be the one to tell them off. I was drenched.

So, what did I do? I took all of my clothes off.

'Well,' I told them, 'go and get me a towel, and please pick up my suede jacket from my chalet bedroom. Thank you.' One ran off immediately.

'Sorry, Joan,' the rest said. They didn't quite know where to look while we waited.

That's when Fritz Fryer walked in. Horslips were the next band in, and he'd come a few days earlier. Thank God the band weren't with him. I would have been mortified.

Fritz didn't seem to mind.

Food Fight Trifle

Of course, I made the trifle, I couldn't help myself, the bands loved it. I know it was a mistake.

shop-bought sponge fingers soaked in sherry (the boozy fingers give weight and sting once thrown).
Bird's custard (it's the easiest custard to give a satisfying 'splat' when chucked at the window between the control room and the live room).
*fresh fruit**

*(I can't bring myself to use tinned even for a food fight trifle, it reminds me of your grandmother's obsession with tinned peaches).

Layer this up in a bowl you don't mind losing.

Top with whipped cream, and hundreds and thousands.

The cream and sherry can cause the most damage, it seeps between the motherboard knobs, and will make the control room stink. That's why Sandra and I were always so quick to run in and clean it down straight away.

15.

Joan's Menu

Rockfield, May–June 1975
DAVE EDMUNDS and Nick Lowe in. John Anthony bringing in Van der Graaf Generator for 3 weeks. Hustler in with Roy Thomas Baker, Pat Moran engineer. Barry 'The Fish' Melton (Country Joe and the Fish) producing himself, Kingsley, Charles, and Dave Charles engineering. Budgie coming back, Pat Moran and Ray Martinez engineering, Fritz, Charles and Kingsley in with them. Starry Eyed and Laughing in with Dan Loggins producer, Bill Aitken engineer. Repair fences, clean out all livestock buildings. Start on cutting and turning hay, all hands on deck. Fritz staying on and available.

A dry thud of wellies echoes; the squelch and suck has gone. Swallows dive under the courtyard awning, their liquid chirps echo on repeat. Summer at Rockfield makes the hedgerows fat, and the crows and the yelling sheep louder than lead guitar. It's heaven and the Happy Hunting Ground here; it's tractors and dogs and kids like me and not like me. It's Brigitte bouncing right at the top of a tower of hay bales on her dad's trailer. She's wearing Marigold gloves because bailer string hurts. It's bands helping with the bales, and following Charles and Kingsley around the farm because they want to watch the milking. It's Mum shelling peas outside the dining room's French windows, a band on the grass around her, a Café Crème in her mouth, and her dress pulled down to her waist and no bra because it's *her* sun and she *needs it*. It's Hustler singing 'Boogie Man', and Barry Melton singing 'Jesse James'. It's cows and chickens you can chase and hug. It's Kingsley setting up the clay pigeon trap outside the dining room, shotguns firing and Mum yelling, 'Chrissakes!' It's making secret tunnels in those hay bales that could crush us, but they don't. It's jumping from the top of the barn down onto an old mattress that winds us. It's playing Action Man and House with Young Charles, and Horses with real horses and Lisa and Amanda. It's doing anything I want because Mum is so busy. It's watching *Basil Brush*, Boom-Boom! on the chalet telly, then later *The Rockford Files*, and sometimes *Kojak – who loves ya baby?* – with the bands in their living room when it's late but still light outside.

Summer at Rockfield is Mum happy. She drives off early to the Worcester wine bar, but she's back here after lunch. She comes to bed late with burns on her fingers and the smells of her kitchen. She's so busy those Biba and Bus Stop dresses still hang from the back of the brown chair. Summer at Rockfield is listening to Corrina's *Young Americans*, her *Ziggy Stardust and the Spiders from Mars*, and being amazed by Brigitte on her Hanoverian stallion named 'Myself'. She tells me he's made up of hands, more than sixteen of them, but I can't find any on his smooth bay legs. Summer at Rockfield is sleeping on the floor between Lisa and Amanda's two single beds in the flat in Bampi and Nana Ward's house and giggling until we're told off. Summer is band after band, and Kingsley and Charles, their shared laugh that's a chortle up then down, and the shock of Charles's strawberry blond hair. Summer at Rockfield is watching Sandra pick vine leaves for dolmades because Sandra is from Cyprus as well as Monmouth. Summer at Rockfield is Mum and Sandra laughing in the kitchen, and Mum telling Sandra how she liked Kieran very much, but he just couldn't cope with her, and she wasn't about to leave this place for him, and anyway when Fritz invited her to his father's funeral in front of everyone, including her parents, in the King's Head in Monmouth, she couldn't say no, could she?

My new words are:
Studer 24-track machine
Picky eater
Engineer
Da doo ron ron
Lap steel
Fascination
Marsala
Lady Grinning Soul
Reverb
Jazz
Vegetarian

Overmonnow Primary has finished for the summer but there is still the routine of Mum's menu. It changes because Mum doesn't have the patience for plans. This week she is determined with fish and there are three pink, liver-sized slabs of veiny smoked cod's roe in the fridge. Last week she was determined with vegetables because Bampi Ward's plot was overflowing. He gives us raw rhubarb dipped in white sugar to crunch. Mum says vegetarians have made life challenging though fascinating for her.

Monday

Smoked trout mousse with cucumber, watercress garnish, home-made Melba toast. *Start easy on the fish*, she says. It goes down well and she's surprised. The main is flattened pork fillets with Madeira sauce.

They say, *What's for pudding, Joan?*

Lemon meringue pie. Also, fruit salad, because she always keeps proper not bloody tinned fruit salad in the fridge. *You can have it with my home-made condensed milk ice-cream*, she says.

Say your prayers, *Van der Graaf Generator, Budgie, Quicksand . . . Amen*

Tuesday

They said, *no more fish, Joan*, so she said, *oh, moussaka then*. She makes a proper lamb one with Sandra.

Ugh, one says, *I don't eat lamb*. She's prepared for this, she has a chicken dish in the fridge, breast with mushrooms in a white wine sauce. The lamb-hater loves it. Moussaka with lentils, plus cauliflower for the vegetarian. A big salad for everyone *because we aren't all carnivore monsters, you know*. Black Forest gateau because *you pleaded*.

Say your prayers, *John Anthony, Barry Melton, BP Fallon ... Amen*

Wednesday

Come on, try my freshly made taramasalata! It's real cod's roe!

The pink slabs have been staring at her from the fridge all week.

And what about monkfish in tomato?

Steaks, steaks, steaks! they cry. *Please, Joan!*

She adds *au poivre*, a big field mushroom and fries the tomatoes in the steak juice. She freezes the monkfish. The band cry into their pillows they are so happy.

I eat taramasalata in front of *The Goodies* and *Are You Being Served?*

Say your prayers, *Hustler, Roy Baker, Be-Bop Deluxe ... Amen*

Thursday

What more steak? she says.

Pleeeeeeeease, they reply.

OK, but boeuf en croute.

Her determination with fish is fading, *just give them what they want, Joan.*

And for pudding? *Apple crumble and home-made ice cream because, in for a penny, in for pound.* She won't bother with fish again.

Say your prayers, *Hobo, Starry Eyed and Laughing, Headstone ... Amen*

Friday

Fish Friday. She can't help herself. Something about the Catholic she once was. Prawns in garlic and butter sauce (OK, so it's *shell*fish). She has to peel them, otherwise the bands won't eat them. The garlic sauce goes down well because she doesn't tell them it's garlic. For main, she compromises with a more chicken-than-usual paella, because chicken and chorizo is not cheating on a Catholic Friday because it's Spanish.

A creamy berry thing in a glass. She's not a pud person.

Say your prayers, *Arthur Brown, Flamin' Groovies, Horslips . . . Amen*

Saturday

The highlight of her week: the lunch buffet.

There are eight salads that could feed an army. She puts an orange in the piglet's mouth because if you touch its teeth you'll cut your fingers. She halves it to cook it, the oven's so small. There's something *Alice in Wonderland* about the browned piglet when she wraps it up in a pink electric blanket to keep it warm. There is a whole (but really two halves) salmon that she puts at the centre of the table. The band, the record execs, the managers, the girlfriends and wives circle it, and finally people fill their plates with fish. Mainly because of her mayonnaise and the horror of the pig, so Mum carries it into the kitchen and cuts off its head with a cleaver. The band, the record execs, the managers and the girlfriends and wives all finish the pig now. The eating and the drinking goes on for hours. Mum is in SEVENTH HEAVEN.

Say your prayers, *Peter Hamill, Nick Lowe, Brinsley Schwarz . . . Amen*

Sunday

Don't get caught picking the crackling off the pork roast, or the crispy fat off the Herefordshire beef before it's ready!

Drink gravy with a spoon it's so good. Cry at the crunch of roast potatoes. If you don't like pork or beef, there's chicken, but don't say it's too 'chickeny', it's from a bloody farm. Tell her if you're a vegetarian, she'll do her leeks, and there are avocados; she knows how to cook them without the mush now.

But please don't come into the kitchen and watch her as she mixes egg yolks, sugar and Marsala for the zabaglione, it's going to curdle if she doesn't concentrate.

Say your prayers, *Ace, Queen, Dirty Tricks, Mr. Big … Amen*

Fish Pie

I wanted to rescue dogs and cats, and men, but I also wanted to redeem fish.

So yes, I did have a thing about fish. I was determined to break through the fish barrier with the bands. Stupid really, as I could have done a steak every night and they would have loved it. I blame my boarding school. For ten years they made me eat fish pie every Friday and it was the most disgusting thing that has ever passed my lips. The bottom layer was the week's leftover porridge, then a layer of boiled, on-the-turn white fish, topped with a grey sauce like water, and on top POM Potato, a revolting artificial potato from the war (the same as wartime powdered egg). God, the stink, the grey horror. The other girls would get in a state and say, 'Oh I'm going to be sick!' Many were, but I'd refuse to eat it. I was forced to sit at the lunch table with the housemistress who had a moustache. It would get dark. I'd miss my lessons, but I would not touch my plate and the housemistress would nod off. I'd creep out and chuck it in the bin. In the end they gave up on me and I didn't have to eat that fucking fish pie.

chunks of turbot (it was cheap then), haddock, cod: me and quantities are a joke, but maybe for a band of eight, 4 lbs of white fish
milk, a little to poach the fish
bay leaf
salt
pepper
king prawns, if the band can take it

For the Sauce

butter, 1/4 or 1/2 pack (always add a little olive oil so it doesn't burn)
flour
fish stock
dessertspoon of lemon juice
salt and pepper
milk and a little cream

Poach fish in milk seasoned with the bay leaf, salt and pepper for about 10–15 mins, cool, do not overcook, flake fish, REMOVE ALL BONES. You can cook a few shelled king prawns for colour and taste.

For the sauce, melt the butter carefully, add the flour, stir and then add the fish stock – just a little for fishy taste, dessert spoon of lemon. Taste. Salt, pepper, nutmeg. Round off with the milk and cream. You want it velvety. Not too thick, not too watery, right? A little bit of parmesan. Tiny bit of parsley. Combine flaked fish with sauce.

For your mash, cook the potatoes in salted water, mash really well, add butter and cream, salt and pepper, taste. Cover the fish filling with mashed potato. The idea is to put the potato under the grill to brown.

You can also do this with raw fish, just chuck it in the dish, pour on the sauce, top with the potato and in the oven.

Do you know what? Serve with peas. As I've already told you, everyone loves peas.

16.

Cordon Bleu

Rockfield, July 1975
HORSLIPS back to mix with Fritz. Gus Dudgeon bringing Solution over from Holland. Need landing strip? Pat to engineer. Barry Melton staying on. Budgie with a new album and Kingsley engineering. Kieran White here, Dave Charles engineering. Joan knows. Hobo in with Pat. Tim Rose in. Bale the hay, all hands on deck for bale hauling into stable loft. Farrier in. Royal Welsh Show, Builth.

The band are Dutch. Their names are Guus, Willem and Hans, and they play jazz. They have saxophone sounds in their songs, and I love saxophones, and they love Mum's food, so she loves them, and I'm washing up badly when one of them coughs at the open door of the Rockfield kitchen.

Mum is cleaning surfaces. This is her most important thing. A cook must not poison.

Guus or Willem or Hans coughs at the kitchen door again. 'Joan?'

She is rubbing and wiping, and 10cc are telling us they're not in love from the cassette player on the windowsill.

'Joan?'

'Yes. Busy!'

'We wanted to tell you—'

'Tell me what?'

'We have a name for the album.'

'That's great.' Mum scrapes leftovers into bowls because refrigeration is her other religion; no one is getting ill because of her food.

Guus or Willem or Hans is either very polite or he's waiting for Mum to straighten up and look the tiniest bit interested.

'Joan, we are calling the album "Cordon Bleu".'

She puts the leftovers bowl down, picks up her cloth and finally looks up at the man. He's tall. Mum says it's because he's from Holland.

'It's "Cordon Bleu" in honour of you, Joan.'

Mum doesn't know what to say. I can see her trying to work it out under her skin. I think she might cry, then she blushes. 'Oh, that is fantastic.' She looks down at the counter and yes, she's blushing redder. 'How lovely,' she murmurs, but she doesn't let go of her cleaning cloth. She carries on smiling at the cloth and the Dutch man laughs and leaves. She gets busier on surfaces she has already cleaned. She's laughing a strange little laugh like she doesn't exactly know what to think.

I pull out the sink plug and plunge my hand in the thick soapy water to claw the gloopy bits of meat and God-knows-what out. In the dishwater I touch the new red scar on the back of my hand. It's a perfect bite shape: top teeth cut a small red smile below my middle finger while bottom teeth make half a moon at my index finger joint on my palm. I'm proud of it. It was Jason, the black Rockfield Labrador (Cherie the poodle, who belongs to Lisa, wouldn't bite me). Jason was fighting Boggle by the stables, and I had to protect Boggle because he's my brother now.

Jason's bite didn't hurt, but there was a lot of blood. Mum tried to press the edges of the gashes together over the kitchen sink, because that's where the First Aid Kit is.

'Tiff, don't you know water is the only thing to stop a dog fight?' she said as a Hobo singer took something from the fridge. 'You put a hose on fighting dogs, or a bucket of water. Shit—' Too much blood was dripping: the plasters weren't working but it still didn't hurt. 'You've gone white, oh dear.' She wrapped a white tea towel around my hand. 'You need stitches.'

Her MGB GT keys rattled into Monmouth. 'Please, in future stay away from fighting male dogs,' she told me from the driving seat. 'Let them sodding tear each other apart.'

I thought of new words to take my mind off stitches:

Gus Dudgeon
Jazz
10cc
Riff
Poached
Country Joe and the Fish

Tetanus
Quadraphonic

Fritz has brought Horslips back to mix. I like him when he's with them, but I'm not sure about him in my mum's bedroom. Because he's her boyfriend now, he sometimes stays in our chalet like Kieran did. If I don't go down to the Lodge or stay with Nanny, I sleep on the downstairs sofa and play with Boggle when he's not growling at me. I'll stand on a chair and hold up bits of meat to see if Bog can snatch them: he always does, even if his teeth have been worn down by sticks. One day Fritz caught me putting a Biba dress on Boggle and he asked me not to. Boggle was trying to hop, but he got caught in the skirt and fell over. At least when everyone goes to the pub and me and Boggle are in the car, Fritz brings us a Coca-Cola *and* Walker's smoky bacon crisps. For the first time since Fritz put a pile of clothes in Mum's drawer and told me *if a job's worth doing it's worth doing well*, I almost smile. I suppose I don't mind him when he and Charles Ward sing 'Hound Dog' and 'Teddy Bear' down at the Lodge with their acoustic guitars. Mum and Sandra, and Brigitte and Corrina hold onto one another and dance in the small hot living room. I jump on Sandra's pouffe, and cheer. Jason the black Lab barks.

Fritz wants to take the stabilisers off my bike. He wants me to be as brave as the other Rockfield kids who pedal down the Trolley track from the bungalow, to skid the turn into Studio Two. When they fall over, graze knees and elbows and their chains come off, they don't cry. Otto will come out of his engineer workshop. 'You will hurt yourselves,' he'll say with his warm German voice, and he'll thread their chains back on. Otto has the best laugh.

Today I line my bike up with them. They pedal off, but I'm slow with my little white stabilisers. I get stuck, spinning in a pothole. Lisa's already wiping the brown dust from her jeans down at the Studio Two turn, and Otto's threading her chain back on. I get off and push.

Fritz comes out of Studio Two. He blinks in the sunlight, shields his eyes. When he's producing, Fritz will be inside for days. Mum sends food down.

He points at me. 'I'll take those ga-ga wheels off for you, Tiff.'

I shake my head.

'You're too old for stabilisers.'

'I'm not.'

He stretches in his blue velvet jacket. 'Don't be wet, Tiff.'

Corrina and Lisa are speeding down the track again. Their wheels skid, gravel dust puffs, and I throw my little pink and white bike to the ground. I storm off: just like my mother.

In the tiny chalet kitchen Fritz is teaching me to make a proper cup of tea with a teabag, not like Mum's tea leaves, and when Mum isn't looking, he lets me try a forkful of his Heinz baked beans. The sweet, red tin taste is something new and forbidden. I smile. But later, when Fritz and his friend Man Horrid are carrying my mattress down the staircase, I go back to sulking. Mum is behind them. 'You're having your own bedroom downstairs, Tiff.'

Fritz and Man Horrid have already moved the sofa under the window, but this isn't a bedroom, it's still a living room and a kitchen. Mum wafts down the stairs in her thin kaftan.

'But the front door is just there, Mum.'

'And?'

'Someone could creep in in the middle of the night.'

'Don't be silly, Tiff, the bands aren't interested in barging in here.' She plumps up my pillow.

'I mean the bogey man. And the boogie man.'

'What?'

'It's dark out there.'

'It hasn't frightened you before. Keep Boggle with you.'

'He doesn't like me.'

'She needs her own dog,' Fritz says as he and Man Horrid plonk my single mattress on the bedframe under the pine stairs. Right now I hate him but I'll remember what he said about the dog.

'Look,' Mum says, 'Fritz won't be here the whole time, but we all need our space when he is, you included. It's not ideal, darling, but there's nowhere else at Rockfield.'

Mum's reasoning with me: I don't like it. She's right about one thing, there *is* nowhere else. The families and the bands sleep in all the houses. I could sleep in the stables with Peter Pan or Orinoco, or the tack room, or in Brigitte and Corrina's, or Lisa and Amanda's bedroom. I'm about to ask my mother when she says, 'We should think about moving.' She's looking at Fritz, not me. 'Tiff needs her own bedroom.'

These words do something: I go up on tiptoes. A 'no!' bubbles out of me, far too loud. 'I will never leave Rockfield!' I yell like a curse and my toes claw into the carpet. I'm a toddler again, a wild animal. I'm a wild animal toddler.

Fritz and Man Horrid look embarrassed; they go upstairs for my things.

Mum says, 'We're not going anywhere yet.'

I don't like this new 'we', and I don't care about *his* smoky bacon crisps, *his* Elvis songs, *his* proper tea with a teabag, *his* baked beans. I run out into the courtyard. Orinoco and

April jig their heads from the stables. The evening sun is hot and milk cows cry out from the fields. A drumbeat thuds from the rehearsal room. I hear the Rockfield kids laughing, shouting, squealing somewhere. Suddenly I'm breathless with excitement, not anger, because I could run from this spot, find them and play: it's as easy as that. Boggle hops out of the chalet and stands next to me. We listen to the Rockfield night. I hear Mum say, 'Who on God's green earth is going to worm and de-flea that dog before he sleeps in my daughter's bed?'

Horslips run into the courtyard and start kicking a football. Boggle joins them. Boggle likes to burst footballs. Dirt clouds up.

Learn your new words, Tiff:

Reel to reel
Acetate
Rickenbacker
Otto
Open plan
Privacy
Hobo
Hassling
Tough tittie
Tape dump

Joan Deals with Complaints

There's a manager down for the week and night after night he complains about the wine, he says he can't drink the plonk the band have, 'those boys aren't wine connoisseurs like me,' he says. So, I buy one good bottle, drink it myself when cooking, and fill it back up with the wine I've been using all week. After supper the manager comes into my kitchen, talks about himself, winks and says, 'Well done, Joan, at last you've got the wine right.'

For the rest of the week I do the same and every night he winks at me and raises a glass at the table, and the band starts laughing, because I told them. He doesn't know why. Oh, and he wears Cuban heels.

I did a pudding a band complained about. The next night I shoved it all in the liquidiser, put it into wine glasses and topped it with a bit of meringue, whipped cream and blanched almonds.

The bass player said, 'That's more like it, Joan.'

I may or may not have dropped a little ash near or on his next meal.

Sandra said, 'Only you could do that, Joan!'

The producers are different; the producers always thank me for feeding their boys. I like the producers. Gus Dudgeon is a sweetheart, as is Mutt Lange. Some nights John Anthony will say, 'You're not cooking tonight, Joan, we're taking you out,' and that's so kind. John is a vegetarian, and he pushes me to try out new things. He loves my ratatouille, my cauliflower, my mushroom bake, but I do remember the first time around my cooked avocados were a mushy disaster fund.

17.

'Bohemian Rhapsody'

Rockfield, August 1975

QUEEN coming into Studio One, Roy Baker producing. Budgie back with Kingsley engineering. Van der Graaf Generator, Dave Charles with them. Dave Edmunds to produce and engineer himself. Dirty Tricks in with Pat. Mr. Big with Kingsley producing. Ace in with John Anthony producing, Joan will be happy. Replace 4 clay roof tiles, first stable. Monmouthshire Show.

Mum says, 'I blame Van der Graaf Generator.'

It's because I overheard her in the dining room asking them if they enjoyed rehearsing at the Vicarage. 'You were there for months!' she said. That's when I started asking about Cleo again.

'Did you see her, a big Great Dane?' I asked a Van der Graaf Generator (I didn't know if he was the Van, the Der, the Graaf or the Generator). 'Are you sure? She's in a half-eaten caravan, or she might have a den in the garden, or the pottery, or—'

Mum pulled me away, 'Stop hassling, Tiffany.' In private she told me that Jackson had gone away.

'But is Cleo still at the Vicarage?'

'I don't think so, darling.'

'Then why were Van der Graaf Generator –' I had to take a breath '– at the Vicarage?'

'I presume Jackson still rents it out to bands, I don't know. Forget it, Tiff.'

I couldn't. I imagined Cleo jumping over Van der Graaf Generator's cables, saxophones and clarinets in the big Vicarage hall; I dreamt about Cleo splayed across their beds, Cleo rubbing her muzzle against their drum kits and the funny parp-y instruments they brought from there, to Rockfield.

Since Van der Graaf Generator left, I've been on the prowl.

It smells of Fritz's cigarettes in Mum's bedroom. Sometimes he leaves his blue velvet jacket on the brown chair. Mum's dresses are hung up now. I pick up my rock 'n' roll dog puppet, climb on the chair and stick my head out of the roof window.

The Rockfield courtyard is bright even though it's evening. Crows float in hot air. Sheep burp in the fields.

My new words are:

Galileo (who Fritz says is a man who saw the stars)
Pegboard
Chablis
Figaro (who Fritz says is the Barber of Seville)
Pavlova

If I push half my body out of the roof window I can see Boggle and Jason the black Lab in the courtyard. They circle each other, hackles and tails up, arseholes out. I feel the sparks of dog-hate as they take measured steps, eyes locked.

It's when the studio doors open that the Galileos escape, and there is Freddie stretching in the sunlight. He squints. I wonder if he'll go into the tack room and play the piano there: at night I hear it pour across the courtyard. Bits of Queen are always running off into the rooms around the courtyard to practise. The hackled dogs break their stand-off to jog to him, tails loose and wagging and Freddie pats their heads. Brian walks out of the studio; still tall and thin as a silver birch, and he stretches too. The dogs copy them, bending their heads and front halves to the ground, bums up. Freddie and Brian blink in the light. They've been in the studio for days singing the same words over and over. Freddie picks up an abandoned Frisbee and they skim it to each other in the hot air.

Since Queen arrived, I can't shake the feeling, or the hope. Mum says, 'Now you're being ridiculous, Tiff. I doubt they even remember you or me, let alone a Great Dane.'

But I have to be sure. Don't I?

Galileo, the playback sings. And again: *Galileo*. The band say it for hours and hours and hours.

Again and again.

And again.

Galileo

The horses jig their heads from the stables, they've gone mad with the day-and-night Galileos; with the Figaros, too.

Freddie rubs Jason's flat Labrador head, and I think of the way he hugged Cleo. Because it could be possible, couldn't it? That a Great Dane has been travelling the world with Queen: from LA to Japan, nestled in the back of a tour bus, an aeroplane, a limousine; stretched out on Freddie's hotel-room bed night after night, her heavy tail thumping out a wag on the sheets. After his nights of hard piano playing, singing with arms spread wide like Jesus, jumping and marching about on stage, Cleo would lick him head to foot until he laughed, his chin up at the hotel ceiling. She'd shove her big nose in his parts because that's how dogs say hello, and she'd stretch down on her front paws and bark because she's been so bored all day in the hotel room, and she just wants to play.

I hear Brigitte and Amanda in the field trying out jumps on their horses, thump-thump. Queen's bassist, John, and the pretty drummer, Roger, walk out into the daylight; they stretch, too, then catch the flying Frisbee. I jump off my chair and I run down the pine stairs to our chalet's front door.

I waited in the kitchen until Queen came to dinner. I put out the crudités and dips, then helped Mum with the king prawn cocktail in a wine glass starter. I heard Queen's, 'Thank you, Joan. Thank you,' because Queen are still very polite and Freddie toasts glasses before they eat. Then, I sneaked out into the studio.

I crept along the parquet corridor outside the control room. Galileos were singing out because the producer was still in there. I kept walking on to the live room. I held out my dog puppet's hand so he could open the doors, not me.

He made me do it, Miss.

The live room is where Queen sing their Galileos and it is absolutely forbidden to sneak in here. The door sucks closed behind me: the air is body-warm, I smell lived-in clothes and grown-up breath of coffee, lemon and honey. Maybe this is what Galileos smell like. Figaros, too. Dim lights spot the long room, and Freddie's grand piano has its big mouth open. A tower of Vox amps wink red eyes at me from one wall. Maybe they're the same amps Queen brought to the Vicarage. Cleo would have rubbed herself on those. The drum room where Roger plays is at the far end. White pegboards make the room look like a butcher's shop. Strange panels hang from the ceiling in a line: Charles Ward built these, and he told me this is where sound reflects. I hug my frizz-haired puppet to me, and I wait.

'Cleo?' I whisper.

She doesn't come bounding out from the drum room, my biscuit-flavoured Scooby Doo. There is only the amp buzz and the lemony ghosts of Galileos. My throat feels stuck.

'Cleo?' I say a little louder. I glance at the control-room window, and there's the producer. The light from the mixing desk brightens his face from below like Christopher Lee as Dracula. I freeze but he hasn't seen me. The playback voices come again: *Galileo.* The tape rewinds. Stops. *Galileo. Figaro.* On my knees, I sniff the rough carpet. It's damp and daps, not dog. I crawl towards the piano and hit against Freddie's stool.

If I put my ear to the floor like American Indians do in Saturday-morning films (with my grandad's red and white Hereford cows screaming across the dusty plains), maybe I'll hear Cleo because when she runs to you, Cleo *is* a stampede.

There's nothing but a rug-heavy silence.

No, it's more than that, it's a thing where sound once was, but now it's an empty hole.

I sneak under Freddie's piano: there's space enough for a Great Dane here. 'Cleo?'

For a second, I smell her.

I do.

I do, and I'm back at the Vicarage and she is lolloping, front legs heavy with the weight of her head, towards Mum's blue sofa in the drawing room – where Freddie is lying, writing songs in his notebook, the emerald hummingbirds in bell jars frozen around him – and Cleo pushes her huge nose into his face, and he laughs.

The light in the control room goes off. The producer leaves. I hunker under the piano and my throat feels tighter. The band will be past starters now, onto guinea fowl or rump steak, monkfish or pike quenelles, vegetarian chilli with fresh tomatoes or leeks au gratin; lemon cheesecake set with so much gelatine it doesn't bounce. Queen are on the Gourmet Menu.

The Vox tower buzzes louder; it spits like Kaa the snake in *The Jungle Book*. I sit up and hit my head on the undercarriage of the piano.

Buzzzzzz, say the amps. *Whiiiiiiine.*

'Cleo?'

I crawl to the amps so fast the carpet burns my knees. I press my face into a mesh front, and I call her. 'Cleoooooo?'

The lattice pattern scratches my cheek.

Hiiiiissssssssss, the amp says.

'Cleee?'

There is nothing but the nothingness of not-her.

Brian's guitar is leaning up against the amps. I lean back too, and I don't care if the tower wobbles and falls on me because now I know Queen didn't take Cleo off to America and Japan, and all those places in between. Cleo isn't lost inside these black amps, whining for me. She's not at the Vicarage and she's nowhere in this room with the ghosts of Galileos and the Figaros.

Cleo is gone.

The Vox hums into my back.

'Cle—' but I can't finish the word because a bolt of tightness twists my chest. I reach out, pick up my rock 'n' roll dog puppet, and I smash his head into the floor.

Figaro.

I look down: his jaw is hanging off. I jump up and run to my mother.

Queen are at the dining table, but they've stopped eating to stare at me. I haven't made it to the kitchen. I'm in the dining room, wailing.

'Please calm down,' Mum is saying. Her striped apron hangs from her neck. My body is rigid. I take a deep breath for my next wail.

'Fritz will fix it. Fritz!'

He comes out from the kitchen, also in an apron. Queen watch.

I hold out my broken-faced puppet.

'Shh, Tiff,' Mum says, 'a bit of Copydex and it will be fine.'

I howl. Mum uses Copydex for everything: upholstery,

photograph albums and the hems on my skirts and trousers. It does *not* work.

'Take her into the kitchen, Fritz.' She looks up at Queen, 'So sorry!'

Fritz kneels and I don't want to, but I fall into his chest. He picks me and the bashed dog puppet up, and my knees tighten into his sides. I see Freddie over Fritz's shoulder. Maybe Freddie gives me a half-smile. Maybe it's indigestion. He puts his knife and fork together neatly on his plate. I have made too much noise in public; I should be seen and not heard.

Fritz puts me down on the kitchen floor. He takes the puppet from my hands, holds him up by the pole that comes out of his back and examines the dangling jaw. 'What happened here, Tiff?'

'I-I killed hiiiiiiim.'

'Well, it needs something stronger than Copydex.'

Mum closes the kitchen door. She walks to her counter and, with her Sabatier, she stabs a pert, purple kidney and begins to pull out the stringy bits.

The only thing that calms me is going down to the Lodge. Fritz takes me. I watch telly with Brigitte and Corrina in the sitting room. I hide under a blanket as the Horror Double Bill on BBC2 plays *The Cat and the Canary* and *The Comedy of Terrors*. I pee myself a bit and finally go to sleep. When Fritz comes to pick me up, I ask, 'Where's Mum?'

'Up in the kitchen with Sandra.'

'Is my puppet better?'

He shrugs. 'We'll see.'

Fritz gives me a piggyback, muttering, 'What am I? Bring me, carry me, fetch me?' but he laughs. We pass Studio Two, and the horse weathervane squeaks as it turns in the summer wind. I grip my knees tighter into Fritz's sides, like I do on the smaller

Rockfield horses. *Giddy-up* I want to say, but I don't. I can feel he won't drop me, and he might mend my puppet, although I'm grown-up enough to know, deep down, it won't work. My puppet is broken, I have killed him. In the Quadrangle, Fritz stands still and in the darkness we both listen. The Galileos are pouring into the night. I don't think they will ever end.

I stop ignoring Fritz. I watch him. While I eat boiled eggs in my double egg cup in the Rockfield dining room, Brian and Fritz chat. Brian says a few years ago Fritz asked him to sing a song called 'April Lady' in a basement studio in London, because Fritz produced Brian's old band Smile. Mum cuts my toast into soldiers and says, 'What a small world.'

Now, whenever Fritz comes down to the Lodge on a Saturday night to fetch me, I pretend to be asleep, so he *has* to pick me up. I ask Fritz to carry me all around Rockfield. I like being carried by Fritz; it's better than walking, particularly when the ground is quicksand or molten lava. Which happens a lot.

Show-Off Crêpes Suzette

I adored the drama of Fanny Cradock and Johnnie. I still have my copy of *Bon Viveur* from 1964. It was the inspiration for this recipe. I came up with my own version to suit the equipment I had to hand. I loved the idea of serving my version of Johnnie and Fanny's crêpes Suzette to Queen. It's such a show-off dish. Fanny even called them 'those blatantly vulgar Dante's infernos of flames' in the recipe book.

Everything can be done in advance, but the last bit in front of everyone. You'll need a portable burner. I'm sure Freddie clapped. Sometimes I did it in the kitchen, I was just too tired.

Precook the pancakes, store between greaseproof paper in fridge. I mixed this in my Kenwood so no need to strain.

Pancake Batter

5ish *heaped tablespoons plain flour*
1 *pinch baking powder*
1 *large egg*
1 *egg yolk*
2 *tablespoonsful of olive oil*
milk for creamy consistency, play by ear

Add milk to rest of ingredients until you have a creamy consistency batter. NOT TOO THIN.

Put in fridge, at least 2 hours.

Add thin coating of batter to frying pan (lightly brush pan with groundnut oil) cook and flip

Crêpes Suzette Butter

6 oz	*unsalted butter*		*orange Curaçao or Cointreau,*
8 oz	*icing sugar*		*half a coffee cup*
	orange zest (two dessertspoons)	½	*cup of brandy*
	juice of one orange		

All this in mixer, minus the brandy and the juice of another orange.

About 4–5 tablespoonfuls of the suzette butter into a frying pan, on LOW, add the strained juice of 2nd orange, let the mixture bubble.

Add a pre-cooked pancake. Flip it.

Warm the brandy in a soup ladle, ignite and pour into mixture, which has been put on maximum. WATCH WATCH.

Flames will burn for about 20 seconds. Flip to quarters. Serve immediately.

What did Fanny say, 'fat out and flavour in'? This is a lot of fun.

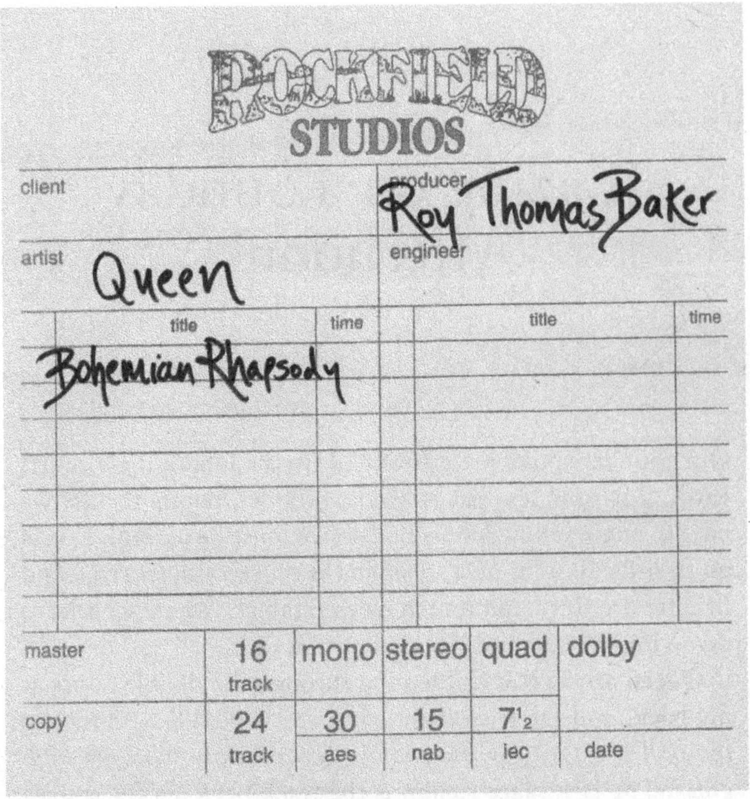

ROCKFIELD STUDIOS

client

producer Roy Thomas Baker

artist Queen

engineer

	title	time		title	time
	Bohemian Rhapsody				

master	16 track	mono	stereo	quad	dolby
copy	24 track	30 aes	15 nab	$7\frac{1}{2}$ iec	date

18.

'Lazing on a Sunday Afternoon'

Our rounders posts are dustbin lids in the Quadrangle courtyard. Our rounders bat is an old wooden tennis racket: we have a single yellow tennis ball so we must be careful. Lisa is on first dustbin-lid post, Amanda is on second, Corrina and Brigitte are third and fourth by the stables. Young Charles is throwing the ball and I'm going to hit it.

Queen are STILL Galileo-ing through the double doors at my back, and the trick is (in between the Galileos) *don't hit the ball too far over the chalet roof and lose it to the high grass*. The best place to aim is the track between the stables and the tack room.

'Hit it, Tiff!' Brigitte says. I think she'd rather be riding her Hanoverian stallion or talking to my mum. She looks so grown-up in her denim flares and black waistcoat with bare arms.

I squint and focus. I love rounders.

Before Young Charles can throw the ball, the doors behind

me burst open and Queen tumble out. They see us, laugh, and run to our dustbin lids. They clap their hands, and say, 'Hit it!' to me.

Young Charles throws, but it's not very hard and I hit a lacklustre lob that Freddie catches. I'm out. Lisa and Amanda back away from their posts. I hand over my tennis racket.

We try to play with them but they're grown-ups and we get bored. We slink off to my chalet, wipe the summer sweat from our top lips and I pour out Robinson's barley water in six wine glasses. We listen to Queen play *our* rounders through the open door.

'You're lucky having your own bedroom,' Lisa says as she looks at my single bed under the stairs.

'It's not a bedroom,' I tell her.

'But you don't have to share, do you?'

We all decide that the barn is the place to be, and we run back outside through Queen's game. We holler and whoop and they stop to watch us, but we're gone, sprinting past the stables and up the brick alley to the old mattress, and the high drop from the top of the barn.

Queen aren't allowed up here. It is ours.

An Underappreciated Squid Recipe for Queen

I get my squid from Milford Haven.

Queen are very ordered and they come in together.

Brian is the politest. If they don't know what something is, Freddie will ask.

To be honest squid is a disaster at the studio. No bands like it and they freak out at tentacles. I persevere. It might end up being fried calamari instead.

2-3	*medium whole squid*	*white wine*
4	*shallots, thinly sliced*	*coriander, chopped well*
8	*or more cloves garlic*	*salt/pepper*
	fresh tomatoes, or tinned if you must	

First fry shallots, then add the garlic in olive oil. Then add the tomatoes. Follow with white wine. To make a rich sauce, add butter.

Cut the squid, include tentacles (best bit). Clear out stomach contents, which freak you out – like the little fish – but you like the glassy cuttlebone.

Put the cut squid in the sauce and gently cook and then leave to rest. You don't want it rubbery, do not overcook!

They are much better left for 2–3 hours.

Before serving, warm up gently, pepper, maybe more salt. Finish with coriander (which I now grow at Rockfield).

19.

'Love of My Life'

It's early afternoon in the Rockfield kitchen and Mum has her hand flat on a squid's white belly. She's cutting into it. I reach up with a finger.

'Have you washed?'

'Yes,' I lie, and I press my dirty nail into it and the squid feels cold, wet and smooth. It's silvery-shiny and maybe like David Bowie's throat-bones on the cover of Brigitte's *Aladdin Sane*. I think of a squid-ish David Bowie seeping up my finger, my arm, and into my heart and brain and it doesn't seem a bad thing.

Mum pulls out the hard glassy sheet from the squid's body and chucks it into the bin.

'Can I have it?'

She laughs. 'What on earth would you do with it, Tiff?' Her Sabatier pierces the milky belly of the next squid, and a baby fish pops out. 'Well, look at that.' She picks up the tiny fish and jiggles it at my face. I don't like the dead-eyed look of it but I laugh, too. Mum has already been to her Worcester wine bar; her face is red, and our bath is full of spitting clams for tomorrow night's meal. I'll have to wash myself at our bathroom sink with a hard flannel and bitter soap.

'Tiff, what's the matter? You're like Velcro, always under my feet.' She slices the squids into strips.

She's right, I won't leave her side: I'm on the lookout, but I can't tell her why.

Early this morning, when the starlings were loud, Freddie saw me and my B-I-G secret on the belt of grass that runs down from the Rockfield bungalow across from the weathervane, and he said, 'What a magnificent creature!'

It was that word again, 'magnificent'. He said it about Cleo at the Vicarage. I say it to the horses in the fields now: 'MAGNIFICENT CREATURE!'

In the kitchen I stick my finger back into a milky white squid. 'Nothing's the matter,' I tell my mother.

Fritz is at the sink by the window. He doesn't need a milk crate to reach. He's helping Mum before 'bombing' up to London for a week. Mum likes to describe Fritz as 'bombing' when he drives off with Boggle in his car. Fritz can pick up heavy pans because his hands are wide and strong, even if he has a green stone ring on his little finger. Fritz still says, '*booogadeeboooogadeeboo*', but now he sings 'Hey,

Fattie-Bum-Bum!' When Fritz takes cold showers he makes a weird noise, and his bottom front teeth are false.

There's a clatter and Sandra trills her laugh from the counter. 'Think you dropped that, Fritz!' Sandra is cutting a pile of fresh tomatoes because Mum hates tins. 'Satellite of Love' plays on the cassette player and Mum and Sandra sing, 'La, la, la!' to the chorus. The kitchen smells of fresh sea and sunlight.

Queen's gourmet menu tonight is crudités with dips; calamari and home-made saffron mayonnaise; monkfish in tomato, roast fennel, ratatouille, mangetout, new potatoes. Mum has also done pike quenelles she's chilling for tomorrow. Pudding is syllabub in a glass. Tonight, I wish her menu was raw deer, pig trotters, an Obelix whole boar, her Robert Carrier terrine wrapped in bacon, beef Wellington, and chicken liver mousse with black pudding. I also wish I was Little Red Riding Hood because I need to steal the sort of food that a wolf would eat.

I know my wolf is a she because I have crawled under her, moved the soft grey hair from her belly and looked. I found her sniffing around the barn very early this morning. I coaxed her into an empty stable, and she drank almost a whole bucket of water. I stole two raw rump steaks from the kitchen fridge and watched her gobble them up in the straw. She threw them up and ate them again. If Oswald scythed graves around here, he'd tell me to put a saddle on her.

It was just dawn and Freddie was walking around the tracks. Maybe he'd just woken up, maybe he was in the studio all night, but when he saw me with my wolf on that strip of grass, he asked, 'What *is* her name?'

'Lady.' I made it up on the spot.

Freddie knelt, and suddenly Lady was taller than him. Then there was that word, 'Magnificent.' She pushed her big black fleshy nose into his face and almost knocked him over. 'She's so strong! How do you take her for walks?'

I worried Freddie would tell, then I worried how I was going to take Lady for a walk; then I worried about how I was going to keep her a secret, but Freddie had gone. Robins and blue tits sang out from the stable roof. The weathervane turned.

At least I know I can feed her from Mum's fridge. Nobody noticed I was off playing with her for the day. Now she's back in the old stable, I hope the girls don't find her.

Mum bangs a pan onto the cooker. I tell her, 'I'm hungry.'

'Go down to the Lodge, love, see the girls,' Sandra says, and she sways her lovely hips in a black pencil skirt to Lou Reed's 'Take a Walk on the Wild Side.'

Do, do-do, do-do

'Yes, get out from under our feet, Tiff.'

'I'm hungry,' I lie again.

'There's plenty of food in the chalet. You're not a baby, you can feed yourself.'

'I want a T-bone steak.'

Mum turns around. She has flour and squid-wet on her fingers: she's cooking a batch for Fritz and Sandra to try. 'I beg your pardon?'

Sandra smiles, and the dimples high on her cheeks deepen. I run to her and hold on tight to her right hip. 'Oh, Tiff, you make me laugh,' she says.

'Listen, Miss Spoilt Child, I can't just magic T-bone steaks,' Mum tells me.

'Beef Wellington?' I murmur from Sandra's hip.

'What about lobster?' Mum says.

I shake my head, fast.

'Truffle foie gras?'

I scowl.

‘OK, Tiff, there’s ham. I’ll cut it.’

‘Can I have ten slices?’

Mum and Sandra laugh, and Fritz looks back at me from the sink. Fritz likes to say I should always tell the truth (*and* ride my bike without stabilisers because I’m not *a ga-ga baby*). He’s about to say something then Brian is standing at the door and Fritz dries his hands and they go out, talking, maybe about April ladies and a studio in the past. If I ever say Fritz *was* a producer out loud because he does the washing-up now, Mum tells me off: *he still is a producer he’s just helping me in the kitchen, you silly girl.*

Boggle trots in: he goes up on his hind legs and nips at a pike quenelle. He chucks it back in one and hops out before a hint of my mother sees him.

At dinner time Queen come in together. Mum likes the fact they are organised. It is just Sandra and me because Fritz and Boggle have ‘bombed off’ to London. I have a plan. After the crudités we start to bring in the starter plates, already dished up. I hover too long at a shoulder. Mum takes the plate from my hand and places it on the table.

‘Thank you, Joan. Can you tell me about this?’ Freddie asks and Mum talks about the squid which is now calamari. She tells him ‘fresh’ and ‘Milford Haven’. She tells him how pure the saffron is in the home-made mayonnaise, and the freshness of the poached monkfish, but Freddie looks tired, although he smiles at the right bits. The band chink glasses.

I sit at the top of the small set of stairs that lead down from the dining room to the courtyard and wait. Queen don’t eat much. Freddie is pushing a squid ring around the plate. I’m hoping Lady will like calamari, and monkfish and red sauce. There’s a nice draught but I wish they would hurry up. Queen are talking about voices and layers, Mum is banging pans in the kitchen, and I know this means that maybe she won't do fish tomorrow. Queen talk softly, and before they have finished I get up and clear their plates, ready for the next course. I make sure to keep all of the leftovers.

It's hard to fit in our chalet bathroom with Lady and my bag dripping with fishy red sauce. Tail to nose Lady reaches from the door to our sink. She jumps on the spot with a thud and barks a deep bark. Lady has eaten the calamari, and a plate of chilled pike quenelles. Now it's monkfish in tomato leftovers, but first slices of Mum's golden syrup roast ham. I sit on the loo, unwrap the silver foil, and Lady gobbles the ham in one, white fat and all.

'Chew it,' I tell her.

I've looked her up in my *Encyclopaedia of Dogs* and I think she is an Irish wolfhound or an extra-large deerhound, or she could be *the* Hound of the Baskervilles. She snatches the greasy silver foil from my hands. Mum taught me the only way to get a dog to drop something is to press the dog's nostrils together. I try but it's hard to get a grip on Lady's huge wet nose.

Someone bangs on the door, but I've locked it.

Lady barks.

'Tiff? What is—' It's Mum.

Lady's front legs lift off as she barks again, deep.

'What the hell have you got in there, child?'

'I want to be private, Mum!'

'What have you taken?'

This isn't the first time I've found an animal and Mum has called it 'stealing'.

'Tiffany, do you have a dog in there?'

'No!'

'Don't lie to me.'

'I'm not!'

'Tiffany, I need to pee!' Mum likes to use her own loo.

Lady backs up in the narrow bathroom because she can't turn.

'Bloody hell, child. I don't have time for this, I've left my syllabubs out of the fridge!'

The front door slams and she's gone. Lady barks that deep throaty bark and I hope she likes syllabub in a glass as well as squid.

'TIFFANY! What the hell is this?'

I wake up, breathe and gag.

'Chrissakes!'

When Lady backed out of the bathroom, we played chase and chew in the chalet, I dressed her up in the only clothes that fit her (a big white nightie), we jumped on the double bed upstairs *and* my single downstairs, and I hid her under my blankets. We fell asleep. It was while I was asleep that Lady woke up and shat.

She's whining now and the light is on: she's still wearing the big white nightie, but it's brown and red with shit and monkfish and tomato at the back.

'What in God's name—' Mum stands on the threshold, hand over her nose and mouth. She's come in from the kitchen. She glares at me and Lady bolts past her through the open door into the courtyard.

'It's a fucking wolf!'

'She's mine!'

'What *have* you done to that poor dog, Tiffany?'

Lady the Wolfhound who is wearing Mum's nightie squats and walks forward in the courtyard.

'Tiff, that poor dog is not yours.'

Lady whines, her back half bent over.

'What *have* you done, child?'

Lady has gone and yet she is still here. Mum cleaned the chalet out with bleach, but we still have to keep the doors and windows open for a through-draught. 'We will never get the stink out,' she says.

Lady had no collar, so Mum put an advert in the *Monmouthshire Beacon.* I had two whole days with her (because she got better; Mum bought her Winalot) but a man came to pick her up. He told me his kids missed her, gave me a pound note for looking after her and said he had no idea how she escaped, but maybe it was cruel of him to keep an Irish wolfhound in a ground-floor flat. Her real name was Wolfy, and I didn't like that. I cried like a banshee and I'm still not speaking to my mother.

Fritz is back from London and I'm watching Boggle and a dog I haven't seen before (but cannot steal) play a strange game in the courtyard. Queen are still singing their Galileos plus a Scaramouche as Boggle jumps off the other dog's back and now they are bum to bum, tails up.

It's not fighting.

They stay like that for so long I creep as close as I can and crouch in the dust. The dogs are just standing there, bums touching and staring out like they've forgotten something. Queen blast out a high-pitched 'Galileo!'

Fritz is walking over to me. He's wearing his blue velvet jacket and a T-shirt that says U C L A. He doesn't wear Jesus sandals any more, but daps.

I point at the dogs. 'What are they doing?'

Fritz goes to laugh then stops, and when I look up, he has

a strange expression, like he's forgotten something too. He looks up at the sky.

'It's nature, Tiff.'

'Why?'

He sighs. 'It's where puppies come from. Your mother will tell you.'

I jump up and start towards Boggle and his friend. The friend wags its tail and walks to me. Boggle is dragged backwards. He squeals.

Queen sing a high 'Galileo'.

'Tiff, don't interfere, leave them.'

'But I want to—'

'It's a private thing.'

'It's not, I can see them.'

'Tiff—'

'I want to the find the puppies.'

Fritz reaches down for my hand and pulls me away, 'If it takes, we'll see.'

I look back and Boggle's friend, a sandy-coloured mongrel, is still following us across the gravel while backwards-Boggle yelps. Queen blast out another high-pitched 'Galileo!'

Later Mum comes back from Monmouth with a WHSmith bag and hands it to me. 'The birds and the bees, Tiff,' she says. 'You like animals, so here's a book about it.'

It's a big glossy book with two tired lions on the front: the boy lion with the mane is on top of the girl lion without. It's called *The Mating Game with 179 Illustrations*.

Robert Burton
THE MATING GAME
with 179 illustrations

Hardback Books

We'd go to WHSmith's in Monmouth. Tiff loved it. After one visit we were walking down Monnow Street and suddenly a hardback book dropped from underneath Tiff's dress. It was *Twenty Thousand Leagues Under the Sea* by Jules Verne. I'm not joking. That's when I noticed the bulkiness all around her middle, back and front. I tried to keep walking, but Fritz had seen the book.

'What is that, Tiffany?' he asked. She went puce. She did in those days. He picked the book up, looked at her dress and that was it. 'You're going back to Smiths.'

Tiff was hysterical. She tried to walk, but those hardbacks made it difficult. Not only did she have *Twenty Thousand Leagues Under the Sea*, but *Around the World in Eighty Days* and *Lorna* bloody *Doone*. I had to lift her dress up and pull them out of her knickers.

In Smith's, Fritz asked for the manager. Tiff kept wailing, 'I'm going to prison; I'm going to prison.' Fritz had just got a member of Motörhead out of prison, so she knew about that. In front of everyone the manager told her she was on thin ice, and next time it *would* be prison, and she burst into more tears. Fritz bought her one book, *Aesop's Fables*. In the car she pleaded with us not to tell anyone at Rockfield. Fritz told her to write her own stories, and I took her to the library.

The Dirty Donkeys

By Tiffany Murray

Once upon a time there were four brothers who were donkeys, Polydor, Parlophone, Polygon and Ned.

Together they were The Dirty Donkeys, the most terrible heavy rock band in the world. They wore leather jackets and motorbike boots which was unusual for donkeys.

POLYDOR

Polydor played the drums (badly),

Parlophone played the lead guitar (awfully)

PARLOPHONE

and Polygon played the bass (and he wasn't so bad).

POLYGON

Ned was the manager, and he tried his hardest.

Ned gave out ear plugs at gigs and unplugged his brothers' amps, but still The Dirty Donkeys were the worst band in the world.

The village hated them so much they banished them.

'Get away from here and never come back!' the mayor said.

They ran away to a cave in the hills. Polydor cried and hit his drumsticks on the rock. Parlophone played his lead guitar but with no amps it sounded funny. Polygon just cried. Ned tried to keep them warm at nights.

The rats of the village were happy the Dirty Donkeys were banished.

The rats were so happy they poured back into the town, they poured into windows and down chimneys and pushed down doors. They stole all of the food, and they took all of the babies.

One day the whole village and the Mayor came to the donkeys' cave. He said, 'Please if you help us, we will love you for ever.'

Ned asked for a fee.

The Dirty Donkeys had to have a helicopter to get into the village, there were so many rats. They plugged in their guitars and drums to a big pile of VOX amps and they played. The villagers had to cover their ears.

The Dirty Donkeys played, and it was the best gig of their lives. The rats ran and the rats that didn't run exploded, and those that didn't explode never came back.

The Dirty Donkeys are heroes of the village forever more and every weekend Ned gives out earplugs, and Polydor, Parlophone and Polygon plug in their amps and they play and it is the worst and best sound in the world.

VOX
VOX

20.

'On Parole'

Motörhead, 1975–6

Rockfield, October 1975
DR FEELGOOD in with Dave Edmunds. The Flamin' Groovies in from San Francisco, Dave Edmunds producing and engineering, too. Hawkind in. Ace back with John Anthony. Stackridge recording. Phil Ryan working with Dave Charles engineering. Start hedge cutting. Joan has asked for a gas cooker. Farrier in.

Mum says she's spent the autumn having her patience tried by Wilko Johnson from Dr Feelgood. Because she dropped a matchstick in his food a year ago, he now says, 'How many matchsticks tonight, Joan?' at evening meals. This means Mum has to say, 'Oh, count yourself lucky, Wilko,' or, 'Now everyone will want one!' when we serve poussin wrapped in bacon. Dr Feelgood don't laugh because they're talking about something else, and Mum doesn't laugh either. Sandra closes the kitchen door to cheer Mum up with their glasses of white and red.

Fritz goes to London a lot and I'm spending my autumn pressing my ear to the studio door as The Flamin' Groovies sing 'Let the Boy Rock 'n' Roll'. They are from San Francisco, like *The Streets of San Francisco.* I love their American accents when they look down at me to say, 'Hey, kid.' What I look forward to most, though, are Friday nights when I sit with Lisa and Kingsley in their upstairs flat in Nana and Bampi Ward's big house. We watch *Fawlty Towers.* I laugh until I pee myself and I think Fritz looks like Basil Fawlty. Mum says, *Only when he's manic.* One night after Lisa has gone to bed, I'm running up Bampi Ward's garden path to cross the dark track back to the Quadrangle and Mum, and I hear Ace playing their song 'I'm A Man'. I already know this, it really is *always* men here at Rockfield. Mum said it's a pity I just missed Joan Armatrading.

Now Rockfield is wet on the outside and inside again, and it's not long until Christmas. Mum and Fritz party at the Lodge, or laugh and drink in the Rockfield dining room with producers. The Galileos and the Figaros are called 'Bohemian Rhapsody' and it's been number one for weeks. It's strange seeing Queen's heads lit up in a dark circle on *Top of the Pops,* and not in the yard playing Frisbee or rounders.

Mum says, 'Well, at least we're not *I Am Sailing* with Rod Stewart any more.'

It was the record label who told Mum they'd pay her extra to get food into Lemmy. She sat the black and silver cloud of him down at the empty dining-room table. 'So, what do you like to eat?' she asked.

Lemmy told her *Jack Daniel's.* She said *lasagne*, and he said *don't be stupid, Joan.* She said, *OK then, boeuf en croute,* and he said *now you're taking the piss.* So she said *what about a bacon sandwich, Lemmy?*

'OK, Joan. But I like the crusts cut off. And the bacon well done to burnt. And Mother's Pride, none of this brown bread hippie shit. And lots of salty butter. And Heinz tomato ketchup. Thank you very much, Joan. And a plate of baked beans.'

Mum says underneath it all Lemmy is very polite; in fact, Motörhead are nice boys. 'Well, maybe the jury's out on the one called Animal – he needs to put some bloody clothes on when he's wandering about outside.'

It's because of the bacon sandwiches that I am in the corridor, leaning against the door of Studio Two. It's my job to deliver a tower of them to Motörhead on a plate. Mum cooks quantity *and* quality. Also, Fritz has to eat and he's inside with Motörhead because Dave Edmunds stopped producing and Fritz started. Fritz works all day and all night. Mum says he's *off his head.*

I've been here so long my arms ache: the plate is heavy. Boggle jumps and snaps at the sandwiches. Drool sprays.

'Stop it, Bog!'

I've been doing this before school for a week now. It's not that Fritz and Motörhead get up early, it's that they don't go to bed. Sounds thud into my back, so loud and hard I think they might be making space between my bones. I could scream in this corridor, and no one would hear me. 'Motörhead!' the chorus from the studio cries,

'Motörhead!'

Melted butter has hardened and mixed with the ketchup on the plate. I wish they'd come out because I don't want to go in: the noise they make hurts my ears, and there are smells in there, like damp mushrooms and Vim. Fritz and Motörhead have been inside for three days straight because Animal the naked drummer has to redo the drums before he goes back to prison.

Inside, Fritz will be sitting on the black spinning chair at the motherboard, pushing Black Jack knobs up and down. Fritz says, *8-track Trident TSM*. Motörhead will be caught in a cloud of smoke, tea-coloured fingers with silver skull rings running up and down the necks of their guitars. I know their growly faces won't say much until I offer them a bacon sandwich and then they will say, 'Thank you very much,' or, 'Cheers, kid.'

Sometimes their skin looks like it has been rubbed in fire grate ash. Sometimes they don't say anything at all because they are staring at the wall. Motörhead don't cover the motherboard in trifle, Fritz said, they set it on fire, and he meant actual flames.

In the corridor, Boggle keeps drooling. I let drum thuds hit me in the back, but I don't go in yet. Knocking on the Studio door is pointless because now they're singing

Vah-vah-vah-vi-brator!

I list my new words:

Spring from prison
Hell's Angels
HP Sauce
Iron Horse
Filthy Animal or P-H-I-L-ty Animal or Phil. T. Animal? I don't know.
Nicotine stain
Speed
Mother's Pride
Vah-vah-vah-vibrator
Skull and crossbones

Out on bail
On Parole

I chuck a triangle of bacon sandwich at Boggle. He snatches it mid-air long before it lands. Boggle really is my brother now. There's bacon grease on my T-shirt that spells out ROCKFIELD STUDIOS in brown letters, and I've missed my lift to Overmonnow Primary with Ann and Lisa, but I don't care because the Hell's Angels are coming.

Mum is up in the Quadrangle kitchen now, making lemonade and picnic sandwiches for them. It was Fritz who rang up the Hell's Angels on Nana Ward's phone. Mum said she didn't know they were listed.

'Yeah, that's it,' Fritz said in the big house hall. 'I want the noise. A real sound for the track. Yup, Lemmy will be there. All of you, bring as many as you can.'

I slump against the studio door; the plate's heavier the longer I hold it. My elbows drop and before I can stop him, Boggle is on the bacon sandwiches, wolfing them all as if he's lapping water. The plate falls but doesn't break. I watch him chuck the sandwiches back like a starving farm collie, which both of us know he is *not*.

There's no reason for me to go in to Motörhead now.

Outside there's a new sound bubbling up from the Rockfield Road. I stand by the hedge with an empty plate and a full dog and listen to the rumble. It's an earthquake, no, it's a sea of motorbikes. They turn, a silver wave, and pour up our rough track. Sandra comes out of the Lodge.

'What has Fritz done now?' She laughs. The bikes pass us, and I can't hear anything but engines.

Some of the riders have to stretch their hands right up in the air to reach their handlebars, like boys do on Choppers in town. I feel the heat off them. Boggle runs at wheels, barking, snapping, but he's too fat with sandwich to bother much and there are so many motorbikes he stops, dog-confused. I run after the tail end of Hell's Angels and Sandra follows.

Mum is corralling the motorbikes in the courtyard. They circle, a nervous herd, huffing and spluttering like my grandad's Hereford bulls (and a few even have horns on their handlebars). I wonder if Hell's Angels have to tie their bikes up like cowboys tie their horses up in the films? I walk through the heat of them, and smell oil, fumes, wet denim, underarm and patchouli. I have no idea how Fritz is going to fit all these people and their bubbling machines into the studio. Sandra's still laughing, but she does look a little worried. The horses whinny from the stables. Most of the men are wearing mirror sunglasses even though it's winter. They look like Motörhead, only wider. And there are women, too.

The bikes splutter and stop: sounds cut off.

The strings of Mum's blue and white striped apron drag on the gravel. Her *Poor Cook* lemonade will not be enough.

'Are you the leader?' She talks loudly with a clipped voice at a man with so much beard I worry it will get caught in his front wheel.

'Where's Lemmy?' he says.

'Yes, yes, they're all down at the other studio. We have refreshments up here.' She points at a trestle table she's set up with plates of cut sandwiches and shop-bought cake. 'But first can the best bikes come down with me?' She sounds like a headmistress.

There is some discussion, then the leader Hell's Angel nods.

'Right then, off we go, the rest of you stay here. Help yourselves!' Mum-the-headmistress tells them.

About ten bikes start up and follow her down the track. The rest do as they are told and stay in the Quadrangle. Sandra stands behind the sandwich table as Hell's Angels take triangles of coronation chicken, cheese and onion, share out a red tin of Rover biscuits, a cut-up Battenberg and bowls of pale crisps. I follow Mum.

Fritz is outside Studio Two in the daylight; he has more hair on his face than usual and an armful of recording cables he's uncoiling. He looks tired and twitchy. We haven't really seen Fritz since he's been with Motörhead: he decided it's better to stay in the bungalow with the band.

'Where's Lemmy?' the big Hell's Angel with the beard asks.

'Sleeping it off. He'll be around.' Fritz tries to smile in the daylight, but it looks like it hurts. He tells the smaller herd of bikers exactly what he's after, how it has to be loud and live and how he'll audition every bike to find the exact sound. The first column line up on the track. The rest shut off their engines. Fritz puts the mic close to the exhaust pipe and gives the orders.

'Right, you fire up first.'

One by one the riders rev their engines, exhausts bubble and pop, then each bike tears down the Rockfield track to the main road. Fritz listens, going from Angel to Angel to find his perfect sound. Nana Ward comes out of the big house and Mum has to tell her that everything is under control, although I'm not sure she believes it is.

Afterwards, the Hell's Angels cram into Studio Two but Motörhead aren't there. I push in between denim and leather legs. Fritz plays back the sounds of each of their bikes. He must choose but he doesn't say anything out loud. They start to chant, 'Lemmy is righteous, Lemmy is righteous.' It's getting louder and louder and smellier, and I wriggle and squirm my way out of the oily denim bodies, back to fresh air.

Later Fritz will tell me he chose the first revving motorbike, and the Hell's Angels had names like, 'Goat', 'Charger', 'Tramp' and 'Blue'. I think these would make excellent names for the next dogs, cats, chickens and goats I have.

The Hell's Angels are lying in the meadow now, like farm workers do in old French paintings. The ground must be wet even though winter sun sparks from the silver of their bikes, parked neatly along the fence. They are still waiting for Lemmy, but he's locked himself in the bungalow, and they won't leave until he says hello. The Rockfield sheep move among them, dirty-white wool through a herd of black leather.

Hell's Angels Picnic

Lemmy's thick white Mother's Pride
butter (no need to soften because they're hard, ha ha)
cheddar
a thick slice of white onion
coronation chicken already prepared with saffron mayonnaise
a shop-bought Battenberg, cut into small slices
open a red tin of Rovers
use Poor Cook lemonade recipe with citric acid
dream of the Kugel cake you had as a young girl
cans of Old Jamaica Ginger beer ... add Lemmy's Jack Daniel's

Lemmy, Jack Daniel's and Joan's Food

I'd never heard of Hell's Angels. I was left in charge of them; everyone else apart from Fritz was scared out of their wits. Fritz came out with his equipment, they had to make an enormous noise, he recorded them, they went into the studio to listen, and then what? They hung about in the meadow and demanded to see Lemmy, but he wouldn't come out of the bungalow. They seemed quite happy. It was cold but it wasn't raining. They kept asking, 'Where's Lemmy? Where's Lemmy?' In the end I had to bang on the bungalow door. 'You're going to have to come out here, you know,' I told him.

He wouldn't so I went in and begged. It took me ages.

'All right then, Joan, but just a "hello",' and he walked out, nodding and listening and shaking hands. It was almost royal. He was very good with them. Lemmy was a gentleman. Then he went back to bed and the Hell's Angels went into Monmouth, got pissed at the King's Head and trashed the place. Which was a pity. They were good as gold at Rockfield.

I thought it would be easy to get *some* food into Lemmy. I remember at the dining-room table one morning he said, 'I'll eat if you drink, Joan,' and I thought, *Well, I've done worse.*

'It's a deal,' and I put a bacon sandwich in front of him.

He filled a half-pint glass with Jack Daniel's and tapped its side with a browned finger (it was like he'd dipped it in Camp Coffee). 'Drink, Joan,' he said, and so I picked up the glass of JD and I did. I gagged on the third swallow.

He laughed. 'Told you.' He didn't touch the sandwich and got up from the table.

I have not touched Jack Daniel's since, although I did try to introduce it into their dishes. I think the JD syllabub and the JD Zabaglione worked. The rest was a disaster fund.

Lemmy's Jack Daniel's Syllabub

1 *pint double cream*
cup caster sugar (if not more? I'm using Jack Daniel's, after all)
4 *lemons, zest*
juice of 1 lemon
10 *tablespoons of JD (or more, I didn't measure for Lemmy, but you don't want to end up with Irish coffee consistency)*
60 g *of amaretto biscuit, crushed, plus extra to serve*

Throw all but JD and sugar into the Kenwood bowl with whisk. Now sugar, JD last. I made Lemmy come in and taste it. He'd almost ruin it by pouring more Jack Daniel's in. It was a rather unpleasant brown colour but at least I got him to eat some food.

The bungalow where Motörhead and Fritz stayed had a tiny electric cooker, but I did my best because I was worried about Fritz: he loved his food, but he wasn't eating. We hadn't been together long, so his Motörhead producing time was certainly a test. From what I knew about his work so far it was Irish bands, folk bands like Stackridge and Prelude, who did 'After the Goldrush' with him, rock 'n' roll, psychedelic stuff, hippie stuff and, once, Stéphane Grappelli (he said that was his favourite producing memory). Motörhead were a change. He told me he had to give in to the vibe (man), particularly when he was up for four days and nights straight, and I suppose that meant speed or whatever. I'm shit with that stuff. Anyway, in the bungalow I tried them on steak sandwiches, and I got, 'I'm not eating that, Joan, there's blood in it,' so I burnt the steaks within an inch of their lives and focused on mashed potatoes.

I did a casserole one night and they hated it, they hated sauce. Fritz had introduced me to baked beans and Motörhead tolerated those.

Lemmy was a bit more discerning than the others and, in the end, I did get him to eat. But the bacon sandwich became the mainstay.

Just before Christmas, Lemmy's mum and stepfather came to visit him. They were very traditional – I think his stepfather wore a cravat and a golf-club blazer. His mother wore twinset and pearls. They were so looking forward to seeing him, but I don't think he could cope. I was panicking because he wouldn't come out of the studio. Sandra kept his parents happy with tea in the main kitchen.

'I can't, Joan,' he said. 'You've got the voice for it, you go.' He gave me £100 cash there and then to take them out to lunch. That was a hell of a lot of money in 1975 and more money than I'd seen in quite a while, so I took them to the Walnut Tree near Abergavenny and we had a delightful time and the seafood platter. When we got back to Rockfield I made him stop recording, come out and at least have high tea with them, which I made. Including sandwiches. Cucumber this time.

Fritz went partially deaf in his left ear producing that album, and then the label shelved it. That's the music business for you.

*

A change was coming. We couldn't all live in the chalet any longer, there was absolutely no privacy and nowhere else at Rockfield for us to go. We needed our own home, and you needed your own bedroom; you couldn't live under the stairs for ever. It was hard for Fritz having no off switch at the studio, too. He told me categorically he didn't want to go back to London, which he probably should have done career-wise. He wanted to stay with us.

So, I would carry on being the Rockfield cook, but we were moving.

My only problem was telling you …

We decided to say you could have a puppy. Boggle had got the record-shop dog pregnant. If we moved, you'd have the pick of the litter.

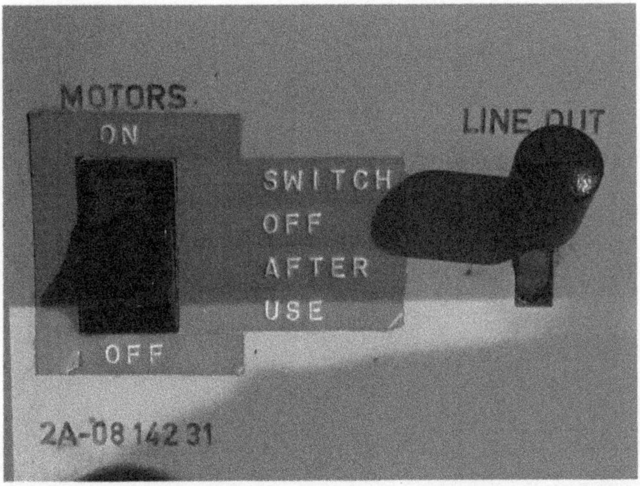

Part 3

Growing Up Is Hard to Do

Primrose Cottage

1976

Dear Tiffany,
Nice to hear from you. I recall your mum and the fantastic dinners she served up at Rockfield which I looked forward to every day. I remember trout being on the menu often and fresh veg always, cooked perfectly. The trout is foremost in my mind, but we weren't short of choice or amount for sure!

Graham Parker

Set List

Old Hag You Have Killed Me, the Bothy Band
Dúlamán, Clannad
Heat Treatment, Graham Parker and the Rumour
Grievous Angel, Gram Parsons
Jolene, Dolly Parton
The Gilded Palace of Sin, the Flying Burrito Brothers
'Save Your Kisses for Me', Brotherhood of Man
Pearl, Janis Joplin
'Juliet', the Four Pennies
'Come Back Beatles', Lipstick
Uncle Charlie and his Dog Teddy, the Nitty Gritty Dirt Band
Rubber Soul, the Beatles
'Take Me I'm Yours', Squeeze
Music from Big Pink, the Band
Stage Fright, the Band
Red Star, Showaddywaddy
The Rockfield Mixes, Ian Gillan
'Old Man', Neil Young
'Old Shep', Elvis Presley

21.

'The Kid On The Mountain'

The Summer of Drought, 1976

Mum has swapped her MGB GT for a beige Audi 100 so stainless-steel trays of her sticky spare ribs can fit in the boot. Fritz drives her food to Rockfield in the evenings, when he isn't producing albums called *Old Hag You Have Killed Me.*

We have moved. Rockfield feels so far away it stings more than my sunburn, but it's only twenty minutes on the dual carriageway.

We rent Primrose Cottage on the crown of a hill, built into the bank of a stupid wood. Primrose Cottage is on an estate, but it's not an estate with streetlights and kids to play with; it's an estate with pheasants and vermin, a gamekeeper, a farmer, a lord and lady.

My new Primrose Cottage words are:

Bailer twine
Grotto

Squab
Missionary
Vermin
Stain of sin
Reservoir
Heatwave
Spoilt cream
Drought
Polecat

If I ride my bike to the cattle grid, before the lane pitches down, sharp, I'm not even in Wales any more. Fritz says it's a border, but I can't see it. Every day I tell Mum and Fritz I'm going to ride to Rockfield and never come back.

'Well, I for one do not wish to see a child with stabilisers pedalling along the A40,' Mum says, and she doesn't turn round from the cooker.

There's no Brigitte, Corrina, Lisa, Young Charles or Amanda here, and I can't hear Sandra's laugh. When I wake in the night, I think I'm back in our Quadrangle chalet, but I hear owls and barking deer, not Hawkwind.

I'm eight and this is a heatwave. Melting tarmac sticks to our wheels and Britain has run out of water. In the day I count the ladybirds that land on my arms. At night dead things hum at me from the woods.

This afternoon I'm sitting cross-legged on the bonnet of Mum's beige Audi in my towelling yellow knickers because Mum and Fritz have forgotten I exist. *They have, they have, they have.* I'm going to sit up here until we all go back to Rockfield or the burning sun and car metal scald me to death. That will show them. A buzzard hovers, mewing. It's waiting for my flesh to sear pink as Mum's T-bones. Bessie, my new pup, pushes beneath my knees for shelter. She whines. She wants to get down, but I hold on to her collar. Boggle and his worn-down teeth pace the gravel below us.

Mum is in the Primrose Cottage kitchen sweating over boiling meat terrines for Ian Gillan or Graham Parker and the Rumour, an elasticated skirt pulled up and across her chest and nothing else. Ice doesn't last in her wine and the water makes it *ghastly*. She is considering salads ONLY.

'At least the cottage has its own water pump,' she says, 'but even that will be dry soon.'

Fritz has opened the sitting-room window and he's playing *Music from Big Pink* by The Band. 'Tears of Rage' blasts into the oaks and beech. The watery guitar and Richard Manuel's voice make my chest tight. The Band do this to me. I know all their names and I love them, but I won't tell Fritz: I am sulking. In the hot nights he'll play 'The Night They Drove Old Dixie Down' and 'I Shall Be Released'. Fritz says The Band are *proper musicians*. I chose the name 'Bessie' because Levon Helm sings about a Bessie in 'Up on Cripple Creek.'

Bess, the light of my life. Bess. Bessie. Bess. When you say her name, you smile on the 'ss'. She's soft and tan and brown with extra skin and big paws to grow into. Fritz said Boggle begat Bess, and Mum said Boggle had his way with the record-shop dog. Bessie is the only one who cares about ME.

Mum is yelling at hot beef fat from the kitchen, I can smell it. It's nearly time to drive the food to Rockfield. Heat shimmers at the hump of our driveway. That might be the Holy Spirit who's popped by to give me a warning because Bess is now panting with a grin. She chews at my fingers with needle teeth but I won't listen, I *will* squint in the bright sun, and I *will* throw up, or faint, or die.

THEN they will miss me . . .

. . . I said . . . .

I have a headache.

'What are you doing up there, Tiff?' Fritz's head is at my level. I hear 'The Weight' by The Band from the open window behind him.

'You're burning, you daft apeth, and Bess needs shade.' Fritz doesn't wait for a reply. He slides his big *make-yourself-useful* hands under me and Bess and carries us both into the cool of the stone house. Boggle hop-follows.

'I ran you both a cold bath.' Fritz still says *baath* not *barth.*

Upstairs he stands over the brown plastic tub and drops me into the water. I cry out it's so cold, but it is a relief. Bess is trying to drink from the loo, so Fritz lifts her into the bath and she flops down to lap at the water next to me.

'You can't make a dog stay in the sun, Tiff. It's your responsibility to look after her, so do it properly.' He wags his finger at me, then he's away downstairs to help my mother.

Levon Helm is still singing 'The Weight', something about Judgement Day. I feel a shiver that's not sunstroke; it's guilt. I am cruel like Cruel Frederick in *Struwwelpeter.* I hug Bess to me, she's still hot. 'I'm sorry,' I tell her, 'I'm so sorry, Bess.'

I'm going to have to find another way to get back to Rockfield.

The 'Old Hag You Have Killed Me' Crisp Sandwich

That summer it was easier when Fritz was in the studio with the Bothy Band. You stopped sulking because we'd stay at Rockfield, sit around the dining-room table, the French doors open. Kingsley still had that rusty clay pigeon trap out on the grass, but I don't think the Bothy Band were into shotguns like Ozzy. I had Dena to help in the Rockfield kitchen, too. I could not have managed without Dena.

One of the Bothys did insist on me making him a crisp sandwich. He had to show me. I couldn't believe it: it was just white bread, butter and loads of crisps.

doorstop white slices
salted butter, thick

a bag of Walker's ready salted
(no, sorry, we don't have
'Taytos')

press together with flat of hand

cut in half, I suppose?

22.

'dTigeas A Damhsa'

I have discovered a new thing about Rockfield: it's not *always* men. When Fritz was in the studio with Clannad putting harps on pianos and layering voices, Mum and I sat on the sofa while a beautiful lady called Máire sang in a way that made me curl up and sigh. The album is called *Dúlamán*, which means seaweed. That's not beautiful, but I've learned the Irish songs by sound. I sing, 'Jiggasadosadom', which Clannad and Fritz spell, 'dTigeas A Damhsa dom', and I dance in our sitting room.

When Fritz was in the studio with the Bothy Band, it *was* all men. Mum had to make crisp sandwiches, but Fritz said 'chip butties' are better and one day he'll treat us.

Rockfield have bought Mum a gas oven for Primrose Cottage. Now she can baste her ducks here, but it's so hot she's gone from 'Chrissakes' to: 'fucksakes', 'fuck off', 'holy shit', 'bloody hell', 'bastard' and 'go to hell'. Mum swears a lot in this heat. She's even given up her Café Crème cigars. Sometimes when she's standing over bubbling pans, she forgets our names: Fritz becomes 'Man', I am 'Child', Bess is 'Dog', and Boggle is 'Get That Fucking Dog From Under My Feet.'

If the heat has turned Mum's mood, it's also turned her cooking days around: she gets up in the dark to pan fry and roast. Cream is off; at last, she's wary of shellfish. I can take a cold bath in peace.

This morning she's already sweating, her elasticated skirt up across her chest and nothing else. 'From tomorrow it's summer fucking puddings and cold smoked trout,' she growls. 'This is the last time I'm cooking!'

Fritz and I keep chopping. He's going into the studio soon to produce a band called Squeeze, but now he's on onion duty at the long kitchen table. I've progressed from garnish to garlic: I have my own knife and chopping board.

Orange dawn lights up the kitchen, vine-leaf shaped, because this house is covered in vines and Mum won't let Fritz cut them back – 'they keep me cool!' she'll say – but they aren't working today. Rockfield also bought Mum a fan, and it purrs at her along with our new cats.

When the opening jingle-jangle of 'Save Your Kisses for Me' plays on the radio I jump up, hook my thumbs at my waist and dance side to side like the Brotherhood of Man did when they won Eurovision. 'Save Your Kisses for Me' has been my favourite song for months.

'Please stop, Tiff.' Fritz sighs. He says he regrets bringing Radio 1 into Mum's kitchen.

Fritz has brought lots of things into this kitchen: fish and chips in newspaper from Wye Fry (Mum is fascinated; she'll hold up and stare at a fat pale chip); tan horseshoes of Matheson's sausages you must boil in a bag until you achieve an oily film; malt vinegar; Heinz tomato ketchup; home-made vegetable curries. He's also taught me how to make scrambled eggs. I must stand over the pot and stir and not stop because *if a job's worth doing it's worth doing well.* Fritz is full of riddles. He'll say, 'your mother's having a do', and, 'you'd make a better door than a window', and 'it's like Blackpool illuminations in here' if I leave on my bedroom light. When he puts on a strong Lancashire accent and says, 'ah'reet, cock?' to his friends, Mum looks alarmed. Fritz asks me mysterious questions like, 'were you born in a barn?' But how can't I remember? He's also taught me a rhyme, YELLOWMATTERCUSTARDGREENPHLEGMPIEALL MIXEDUPWITHADEADDOG'SEYE, and told me if I want to spell 'Egypt', I should say EGG-WIPED out loud, then write it down. It's a revelation. Since Fritz, I have learned new words:

Revelation
EG-Y-PT
Bodhrán (which sounds like 'barren' when Mum says it. For example: 'Stop playing that *barren* drum with my pestle, Fritz.')
Manic
Snare
Depression
Bothy
RPM
Duraglit
Equaliser
EMI
Philips
Sneaky Pete
Squeeze with a capital 'S'
Acetate/Test Pressing
Mate-us

Brasso
Odd job
Dixie Down
Kindling
Nudie suit

Mum lines up fat white duck breasts at the cooker: gas burners pop, she's ready to sear and brown before reducing the port wine sauce. Fritz directs the single fan closer to her, but it blows the burners out.

'*Please*,' Mum says. She wants us from under her feet, she intends to shout at humidity. Fritz clears up, delivers the cut onions and my garlic, tells me to wash my hands and says we're going into the living room. Bess and Boggle follow. Fritz closes the door, quietly.

'Right, Mate-us,' he quacks like Daffy Duck then asks, 'What do you want to play?'

He doesn't mean Hide and Seek or Battleship; he means his records.

The first album Fritz played to me in this room was *Stage Fright* by The Band. I was getting over chickenpox, Mum was working, and Fritz was on duty with a bottle of calamine lotion. 'Look, Tiff,' he said, and held up a cover that was a rainbow, 'Listen.' Cats scattered when the accordion played and Levon Helm sang 'Strawberry Wine' in a cartoony voice. I giggled from my sick bed on Mum's Chesterfield sofa because I thought Levon was perched on the arm, grinning and singing at me. Fritz said it was *delirium*. When he turned the record over and I listened to the words of 'Daniel and The Sacred Harp', it was a bedtime story. Fritz sat on the carpet and we both closed our eyes to 'The Rumor'. Mum came home and said, 'You look better, but please don't scratch your face, darling, you'll leave holes.' Fritz looked exhausted.

Now as he opens the dark wooden lid of his record chest, Fritz is Long John Silver standing over his gold, *Ahoy there, me hearties!* His records live under the south-facing window in the chest on legs because even in a heatwave our cottage is damp (my bedroom walls are black with mould, and I found a mushroom growing in the back of the telly when I couldn't get a picture for *Kizzy*, my favourite programme). Fritz battles **THE DAMP**. He lectures us on keeping windows open for air circulation. He bleaches walls. 'Religiously,' Mum says.

She also says his way of playing music is as complicated as a tricky Robert Carrier recipe. Fritz's rules of vinyl are:

Taking Records Out

1. No sticky fingers.
2. Never leave a record on the turntable. *Joan*.
3. Never touch the front of the vinyl with your hands. Fingers on the edge, thumb at the centre label.

Putting Records Away

1. Pick it up from the turntable, edges only.
2. The vinyl goes in the white inner sleeve first.
3. Remember which record goes in which outer sleeve. I don't want my Stéphane Grappelli in my Skin Alley, my *Band on the Run* test pressing in my Steamhammer or Prelude. Put them back in the chest, spines up. They are alphabetical.

My hand span is too small to hold a record with my fingers at the edge, my thumb at the centre, but I have learned the difference between 45 rpm and 33 (I still laugh at the sound when I get it wrong). Fritz has taught me Dusty Springfield and Buffalo Springfield are not the same; and the Flying Burrito Brothers wear 'nudie suits' embroidered with marijuana leaves, stars, dancing girls, peacocks, pills and poppies on the cover of *The Gilded Palace of Sin.* I can see for myself that Aretha Franklin, Otis Redding, Gene Vincent and Sam Cooke have album covers with their mouths wide open and singing.

The Nitty Gritty Dirt Band, *Uncle Charlie and his Dog Teddy* has a black and brown dog on the cover, I love to hear Teddy howl to 'The Old Rugged Cross' before they sing 'Mr Bojangles'. The Bonzo Dog Doo-Dah Band have two Irish wolfhounds on the front of *The Doughnut in Granny's Greenhouse*, and that makes sense – they're the *Dog Band*, after all.

I get a thrill when Horslips grin at me from the cover of *Dancehall Sweethearts.*

Fritz's wide fingers tick-tack-tick through albums in his wooden chest. When Fritz is 'with his records' – which is what Mum calls it – he might sit in here for hours, for a day. The room will be hot and musty and loud. Afterwards Fritz might paint the water pump bright red and blue, or the legs of the metal garden furniture Mum brought from the Vicarage yellow and green. Once Mum and I came home to the front door half orange, half red, with a black stripe down the middle. She said, 'Oh, that's interesting.' The next afternoon the door was back to one colour: green.

She says it's hard for Fritz; Motörhead and so many other things that didn't work out; *but who knows what might happen with this new band, what are they called, Squeezed, Squeeze?* Fritz says the music business is giving him up, *but I can't stand idle, Joan.* He's bought ladders and paintbrushes and rollers: in between bands he's going into painting and decorating, starting with Primrose Cottage and **THE DAMP**.

He hands me albums. 'Take these, Tiff.'

They're heavy. I spread them on the rug and he adds more. He winces at my sticky-garlic fingerprints. I see one of Bess's poos under the table. I don't say anything because I don't want to clean it up.

'Pick one,' Fritz tells me.

There are a lot of heads:

Rubber Soul, the Beatles (heads)
Grievous Angel, Gram Parsons (a head floating in blue)
Imagine, John Lennon (a cloudy head)
Rains/Reins of Changes, Marc Ellington (a grumpy head)
Little Richard, Little Richard (a screaming head)
Pieces of the Sky, Emmylou Harris (a head so pretty it makes me want to brush her curtain of dark hair with Nanny's red-glass brush)
Pearl, Janis Joplin (but there's all of Janis, she's sitting on a sofa, smiling, a pink feather boa in her hair; she looks like a messy version of my mother)

Fritz has chosen animals, too. There is an album with a white goat, *Pet Sounds* by the Beach Boys, and I think of Nanny my goat and I can't remember where she is now. *Stackridge* by Stackridge has a cluster of painted seagulls nipping the air and Fritz's name on the back. I'm not surprised there's a gorilla on the front of *Gorilla* by the Bonzo Dog Doo-Dah Band, and J. J. Cale's *Naturally* is a giant racoon with a cane and a top hat on his racoon-knee. The Band's *Music from Big Pink* has a kid's painting of an elephant on the front. Fritz points and says, 'That's Bob Dylan.' I look at the elephant. On the album *Oobleedooblee Jubilee* there's a cartoon of a bumble bee. On the back of the sleeve, it says 'Kingsley Ward, Piano & Hysterical Laughing on 'Too Much

Monkey Business", and 'Produced & Engineered by Fritz Fryer for Boggle Productions.'

But I'm staring at *Jolene* by Dolly Parton. Dolly looks like she's sitting for a school photograph, neat and brushed but cross-legged on a purple cushion in blue striped pyjamas. I was neat like that when I lived with Nanny.

'Well?' Fritz says. A pregnant cat sways into the living room from the garden.

I point at Dolly Parton in her yellow and blue because I know Fritz loves her. 'Will she come to Rockfield?

He laughs. 'Don't think we'd be that lucky. Right, up on the sofa and listen.'

I perch on the Chesterfield next to Bess; it's covered with towels because Boggle gets his willy all over the blue velvet roses.

Fritz slips *Jolene* out of her sleeve. The label is RCA-Victor-orange.

The stylus crackles and a cantering finger-picking guitar makes me shiver. I lie back, ready to follow the track list on the sleeve.

'*Jo-lene*,' Dolly sings, and I settle into the story as the guitar runs like a river.

Soon Dolly is singing 'When Someone Wants to Leave', 'River of Happiness', but 'Early Morning Breeze' is my favourite. I want one in our sitting room right now. Fritz and I listen to a whole side.

'Side B or something else?' he asks.

I point at Gram Parsons's head floating in blue on the cover of *Grievous Angel*.

Fritz smiles. 'Great choice.'

'Will he ever come to Rockfield?'

Fritz shakes his head. 'No,' he says, and I wonder what colours he might paint the garden furniture today.

Mum is at the door. 'Please could you put on Lou Reed's *Transformer* very loud and clear the decks in my kitchen?' She says, 'Lou Reed's *Transformer*' and '*my* kitchen' because she likes to be exact.

What Fritz doesn't know is, I sneak down to the sitting room in the middle of the night, open his pirate chest of albums and pick up his records one by one. I know that Fritz has all the Beatles, and all of Elvis: Elvis at Christmas, Elvis in a Jumper, Elvis on Skis, Elvis with bad skin and a smile, Elvis in leather and lights; Elvis, Elvis, Elvis! Fritz has had some of these albums since he was a kid: they're coming apart where the glue was, their inner sleeves yellowed. These records are glossy and holy.

Breathe into me Holy Spirit, that all my thoughts may be holy.

Fritz's past is in this chest, too. Albums with his name and 'Boggle Productions' on the back and the label; reels and test pressings with no writing at all. There are albums and singles with his picture on the front, with three other men, but he doesn't look like Fritz; he doesn't have a beard and his hair is brushed and he's wearing a suit. Mum told me Fritz was eighteen when he was in that band, the Four Pennies, and nineteen when he had a number-one hit single. She said he did a Lead Belly song that she calls, 'In the Pines' and Fritz's band called 'Black Girl'. She said his band supported the Beatles in the Cavern, or was it Jacqueline's in Ross-on-Wye? Fritz says he can't remember.

'The Four Pennies were years ago. I wrote "Juliet" on the back of cigarette packet in the loo.' He makes it sound like it doesn't matter, but on the days when he paints the garden furniture in different bright colours, and on the day he painted and repainted the handle of the water pump blue and the body of it red, I think perhaps it does. Fritz doesn't play these albums. He's like Mum; he says *the past is the past, don't think about the past.* Fritz does have a blue scrapbook, though. It's called 'The Four Pennies' and it lies flat and hidden on the top shelf of our bookcase. It's handmade with letters cut out of white paper that spell out THE FOUR PENNIES on the cover.

Fritz told us it was made by a girl who loved his band and she was a 'fan'. Like the thing that blows air in Mum's kitchen.

When Fritz gave me his carry case of singles, I was happy because my hand span could reach from the record edge to the label without touching the vinyl grooves. I love the Beatles' labels best; a wet and green Granny Smith apple that looks crunchy enough to bite into.

Joan's Hot Summer, 1976, Part One

You're not entirely right. I cooked in both kitchens after we moved to Primrose, but that summer I nearly died in the Rockfield kitchen. I'd never known heat like it. I was obsessed with cold baths, and at Primrose I could just go upstairs and jump in. Have you ever cooked in heat? You are, no matter what, smelly.

I don't think I ever worked as hard. I loved it. The Worcester wine bar was so successful I was now setting up two more with new chefs. I'd get up in the dark, half cook for Rockfield, cold bath, drive to Worcester, plan menus, oversee them cook their lunches and set them up for the evening. Drive home, cold bath. And if the food needed me, on again to Rockfield and Sandra and Dena. Yes, I was bad-tempered in the heat, but wouldn't you be? No one had even heard of an 'air conditioner'. I was so lucky you took to Fritz, even if you didn't admit it.

You were in a state every time you left the studio. When the Rockfield kids came to Primrose for barbecues they told you how lucky you were to have your own room, the biggest bedroom I may add, but you wouldn't listen. I did try to stop you going in with Fritz and the food, but it was impossible.

I missed Sandra and she missed me. 'We don't have our laughs in the kitchen every night, Joan,' she said.

23.

'Take Me I'm Yours'

There's one lane on the Primrose Cottage estate. It starts at the cattle grid, passes us, then at the far edge of the hill circles a mission house filled with missionaries, Brothers with a capital 'B', Fathers with a capital 'F', and nuns.

The missionaries, Brothers, Fathers and nuns sing, 'Keep me, my God, from stain of sin, just for today' in their holy chapel. They don't sing, 'Va-va-va-va-vibrator' like Motörhead.

I ride my ga-ga bike with stabilisers past fences lined with dead magpies, crows, squirrels, stoats and polecats the gamekeeper strings up with orange bailer twine. I ride past the derelict Sunday School chapel where he also hatches pheasant eggs in warm trays under bright mother-bulbs (I like to watch them crack out and peep-peep). I pedal faster but hold my breath so I don't smell the foxes he's hung in a circle in the pine bit of the wood (if you jump you can touch their tails: some are fresh bright orange, some are black with rot, others are greasy bone; the gamekeeper adds to this circle, but he doesn't take away). I ride our looping lane round and round to the churn of the factory in the valley. There's no new school yet.

The beginning and the end of our lane is the same, and that sounds like something the mission Fathers say in their chapel. I know this because I sneak into the cool back with Bess to escape the sun. I also sneak into a grotto hacked into the stone beneath the mission. I leave gifts – a magpie, jay or wood-pigeon feather – for a statue of blue Mary, Mother of Jesus. Sometimes the darkness and damp of the grotto makes me think of Studio Two, but the nuns who come in to shoo me away are much quieter than Motörhead or Judas Priest or Budgie, or the Cardiff Chapter of the Hell's Angels.

Nuns look like Mum's new guinea fowl birds that shriek in our garden. Nuns sing sweetly, 'See our Saviour bleeding, dying on the cross of Calvary, to that cross my sins have nailed him, yet he bleeds and dies for me.' I think Lemmy would scream that.

I turn around at the cattle grid and pedal my bike back along the lane that loops the mission like a hangman's rope. In their yard the Fathers and Brothers with capital 'F's and 'B's dart like black and brown minks as I tring-tring my bell and bounce in and out of their potholes. Sometimes I think I can see heaven up here, although it's as hot as hell. This must be how hot America is, where you can cook eggs on pavements called sidewalks, sunny side up. Fritz told me that; he's been on a Greyhound bus, just like Simon and Garfunkel in their song.

When I get home that heat is shimmering at the hump of our driveway, and Fritz is loading the car. I drop my bike in the tall grass and I sneak into the Audi; I still fit behind the driver's seat.

*

Sauces tip over the lips of jugs as Fritz drives down our hill. I smell chicken and tarragon, watercress and orange salad, and the sharp cherry of Black Forest gateau (the cream waits, cool, in the Rockfield fridge). This food is for Paul Brady and Andy Irvine, or Graham Parker, or The Rumour, or Graham Parker *and* the Rumour, or Ian Gillan, Sassafras, Van der Graaf Generator *again*: I don't remember. My cheek presses into the back of the driver's plastic seat. This footwell is where I hid the tortoiseshell cat I stole from the aisle of the cash and carry. I named her 'Tramp' after one of Motörhead's Hell's Angels and my favourite film, *Lady and The Tramp.*

When Mum notices I've gone, she'll *freak.*

Can't deal, can't cope, I'll freak. It's the heat, she says.

Fritz glides onto the dual carriageway and I whisper a prayer from behind him: *Dear Budgie's IF I WERE BRITANNIA, I'D WAIVE THE RULES ... please let us live back at Rockfield.*

I know we won't. I gasp at the hot poultry smell and feel car sick.

By the time Fritz is turning into the Quadrangle I'm so sweaty that if he tried to pick me up I'd slip out of his hands like a greased piglet. When he does open the back door, I'm relieved at the fresh air. Fritz laughs. 'What are you playing at, Tiff?'

I unplug myself from the footwell.

'Well, make yourself useful.'

There's a singer, a drummer, a guitarist, a bodhrán player or a roadie in the middle of the courtyard, squinting in the sun. He's tall and thin, and I'm sure I recognise him but I'm too hot and sad to pay attention. The horses aren't poking their heads out of the stables; I wonder if birds pant. The tall man is walking away now, towards the studio, and it's Nick Lowe, and I haven't said a thing like, 'LOVELY TO SEE

YOU, NICK!' or 'WOULD YOU LIKE SOME ORANGE SQUASH, NICK?' He disappears into the control room. I sigh and search for new Rockfield words because I have to keep it alive:

Mutt Lange
Graham Parker
The Rumour
Neve mixing desk
Fender
Acid
Hag

'Fritz, it's too hot for food!' Sandra comes out, laughing her laugh, and I run to her and squeeze into her hips. 'Too hot for that as well, Tiff. What have you been up to, girl?'

I want to tell her *Tiswas, Starsky and Hutch*, running in the woods with Bess and finding five dead foxes hung up in a circle from the pines. 'Nothing,' I shrug.

'Oven's on, Fritz, more's the pity. How's Joan?' Sandra helps unpack the car because Sandra is still the kindest person in the world.

The door to our chalet opens, and I expect it to be Mum, or another me, but it's Graham Parker in a black T-shirt and sunglasses.

'Brigitte and Corrina are down at the Lodge,' Sandra says, a stainless-steel tray in her hands.

Fritz reaches for the cream-less Black Forest gateau. 'Not tonight, Tiff.'

I want to be angry but it's too much effort. They walk towards the kitchen, arms full of Mum's food. I haven't made myself useful. The studio door opens, and I hear a blast of a song. '*Waaaa-oooooh*,' it cries, like one of the 'la-la-la' rock

’n’ roll songs Fritz plays. I hear the words ‘Back Door Love’ and I twist on the spot in the dusty gravel, determined to join in with the ‘waaaa-oooohs’. I dance, a bit floppy.

I realise I miss Rockfield even when I’m here because it’s not the same. I can’t run out of my chalet door to play rounders with dustbin lids or sneak into the studio to listen to songs and bother the bands with my dog puppet. I can’t wriggle under Sandra’s blankets next to Brigitte and Corrina in the Lodge, as Christopher Lee does his Dracula hiss for the BBC2 Horror Double Bill.

I could run down to the Lodge now. Or I could find Lisa and Amanda in the cool of Nana and Bampi Ward’s big house and ask for raw rhubarb dipped in white sugar. But then Fritz would find me, and I’d have to say goodbye again, and that would make it worse.

I plonk down on the ground, bum first and I cry. ‘Back Door Love’ plays, and a roadie walks past me, chains and keys jingle-jangling. ‘You a’right?’ he asks.

Even though it’s not the same, I don’t stop sneaking down to Rockfield. On our Primrose Cottage hill, the sun is silent and there’s no wind, so the woods are silent. The foxes, the pheasants, the stoats and weasels are too hot or dead to shout their feral shouts. I read *The Wind in The Willows* in cold baths. Whenever Mum and I drive over the cattle grid, *dddrrrrrrrrrummmm,* the sound means we’re almost home and I must check the field fence for her guinea fowl, her new fantailed white doves or, God forbid, cats, that might be hanging with the gamekeeper’s trophies.

‘I just can’t bear to look, Tiff.’ Mum says it’s *pastoral* but brutal up here on this feudal estate, and sometimes she admits that living with rock bands was gentler. ‘I mean

Lemmy was kinder than that,' she says at the gamekeeper's grisly fence. 'But never look back!' she tells me, even though she's driving.

One day we drop the food *and* Fritz off at Rockfield: we leave him with a little plastic suitcase to work with the band called Squeeze. He waves at us from the track outside Studio Two and I suppose that's Squeeze waving too, so I wave back because it's polite. I go and stay with Nanny, but Fritz isn't gone long. When he comes home, he tells us stories of plunging bells in buckets of water all night for a sound effect. He plays me the five Squeeze tracks, and I love 'Take Me I'm Yours'.

This time when the record company won't release the songs, Fritz doesn't paint the garden metalware or the front door in different colours; again he says, 'I can't be idle, Joan,' so Mum buys him a Morris Minor red post-office van with her catering money. He spends two days painting the van green with a single brush, two coats, because *if a job's worth doing it's worth doing well.* Mum and I are both surprised and relieved it's one colour. Fritz puts a roof rack and ladders on it, and he drives down the hill to the village to ask if anyone needs a painter and decorator.

Nanny comes over with a boot full of Marks and Spencer's cooked food: chicken breasts, Scotch eggs, ham in packets. Mum asks, 'Why?' When there isn't space in the fridge or the freezer, we give Bess and Boggle the potato salad and sausage rolls.

It's so hot the missionaries at the big house whisper their sin and suffering hymns. The only other sounds come from the buzzards keening, the crunch of brown grass, the factory in the valley and Fritz's songs: 'It Makes No Difference' and

'King Harvest' by The Band; 'Gimme Some Truth' by John Lennon and 'In My Hour of Darkness' by Gram Parsons.

I miss the voices of Rockfield:

Oh, Joan!
You're a diamond, love.
Hey, kid.
What are you up to, girl?

Fritz Fryer was our producer on this recording, and he too was a dear fellow . . . We did a great version of 'Take Me I'm Yours', for which he set up this fantastic sound effect of a bell being rung as it was being lowered into a bucket of water . . . it took us all night to get this effect and, rather typically, the final version was never released or used.

Jools Holland, Barefaced Lies and Boogie-Woogie Boasts

A Squeeze Surprise

Squeeze came up to the cottage before they went into the studio with Fritz. I had no warning, but a man had dropped off a whole salmon that morning, so I didn't panic. It was so hot we had to go under the plastic awning outside the kitchen. I brought my fan outside.

I think Fritz picked them up and dropped them off, but I did have fennel in the garden. I stuffed that and butter into the salmon cavity, a little white wine, loosely in foil and served it with my lemon mayonnaise and green leaves. Fresh bread.

So yes, after that Squeeze recorded with Fritz at Rockfield. Tracks for RCA, I think. He loved the songs, and them. But it was Motörhead all over again: RCA shelved it and that was that. A few years later those songs were everywhere, with a different label and producer. 'Take Me I'm Yours' and all that. The music business is cruel. Fritz was certainly single-minded, but he didn't have much luck. Punk was here, too. It was even on the television. I don't think Fritz took to punk. He was more of a harmony man.

I do remember after the lunch I still had to cook for Rockfield, and I no longer had a salmon.

Some days Fritz was very happy fishing, but the river was so low all he brought back were eels.

Poached Wye salmon has a completely different taste to farmed salmon. I had a fish kettle so sometimes I cooked it in a court bouillon. I could never say what size I would get; I got what I was given.

Serve this version with new potatoes and my home-made mayonnaise and chives.

My court bouillon is:

2	*sticks of celery*
1	*onion, sliced*
	large bunch of parsley
4	*bay leaves*
	small bunch of thyme
	about 15 peppercorns

add enough hot water to poach a salmon, simmer for 45 minutes or more, sieve, and cook as per Whole Poached Salmon page 1

24.

One Flew Over the Cuckoo's Nest

Before she leaves for Rockfield or the Worcester wine bar, Mum tells me, 'Watch out for snares in the woods, don't go near the youth hostel in the valley there might be weirdos. And no swimming in the Wye, you'll drown. Please listen to Fritz while I'm gone.'

'Can't she swim?' Fritz tut-tuts at me.

'Yes, but doggy paddle only. She's a seal, apparently.'

'Joan, she can't swim, she still has these ga-ga things on her bike. She can't make a proper fire or clean her own room—'

'She'll learn—'

'She needs systems.'

'Well, you teach her if you're so bloody perfect. I have a thousand sodding meals to cook, and in this HEAT!'

I tell them both there's no water in the river anyway.

Fritz packs my swimming costume and takes me to Ross swimming baths to turn my doggy paddle into crawl, my widths into lengths. He stands me at the bump-hard lip of the swimming-pool edge and shapes my arms and hands into a dipping arrow. 'Dive,' he says, and he shakes his head at my belly flops.

In the humid foyer we sip machine beef soup and squint through chlorine-red eyes. After one swim Fritz takes me to see *Jaws*. After that I refuse to get into the water at all, and I stop having baths. He drags me back to the pool but buys me goggles at the kiosk and says, '*Be* the shark, Tiff.'

There are a lot of hours in the day while Mum's away working and Fritz isn't, so the next plan is: INDEPENDENCE.

He unscrews the stabilisers from my bike, holds my saddle then let's me go. I wobble along the lane as he shouts, 'Balance!' Now I glide smooth as a trout through the missionary courtyard, scattering nuns. 'I knew you weren't a wet southerner,' Fritz tells me, bringing back his Blackburn, Lancashire accent. If I do complain he says, '*Ahh*, did a-Mummy rub a-botty with a rough towel?'

INDEPENDENCE also means defending yourself, particularly from weirdos. Mum says they could be anywhere, just look at the paper. So, on the brown lawn in the afternoons, Fritz holds out his big fists and shadowboxes down to my height. 'WONAFIGHT?' he says.

I know I must say 'seven', because if you say *wonafight?* in a Blackburn accent it sounds like 'one off eight', which comes to seven. I don't really get it but I shout, 'Seven!'

Fritz laughs and drops his fists.

The story goes he lost four bottom teeth because he was brave enough to say 'seven' to big boys who *wanted a fight* at school. Also, his real name is 'David' but they called him 'Fritz' at primary because his older brother wore a balaclava and it was after the war. I don't understand this bit, but I do know that 'David' sounds silly on Fritz.

Fritz's next plan is RESPONSIBILITY.

He says I must *pull my weight*, and he gets me a Saturday job at a fish and chip shop in Ross, but the next day the shop burns down.

'You're a witch, Tiff.'

But it wasn't my fault, I only wiped down Formica.

His next plan is 'odd jobs' (which is different to the things he calls 'jobbies'). On Saturday mornings I must polish the candlesticks with Brasso, two silver vases with Duraglit, hoover the sitting room and roll up sheets of newspaper for a fire that won't be lit yet. Only then can I watch *Champion the Wonder Horse* or *Robinson Crusoe*, *The Courage of Lassie*, *Laurel and Hardy*, *Tarzan* or *Tiswas*.

'You watch entirely too much television, Tiff,' Mum says. She also says Fritz is trying to keep me occupied so I don't kick him in the balls again. I only did this once, the day we moved into Primrose Cottage. I wouldn't dream of doing it again because it wasn't what I was expecting at all.

I was curious. Would it, or them, make a Dennis the Menace *thoc!* or a Minnie the Minx *thud-d-d!*? Maybe a Katey Dan hard-chin *crack!*?

But it or them felt soft on my welly.

Fritz writhed on the rug, a patterned one I recognised from the Vicarage. Mum ran in from unpacking her kitchen. She knew right away what had happened.

'Why on earth did you do that, Tiffany?' The strings of her striped apron were dangling, untied as usual.

I didn't know. Fritz had only been standing in our new sitting room, maybe wondering where to put the sofa, his vinyl, his turntable. Boggle's balls looked so black and tight I think I was just interested. Would they pop?

Mum knelt on the rug; she had to help Fritz up. He made a strange noise.

'You'd better not do that again, Tiff,' she told me, and I

agreed. She gave him warm milk at the kitchen table and told him it should stop hurting soon. How she knew, I couldn't tell.

Since then, Fritz can be twitchy with me. When I'm close he sometimes sits like Nanny does in her front Church of England pew; legs crossed, hands folded over his lap.

If Fritz has a bad day when Mum is working, I sit in a cold bath with Bess until her half brown half black hairs film the surface and I've read all of *James and the Giant Peach*. Mostly, though, Fritz makes me laugh. He'll open a door to shout, 'Fernando!' because secretly he likes Abba. Fritz keeps promises, even if they're boring like taking me fishing. He buys me *The Dandy* and *The Beano* and calls me Katey Dan. He's Desperate Dan, of course. When he says, 'cow pie', Mum replies, 'oxtail', and cooks it for him in a red wine sauce.

I don't tell him I prefer *The Beano*, with Minnie the Minx and Dennis the Menace, even if Bess doesn't look like Gnasher at all.

Sometimes he'll drive me in his green Morris, and we sing 'Love Me Do' and 'Day Tripper'. Fritz hits a rhythm out on the wheel and dashboard. He buys one-scoop fudge ice cream from Gwalia in Ross-on-Wye and I'll have a cider lolly. They melt down our hands in the hot van.

There is a fourth plan: It's DOING THINGS AS A FAMILY WHEN YOUR MOTHER ISN'T WORKING.

The only time Mum isn't working is Saturday after the buffet at Rockfield, so tonight we're going to *One Flew Over the Cuckoo's Nest*.

Ross cinema is the only cool place this summer. In the foyer, the box freezer is bright with popsicles. By the intermission of *Jungle Book*, *Lady and the Tramp*, or *Freaky Friday*, my lips, tongue and teeth will be green, orange or red. But *One Flew Over the Cuckoo's Nest* is different. I cannot ask for a popsicle and chew on the plastic sleeve because this is a grown-up film. I've put on a Fenwick dress of Mum's, and lipstick and blusher because sometimes she wears make-up now. In the car she said I look like mutton dressed as lamb, but Fritz said the problem is *I am* the lamb. Because it's an X-rated film, they tell me to hide behind them at the kiosk but the girl with the stiff hair flicks doesn't even look up. Three green paper tickets push out of the flat silver top. Three adults.

You must walk through a Kia-Ora-sticky tunnel to get to the dark chill of the auditorium. It's packed and lit with the glow of cigarettes. We scuttle up the steps in the smoky dark, and I trip on the hem of Mum's dress. Her lipstick tastes lardy and the seats are scratchy. Jack Nicholson is staring out at me, grinning.

Billy Bibbit. Billy Bibbit. B-Billy B-b-b-bibbit and Nurse Ratched with eyes like a dead trout, and the men from the institution are out on a boat. One is hooking a fish through the eye and the cinema laughs, *hahahahahaha*.

The open back window of the Audi makes a judderjudder sounds as Fritz speeds up our single-lane hill and I stare up into hot oaks. I can't stop crying about *One Flew Over the Cuckoo's Nest* and Mum and Fritz are pissed off. I think of the Chief crashing out of the insane asylum and running free into the night, into the woods, and I want to do that now; the car door isn't locked. Instead, I gulp down a sob.

'Oh, dear, Tiff,' Mum says, but I can't stop because Billy Bibbit, Billy Bibbit, B-Billy B-b-b-bibbit, and Nurse Ratched with her eyes like a dead trout: and they made a hole in Jack Nicholson's head.

‘A lobotomy, Tiff,’ Fritz told me. ‘He’s a vegetable,’ and I think of Mum’s mangetout, her fennel au gratin, her creamed spinach.

I watch the headlights on the tree trunks. We’re at the top of our hill now. We rattle over the cattle grid. *Drrrrrrrrrrrrrrrrrrruuuum.* The judderjudder sound of my open back window fades as Fritz slows down. The fields are lined with the gamekeeper’s hanged trophies: magpies, rooks, crows, polecats. I sob for them, and the hot sheep with only dried-up grass to eat. Mum says, ‘No more grown-up cinema for you, Tiff. It’s Jodie Foster films from now on. They’re always fun and you love her.’

Now if Mum and Fritz go to an X or an AA film, or the pub on Mum’s precious Saturday night, they leave me with Heathcliff and Hindley. That’s what Fritz calls the babysitters Mum found in the village at the bottom of the hill.

‘He looks like a bloody werewolf, Joan, and she’s—’

‘Don’t be ridiculous. It’s simply an unfortunate bottle-blond cut.’

Heathcliff and Hindley don’t say much: they smoke. He is thin and so tall he must crouch down beneath the beams in the cottage. He doesn’t look like a proper werewolf but like the werewolves in *Carry on Screaming.* Even in the heat Hindley never takes off her floor-length black leather coat that’s tight around her pregnant belly. Mum said her real name is Kirsty and she’s fifteen and that’s how the village goes, and those kids need an outlet. ‘What about a youth club? I should start a youth club, Fritz.’

‘Joan, you don’t have the time.’

‘I’ll find the time.’

When Heathcliff and Hindley knock on the door, I run

upstairs with Bess. I lie on my bed and listen to the hot wind in the treetops, the long cry of foxes in the gamekeeper's snares.

One night they play Fritz's records and leave the vinyl out of the sleeves. Fritz says, 'OK, that's it.'

From then on, I'm back to certificate AA at the cinema, though no Xs. When Mum and Fritz go to the pub, I'm in the back of the car with my sheet, my *Asterix* books and both dogs. Fritz parks in the shade because the sun doesn't go down much this summer. I thread my sheet through the grip handle, make a den and demand Coke and animal-flavoured crisps. Sometimes it's so hot I take the dogs to swim in the trickle of the river. I listen to the distant bells and whirrs of the pub fruit machines. 'The Boys are Back in Town' plays on the jukebox, the snakebite-and-black grown-ups roar from the bar.

On a Saturday night in the car park of Ye Olde Ferrie Inn, I spy through the gap of my sheet-tent in the back seat, and I see two girls. One has short black hair and hard flicks, and she looks about the same age as Hindley. The other seems older because her hair is deep red, also big and wavy like Crystal Tipps in *Crystal Tipps and Alistair*, or the women in Mum's print pictures she calls Pre-Raphaelites.

What's interesting, though, is they're taking off their cheesecloth blouses and unhooking their bras. They put the blouses back on, but they crouch over the squid-coloured bras and strike matches. I know it's bad to light matches right now, 'the whole place could go up,' Mum said.

I creep out of the car to watch them.

'What are you doing?' I ask.

'Burning our bras.' They don't look up at me. The one with

the short black hair is lighting another match because the fire won't take.

'What's your names?'

'I'm Mandy, she's Cheryl,' she says.

Cheryl is the one with the deep red hair down past her bottom. Because she looks the oldest her bra must be the biggest.

Mandy lights another match. 'Bugger,' she says, 'it won't take, Cher.'

The bras sort of melt. Small patches of them smoke on the car park tarmac.

Mandy kicks the bras. 'Women's Lib!' she cries.

'C'mon let's go back inside,' Cheryl says.

They leave me in the car park. I watch the back of Cheryl's red hair; it moves with her but like another body, too. The bras smoke and then they are simply there: grey entrails now.

I go back to my *Asterix* books, the dogs and the car.

One morning Mandy and Cheryl appear at our kitchen table to help Mum cut up peppers and tomatoes. I learn they are sisters. They met Mum in the pub and they think she's brilliant. Another night they cross the river footbridge from the Forest of Dean, climb our hill and tap on the kitchen window. In the morning I find them in the spare room. Mum tells them they're welcome to run away to our cottage any time, she won't tell me why, but I know it's serious. 'There's an arsehole in their house,' is all she says, and that is that.

As well as helping Mum and sometimes sleeping in the spare room, Mandy and Cheryl become my babysitters, and I don't see Heathcliff and Hindley again. Before Mum and Fritz leave for a night out, Mum gives us all clean sheets of paper and Bic biros and we sit at the long kitchen table. Mandy and Cheryl write MARC BOLAN & T REX and STATUS QUO over and over again in bubble letters. I write 'Bessie', 'Boggle', 'David Bowie' and 'The Brotherhood of Man'.

Sometimes if Cheryl looks white and groans, Mandy will say, 'You got the curse, Cher?' and it sounds frightening and eternal.

Sea Trout for Graham Parker

I served this with mangetout and new potatoes. My mayonnaise. Graham loved it, as did The Rumour. Didn't you hear from him recently, Tiff? Didn't he say he remembered the trout? What a lovely man.

The bands didn't always come to the table at 7.30 p.m., so I put the veg on once they were almost done with starters. I plunged the mangetout in hot water for a minute only. I steamed the rest. Boiled the new potatoes. Butter, salt and pepper.

1 whole sea trout (they look like salmon but are half the size, much tastier)

Simply gut, descale, and wrap loosely in foil with salt, pepper, butter.

If a fork comes out clear, it's cooked. Better to undercook than over, but no more than 20/25 minutes at 375F.

25.

Heat Treatment

Mum says there isn't much you can do about the heat in the Rockfield kitchen. Fritz has brought the fan from the cottage and I'm here to aim it at her, but she says, 'It means nothing, Tiff, it's just hot air!'

She keeps going to the cold tap, wetting a tea towel and draping it across her neck. Fritz doesn't mind the heat. He's wearing a New York City T-shirt, cords and daps and he's happy to run in and out with plates and use his elbow grease over the sink. Sandra and Dena are in the kitchen. Dena has beautiful long hair that bounces at the ends, and she loves Bess, so I love Dena.

'Fritz, you're making me dizzy just watching!' Sandra laughs. 'You can't rush in this heat.' Fritz is dark like Sandra, where Mum and I are pink.

In the dining room I know which one is Graham Parker, but I don't know the names of The Rumour. They're chatting but Nick Lowe has gone. Mutt Lange is still here. There's another band in Studio Two and they're Irish. I've run down the track to check if they are Horslips: they're not.

Dena wraps the big sea trouts in silver foil as Graham Parker and The Rumour eat their starter of prawn cocktail, iceberg lettuce and home-made Marie-Rose sauce in a wine glass. Graham loves Mum's vegetables, so she'll make sure to keep the mangetout crisp.

Because Mum is suddenly laughing in the hot kitchen, I think she'll let me go down to the Lodge and listen to *Station to Station*. Maybe on this hot fishy night I can stay over on Corrina and Brigitte's bedroom floor, as thirsty cows low in the brown fields.

It didn't work out. Mum said, 'We have to go to your grandmother's tomorrow, so no, Tiff, you're coming home.'

The quick glide of the A40 made it worse. I was leaving Rockfield again. When Fritz rattled over our cattle grid, I hiccupped quiet sobs and Mum turned up 'Andy's Chest' on the Audi tape player, because anything to drown me out.

'We're both too old for this, Tiff, you're a broken record,' she said as Lou Reed sang about missionaries and rattlesnakes. 'If you're going to make a scene, you'd better stay at home in future.'

In the driveway I refused to get out of the car. After he unpacked the boot, Fritz tapped on the Audi window and did a 'what's going on?' face.

The summer-late sun has set dark red. I still won't go inside the house but Fritz has taken the ladders off his green van's roof rack, and I am lying on it, belly down. 'Hold on tight,' he says. Bess is in the passenger seat, her head out of the window.

Fritz pushes in a tape and the Flying Burrito Brothers sing

about a 'Sin City' as he lets the hand-painted Morris Minor crawl down our steep drive. I fall forward, head over the end of the roof rack.

'I said, hold on, Tiff!'

We turn left onto the lane. I have to right myself as Gram Parsons sings, and our woods crackle with heat. Fritz bangs the driver door, 'Ready? We're off!' and the Morris catches on gears and verge nettles. I giggle in pleasure and fear, my cheeks tight with the salt of crying and sweating. We drive past the derelict Sunday School chapel at the bottom of our garden (or at the start of the wood, depending on how you look at it) where those incubator trays stand like pinball machines, warming pheasant eggs. Fritz changes gear. The van climbs and I must wedge my feet between the roof-rack bars to stop me falling off the back. This is the part of the lane where you need to hold your breath, but I forget, and the stink of dead fox hits me. Fritz speeds up; he can smell it, too. Gram sings about Satan as we zip past the gamekeeper's cottage where hunting dogs bounce and bark from tall cages.

We drive down the small sharp hill towards the mission: I hold on extra tight. The dogs howl behind us, and Fritz turns up the music. We take the tight bend and roll right into the nuns' and Fathers' and Brothers' courtyard, as the other brothers – the Flying Burrito Brothers – cry out about their city of sin. When I look up, nun-faces are gazing down from open windows and Fritz cries, 'Yeee-haaa!' We drive on through the mission arch: a green hand-painted Morris Minor van with a little girl on the roof, and Cosmic American Music blasting.

I shout, 'Yeee-haaa' too.

We're over the mission cattle grid, we've looped the knot of the loop, and we're onto the thin straight stretch of road that leads back to our cottage. The red sky is turning dark.

Gram sings about a 'Do Right Woman' and a pheasant in the fern shrieks.

Fritz drives the loop again, and again. Past the pheasant-egg chapel, the fox stink, the bouncing hunting dogs; past the nuns hanging out of their windows like teenage girls now. Gram sings 'Dark End of the Street', and we rattle the mission's cattle grid until Fritz slows the van and leans out of the driver's window.

'Turn on your back, Tiff, look at the sky.'

Maybe it's safe to do this, maybe it isn't, but I turn on the hard metal. The night sky is clear. It's hot, and the stars above me might be brighter than anything on Gram Parsons's nudie suit.

This becomes a habit. When we get back from delivering food to Rockfield I climb up on the van roof rack, the metal still warm from the day, and Fritz works through the gears, loops our lane and plays The Band, the Flying Burrito Brothers, Gram Parsons on his own, J. J. Cale, or the tracks he records for me: 'Old Shep' by Elvis, and 'Me and Little Andy' by Dolly Parton.

And once it's dark, Fritz will slow the painting and decorating van he doesn't truly want, and he'll tell me to look up.

It is astounding, all those stars so far away but so close. The more you look the more you see. Fritz stays in the driver's seat as The Band harmonise on 'Acadian Driftwood' but I'm lost in the night sky and the universe or universe-es, and it's hot and the stars here will *always* be brighter than anything on Gram Parsons's nudie suit. I wonder if the nuns at the mission are sleeping, and if we are really getting another dog, a red setter, because Mum said, why not? Fritz doesn't like the sound of a pedigree.

'Ready?' he says, as he hits the driver's door with the flat of his hand, and I hold onto the metal bar of the roof rack, face still up at the sky because I'm getting good at this. I hold on for dear life, and we fly.

I don't wonder what Fritz thinks about on these hot summer nights when he crunches gears on his knackered gearbox to entertain a child he barely knows, while the woman he's grown so attached to sleeps off her hot, hard work at home.

Joan's Hot Summer, 1976, Part Two

We might cater a wedding or a regimental dinner on a Saturday if Dena and Sandra could do the Rockfield buffet. That's when Mandy and Cheryl come to help. At one regimental dinner the on-site cooks didn't want me there and tilted the oven, so my ducks went on fire. A disaster fund, but we coped.

I do remember driving you home after a double Rockfield cooking session (I'd done Studio One and the Old Mill with Dena and Sandra). I was exhausted and you were in the passenger seat saying, 'Mum this isn't our house, Mum this isn't our house' over and over. I didn't know what you were on about, but I'd turned off the A40 into some stranger's drive.

It scared the life out of me when Fritz took you out on the top of his van. 'Fritz, I've only got one!' I told him, but you refused to get down. Fritz's favourite dish of mine that summer was cassoulet. Can you imagine, in that heat? He'd say to guests at our long refectory table, 'It has duck in it,' and I would think, 'Shit, I didn't put duck in it.' It didn't matter.

My Cassoulet in the hot summer of '76 was:

Get up before the sun rises, open all doors.

Check your poultry; it doesn't have to be duck.

Smell it. This summer means check the meat with your nose.

Squeak, the Rajneesh gardener who dressed in orange, grew brilliant veg and dope (it was for him – I didn't smoke but your grandmother loved the look of it and asked for cuttings!). We had water from our own well otherwise the veg would have shrivelled. We also had a young boy from the village to help in the garden but one day you came running in telling me he'd shown you his willy. It may have been harmless, but he had to go.

I was bloody thankful when the rains came.

VPL 328M

26.

'Chirpy Chirpy Cheep Cheep'

Countdown to Christmas, 1976

Christmas comes early at Harrods. It's golden: a birthday-cake castle with turrets, imprisoned princesses, ogres and monsters. Also, a food hall, a toy department, and 'Pet Kingdom' on the fourth floor.

Fritz has a meeting at Philips, and Mum and I are in Harrods staring at animals in cages. She tells me she remembers lion cubs for sale here, and she's sure Noël Coward bought an alligator, and someone else a poor baby elephant. 'Terrible,' she says. 'All I did was leave you here and go to lunch at San Lorenzo on Beauchamp Place. They didn't allow children, you see.' She leans over, strokes a kitten: it mews a silent mew. 'I'd give the lovely boy cash to keep an eye on you for a few hours. I knew if I left you with him and animals, you wouldn't go far. He was such a kind, gentle boy.'

I remember being allowed to play with puppies and kittens for hours.

She looks up. 'I wonder if he's still here?'

I watch a watery-eyed miniature poodle. I think of the bouncing gamekeeper's dogs in cages. I've gone off the pet department.

'When I came back from lunch, you'd refuse to leave. You were glued to a guinea pig or a cat. You wanted to work here.' Mum is reminiscing.

I touch a fluffy-sad German Shepherd pup. It licks me, soft and hot.

Mum slips off her rabbit coat, brushes it down, and I worry for the live rabbits in here.

'Birds, Tiff. I think you should try birds.'

I've saved Nanny's birthday money, and if I choose small birds, I can get more than one. Mum agrees to a tall bamboo cage as my early Christmas present.

'It does smell of sawdust and piss in here,' she mutters as she clutches her small green Harrods bag of Ardennes pâté, pitta bread and a brown sausage of smoked cheese. 'Come on, hurry up. This is another lifetime.'

I think of the soft pheasant chicks growing in trays in the derelict Sunday School chapel. The speckled chicks go into a pen in the woods after that. I don't like the idea of birds in a cage, but we have too many cats with multiple toes. I learned my lesson with my two long-haired guinea pigs from the Cotswold Wildlife Park, when a visiting dachshund bit off their heads.

Sometimes cages work.

They are zebra finches. They come in clusters of six with orange beaks and stripes, and they are the prettiest, tiniest things I've ever seen. They cheep-cheep in the bamboo cage next to me in the back seat as Mum drives the Audi away from bright London. Mum and Fritz are quiet, their pasts are in London, and they never seem quite happy on the ride home. I watch streetlights and hug the cage in case the birds get car sick like me.

'Put my coat over it,' Mum says, 'they'll go to sleep.'

When I wake in the early morning dark in my bedroom, I remember the birds. My stomach flips with the thrill. The bamboo cage hangs at my window. They must be sleeping because they don't make a sound, not even a flutter. I shouldn't but I run to my light switch and turn it on.

I stare into the cage. It takes a minute. My eyes adjust.

I scream.

I scream again just in time for the last tiny bird to drop off its perch, dead.

It takes a lot to wake Mum and Fritz but soon they're staring at the pile of bird-bodies on the cage floor. Fritz confirms death in his towelling robe and Mum says all small animals are a pain in the arse.

'What did you feed them?' Fritz, Animal Detective, asks.

'The seed, the seed!' I point at the tub.

'And water?'

'From the bathroooooom!' I howl on the '*oooom*'. Bess slinks off.

'Did you give them water from that cup?' Fritz is pointing at the blue plastic beaker on my table. It's from the bathroom. He picks it up. 'My bottom teeth are in here.'

'Oh, shit,' Mum says. 'You gave them Steradent, Tiff.'

'What's thaaaaat?' I howl again on '*aaaaaat*!' Bess trots downstairs.

'Fritz soaks his teeth in it, you know that.'

No, I don't. All I know is Mum takes her top teeth out, brushes them, then pops them in her mouth.

Fritz takes the blue mug back to the bathroom.

'Tiff, there's nothing you can do, calm down.' Mum touches the cage and it swings on its chain. 'These things happen, it's not your fault. Small animals really are a pain in the arse.' She gazes down at the dead finches. 'Poor things. Fritz will deal with them.'

Just a few hours ago he'd fixed the cage in the prettiest spot, so the birds could see our view. Now the cage will sit downstairs, empty, or at times trailing spider plants.

There's a Steradent advert on the telly, and I sing along to it with my own words now, '*Steradent, every day, kills little birds in every way!*'

It doesn't make me feel better.

The birds are a disaster fund.

Mum says I'm so miserable after the birds, anything to cheer me up. I can't believe my luck. We're in HTV Studio West in Bristol. They've made the TV studio look like a pub in a barn. Fritz says this is a 'pre-record' for a Christmas special. I don't need to underline it in the *Radio* or *TV Times* because I am here.

Pretty women in tight pink or blue gingham dresses walk about with white tankards on trays. Mum has to help the woman with our tray. I sip from a tankard. It's cider and I love the fizz and tang.

Because Fritz doesn't want to be filmed, we're at the back, next to a small tower of hay bales. I wear a red spotted hanky at my throat. Fritz knocks the stone wall with a knuckle and tells us it's not real. 'Paint's still sticky,' he says. His painting and decorating is going well.

The Wurzels will be here soon and I'm bursting with excitement. Instead of dancing to 'Save Your Kisses for Me', I've been dancing to 'I Am a Cider Drinker'. The dance is: shoulders up then down, knees out to the side, then in and out and in like a squeezed harmonium.

'Christ, light a match in here and they'd all go up.' Mum is glaring out at the audience. I think she means the people in this TV studio are not wearing cotton. They are quite old.

When Mum and Fritz take me to gigs in London, it smells different to this, and people wear colour and leather and maybe feathers, and knee-high boots not wellies. I'll fall asleep in Hammersmith Odeon, Crystal Palace Bowl and the Marquee Club, then later I'll fall asleep on Fritz on a backstage sofa next to a single bowl of oily crisps. Fritz says any hint of a loud guitar solo and I'm out for the count. 'No Led Zeppelin for you, Tiff.'

The Wurzels are different. You can't sleep through their *ooh-arrr* songs.

They walk on stage and I jump up and shout. A man with a clipboard tells me to be quiet. It's hard because there are three whole Wurzels and I'm bursting with the thought of them and the cider, and they wear moleskin trousers and I think, *how many moles?*

I jump up again, clapping. The clipboard man says, 'Be quiet, Miss!'

The main Wurzel with dark hair plays a banjo. The Wurzel accordion player is always smiling, and the bassist is big. The room claps along to the Combine Harvester song and we make the farmer noises, *ooh-arrr.* Fritz sinks in his seat but I'm out of mine doing the Wurzel dance, knees in and out, and the man with the clipboard doesn't tell me off now. The lead singer winks at the camera, and this is the best Christmas present I have ever had.

In the breaks between songs Mum turns to me. 'You have the oddest taste in music, child.'

On the way home across the Severn Bridge, we sing 'I Am a Cider Drinker' with red faces. The Wurzels have almost let me forget the dead birds. I have the back window open; December cold makes my cheeks numb and I love the feeling as much as I love the Wurzels and their trousers made of moles.

Fritz says that Wurzel song is based on another song, 'Paloma Blanca'. Mum says, what's unusual about that, Fritz?

27.

'Under the Moon of Love'

I'm not just delivering food to Rockfield tonight, I'm on a mission. We're in Little Ancre, the white house on the hill, and my hands are shaking at the kitchen sink. Corrina laughs: 'You'll be all right, girl, they won't bite.' Corrina has her black hair short now, and she wears safety pins in places she doesn't need them. Brigitte is talking with Mum and Sandra at the electric oven. I love Brigitte's shiny lip gloss that goes on with a rollerball and smells of marzipan.

Sandra's hung tinsel and Christmas lights around Little Ancre dining room, and I serve Showaddywaddy a starter of pork terrine and cranberry, a radish salad. I think of my *Trocadero* album, the cover a painted picture of the band as kids, maybe my age, playing and fighting in the street.

Showaddywaddy line both sides of the long table, but Showaddywaddy in the flesh aren't the Showaddywaddy I was hoping for. I love the Showaddywaddy who sing 'Under the Moon of Love' and 'Three Steps to Heaven' on *Top of the Pops*, in green, red, pink, yellow, blue or purple Teddy-boy jackets and matching drainpipe trousers. *This*

Showaddywaddy are working their way through Mum's meaty Melba toast in T-shirts, sweatshirts and jeans. They aren't even wearing brothel creepers. They are just grown-up men.

I've never loved a band *before* I've met them at Rockfield. I'm not sure it works.

I'm at Romeo's shoulder – he's the drummer. I linger in his king-li-ness, hoping that if he talks to me, he'll have that 'Under the Moon of Love' low voice. And if I do the Showaddywaddy dance for him – that step in a circle, one foot over the other, round and around – will Romeo run up to his room and come back down in his red Teddy-boy suit?

'How are you doing, girl?' Corrina walks past me with a plate of chicken in a mushroom cream sauce, scallop potatoes, caramelised carrots and mangetout. I should have cleared the empty starter plates by now. Corrina is thirteen, and she is all grown-up. I'm not sure Corrina loves Showaddywaddy as much as I do. Corrina loves the Sex Pistols, but she and Brigitte still prefer David Bowie to almost anything.

My aqua blue zip-up book has the word 'Autographs' written on the cover in swirly writing. Fritz and his musician friends who bang bongos in our kitchen have signed it, but that doesn't count. I've never asked for an autograph at Rockfield – it's not allowed – but the truth is I've never wanted to, until now. Sandra said, 'All right, Tiff, if Showaddywaddy don't mind.'

Mum walks into the dining room, clears her throat. 'I'm so glad you enjoyed your meal.'

Showaddywaddy are finishing off blackberry and apple crumble with custard, like we do at school, scraping the sides. Mum folds her arms and waits for them to clap. When they do, she smiles.

'My daughter has a favour to ask. Tiffany?'

She gestures at me to walk forward but I've lost the use of my legs and the power of my voice; my hands sweat holding the blue autograph book and I hate its cheap plastic cover. I swallow, look down at the carpet and whisper, 'May I . . . may I have your autographs, please?'

It's Dave the lead singer with the dimples who opens his arms and tells me, *Of course, bab, we'll all sign your book.*

I get every signature, but as we pitch down Little Ancre's steep drive and winter branches hit the Audi, I can't read their names under the back-seat light of the car. It smells of chicken and pork in here and, as much as I love Showaddywaddy's autograph (and I will unzip my turquoise book and trace the signatures with my finger for years), I am never, ever, asking for an autograph again.

Apple and Blackberry Crumble With Custard for Showaddywaddy

You adored Showaddywaddy, you played 'Under the Moon of Love' until the grooves wore out (or whatever they do, don't ask me, I just cook here).

If bands were recording all night, I'd leave my crumble in the fridge, and it would be gone by morning.

My custard was always Bird's powder custard, sod it. I told you I am not good at puddings.

2 lb *apples, peeled and cored, probably from the Rockfield orchard*
1 lb *of blackberries (wild, we'd pick them and freeze them)*
8 oz *sugar*
8 oz *flour*
2 oz *muesli*
4 oz *butter*
4 oz *soft moist brown sugar*
3 *teaspoons of cinnamon*

Cook apple and blackberries with the sugar for about 5 minutes.

Mix flour, muesli if you want, cinnamon, softened butter and soft brown sugar either by hand or in a mixer.

Spread on the top of the half-cooked fruit in an oven dish, bake for about 20 mins on Reg 6/400F or when the crumble is beautifully brown.

For the custard:

3 *dessert spoons of custard powder*
1 *pint of full cream milk*
4 oz *sugar*
1 teaspoon of vanilla essence

Mix the custard powder with some of the cold milk making sure you have no lumps, boil the remainder of the milk.

Once it has boiled, mix a little amount into the cold custard mix, stirring all the time, then transfer all of it to a saucepan always stirring, add sugar and some vanilla essence, stir until it comes to the boil, then simmer turn off.

Cover with a piece of greaseproof paper. Warm up on a low heat when you need to serve it.

28.

'When A ~~Child~~ GIRL is Born' (with apologies to Johnny Mathis)

It's not Christmas yet but it was Fritz's thirty-sixth birthday and Mum said his present was a mid-life crisis. They locked themselves away in the sitting room *to talk* and wouldn't let me in. Fritz stayed in there and I missed *Rentaghost* and *The Muppet Show*. Mum suggested having his friends down from

London. When they arrived with guitar cases and bongo drums Mum said, 'Chrissakes'. Five days later they're still here.

One is crying in front of our Christmas tree. Mum and I watch him from the kitchen threshold. I call him Crying Man and right now, I want him out of the sitting room so I can play my single on Fritz's turntable; 'Jingle Jangle' by the Rockfield Chorale. I sang the chorus with the rest of the Rockfield kids ages ago, for Dave Edmunds and Kingsley.

Crying Man's shoulders shake. The lights of the tree flicker. We have regular power cuts and Fritz bought me a stepladder and showed me where the trip switch is. *No wet fingers*, he said. He filled the back of my red torch with batteries and put it by my bed.

Crying Man is howling now. Bess and Boggle jump off the Chesterfield and trot into the kitchen: they can't put up with him, either.

'What's the matter with him, Mum?'

She shrugs, then walks to the draining board and goes back to gutting a milky squid. The kitchen smells light and clean like sea spray, and I close the sitting-room door. I should be kind to Crying Man. I should give him a hug and say, 'there, there,' but I can't even do that when Fritz cries.

'Tiff, can you peel the garlic, please?' Mum points at my chopping board.

I sit down at our long refectory table and do what I was born to do. The kids at Goodland Primary, my new school at the bottom of Primrose Cottage hill, say my fingers smell.

Two more men are staying upstairs in the spare room. One likes to put his fist in the air and tell me it's Black Power when Trevor McDonald reports the news on the telly. He's a guitarist but he strums an electric guitar that isn't plugged in so the chords sound tinny. The second man drums surfaces and objects with sticks he keeps in his pockets. If he sits on the squat leather pouffe he drums that, if he sits in the bath, it's the taps . . . etc. etc. Mum says these men cheer Fritz up, but she's having second thoughts about Crying Man, *and for that matter the whole bloody lot of them.* When she gets home from Rockfield late at night, tired and smelling of boeuf en croute and buttery scallops, she'll say, 'For Chrissake,' and open the kitchen windows to let out the blanket of dope smoke and noise. She will then cook for the men, even though she's bone tired. 'A guest is a guest,' she says. Fritz helps. After wine Mum will get 'a second wind', and dance and laugh.

There's a fourth man in a tent in the garden; he isn't from London because he's Man Horrid. He still has the sweatshirt with MAN HORRID transferred on it, but the transfers have half peeled away.

He is now, AN HO R D.

AN HO R D says he's tough like Fritz because they're northerners, not wet like us southerners, but on cold mornings I see him on the camp bed in the sitting room. Anyway, Mum is always the first up, and I think she is tougher than them all: Fritz does say she has asbestos fingers.

In the evenings, while Mum is at Rockfield, I light the candles on the kitchen table and sit with Fritz's friends, Bess at my feet. They play instruments and sing and call it 'jamming'. Sometimes it's just playing the bongos, although drumstick man does hit out rhythms on Mum's brass candlesticks and the pepper mill. I shake a maraca. Fritz slaps the tabletop like he slaps the dashboard of his van in the cold mornings when he drives me to school.

I like sitting between the men. They smell of sweat, tobacco and fruity white wine as they 'jam', drink and laugh. It's almost like being back in the Rockfield dining room. They tell me my small hands are good for rolling joints. They lick the gummy edges and stick Rizla papers together like we stick bright tissue paper onto card with Gloy glue at school. You must make a double Rizla first, then another paper at the end, then you sprinkle it with Golden Virginia, dope and a bit of cigarette packet or Rizla packet curled up at the end. That's when they give it to me: it's my job to roll it into a cigarette with my small fingers. When I hand it back, they suck on it like orphaned lambs, and I wait for the seeds to pop in their faces. I love this bit because the seeds flare like a sudden sparkler on bonfire night. Some nights Fritz sings 'Cut Across Shorty', or 'Old Shep' until Boggle howls, and I dress Bess as Elvis (if Elvis ever wore my blue cords, red and white stripy socks, Fritz's one tie and a Rockfield T-shirt). The men cheer and sing 'Hound Dog' at her. I lift her front paws and we dance. I know when I fall asleep on the hard settle at the head of the table, the men will still be 'jamming' and Bess will be beneath me in my T-shirt, the striped socks lost to the kitchen floor.

It's the same every night.

I'm a bit bored of it now. It's not Christmasy at all.

I've noticed the men play bits of instruments in annoying ways that don't begin or end. I want them to sing 'Away in a Manger' and 'Hark! The Herald Angels Sing.' And I don't like passing the joint when I'm sitting between them because I get the wet touch of their licked papers on my fingers. I let my hands hang under the table for Bess to lick the germs away.

There's also a problem with Crying Man: he doesn't just cry in front of the Christmas tree. Crying Man spends hours in our little hallway talking on our phone, crying at his reflection in the pitted mirror and making our telephone bill bigger. Fritz says, *Don't be a Nosy Parker, Tiffany, friends are welcome, don't question friends, and don't bother bother till bother bothers you*, but I've seen the red bills in the drawer. Mum says, *If the electric didn't trip, we'd probably be cut off anyway*, and there's a new frown to her face.

I make the decision on my own. I must *pull my weight*. It's early morning when I sit up in bed and I write my rhyme in my neatest joined-up words. If Fritz wrote a number one song on the back of a cigarette packet in a loo, I can do this in my bedroom. I've had to tear a piece of lined paper from my school exercise book, and that hurts, but this is important.

The men, Fritz and Mum and the dogs are still sleeping off their work and their jamming when I tiptoe down the soft, white shagpile stairs. In the hall I take the pampas grass out of the demijohn bottle and walk out into the frosty garden. It's half-dark. A fox screams. I chuck the fluffy pampas into the brambles. AN HO R D will be on the camp bed in the sitting room by now.

Back inside I rub my cold feet into the white carpet and drag the empty demijohn to the table where the beige phone sits. I find the end of the Sellotape, unpick it with my teeth and stick my rhyme onto the demijohn's side. I tape it and tape it so nobody can peel it off. I read it out loud.

Telephone bills cost a lot
So please put some money
In the pot.

What I want to say is GO AWAY, but I can't because a child must say *please*, *thankyouverymuch*, write thank you letters, be seen and not heard but also do something entertaining like dress her dog as Elvis, or be good at darts. I just want Crying Man to stop using the phone, and crying, and hogging the sitting room.

Want, want, want, Fritz says.

Tonight, everything is better because I saw a 10p piece and some coppers in my demijohn, and Keith from California has arrived. Keith doesn't play the bongos; he plays the banjo. He's Fritz's best friend and they record together, go on tour together and tell stories about getting trifle all over the Rockfield motherboard together long before Mum was 'on the scene'.

'Hey, man,' Keith says.

'Hey, *maaaan*,' Fritz replies with a bad American accent.

Keith wears metal hooks on his thumb and fingers to play a banjo patterned with mother of pearl, and his fingers whizz up and down the fretboard in a blur. I'm hypnotised: I hold my breath as his banjo talks.

When we stay in Greenwich with Keith's family (because Mum loves Keith, too), he, Fritz and Albert Lee play guitars and banjos inside, while I play hopscotch with Keith's daughters on the pavement. Red London buses roar. I search for Greenwich Mean Time, and I wonder how mean is it? I hop over cracks and chalk squares, I hear loud ting-ting buses, and I think Keith's daughters are the best thing in the world.

Mum is home and she's brought me out to the garden for fresh air. 'Dope is so very boring, darling. I can't inhale,' she's telling me or the brambles.

The woods around us crackle and splinter with night-animals. Inside the men are playing 'Old Man' by Neil Young, and I can hear Keith's banjo: the music has improved since he arrived. There's frost on Mum's winter greens. It's cold but here they say 'bitter'.

I walk over to the water pump that Fritz has repainted yellow and red. A twelve-bore fires over by the mission and I imagine Fathers and Brothers, nuns and foxes, scattering to the gamekeeper's smile. My new schoolfriend Charlie lives on this hill. She's Charlie like the orange cat in the public information programmes, *Charlie Says*. Charlie is strong: she has long curly blonde hair in a thick plait, and she wears black nylon slacks and wellies. Charlie has taught me how to pinprick the two ends of an egg and blow out the guts without breaking it. Together we spy on pheasants, hedgehogs and nuns, because the woods have endless possibilities.

I like to think of Charlie out there, asleep with the grass snake she keeps in a glass box in her bedroom, 'his name is Fred,' she told me. At the oak by the crossroads is Darren Turley's house. He's from my class, too, and Darren has Elvis on his wall, on his mind, and in his lip curl.

There are other children out there on this hill, waiting for Christmas just like me.

'Come on, bed.' Mum takes my hand. 'It will be easier when our guests have gone.'

I tell her I really don't want Crying Man to stay for Christmas. I want the sitting room: I've underlined *Dr Doolittle* in the *TV Times* and I need to watch it.

The men go home the next day.

Food At All Hours For Guests

One guy who stayed with us insisted I bought him a bottle of gin every day. I dutifully went down to the village shop at the bottom of the hill then back up before driving to set up the wine bar in Worcester, then on to Rockfield. Madness. One day I simply thought, *What are you doing, Joan?* So I told him to get the gin himself. He said every woman he'd ever known had bought him gin every day. I told him, *You've got the wrong one here, dear.*

I'd keep lasagne, or chilli con carne, in the fridge, so they could try to help themselves. I enjoyed cooking for them, particularly Keith, who loved my Sunday lunches. It's what I did.

Chilli Con Carne

Very easy to make.

This for 10 people and there will be plenty left over.

4 lb good minced beef
2 large onions
6 cloves of garlic
2 tablespoons of ground coriander
2 dessertspoons of ground turmeric
a teaspoon of chilli powder
2 fresh green chillis medium. One and then taste for hotness
2 lb fresh tomatoes skinned or 2 tins of good tomatoes
fresh coriander
olive oil
salt
pepper
dried and soaked, or tinned red kidney beans

Slice onions, cook in oil, add garlic, translucent, then beef mince, turn the beef with a spoon, cook for about 5–10 mins and add the spices, turning with a spoon all the time. Then tomatoes.

Let it bubble away as you add the fresh chilli (medium hot), salt and pepper, TASTE, and if you like it fairly hot, add second chilli.

Cook this for about 40 mins.

At the very end add fresh coriander. I used to grow coriander in my garden, or inside in the winter.

29.

'All Shook Up' for Christmas

When it arrives in our kitchen Mum says, 'What the hell, Fritz?'

It's a spaceship, a Tardis, a giant boiled sweet. It's curved, bulbous, in glass and plastic. It is red, orange and it's neon. Fritz says it's his early Christmas present to us.

Mum says, 'We are getting entirely too many presents,' and she looks at me.

'I'm plugging it in, Joan.'

The thing whirrs, purrs and clicks. It flashes into a warm orange glow. It looks like something the nuns would bow down and pray to in their rocky grotto, *oh glory be.*

'What on earth, Fritz?'

I run to the see-through front dome and read a word in pretty writing.

Wurlitzer

'It's an original. It only works with these.' Fritz holds up a plastic bag of golden coins.

Mum says Fritz has spent *all* of his Clannad, Bothy Band, Squeeze and painting and decorating money now, but maybe the jukebox can keep us warm this winter?

It takes me a morning to learn that 'Blue Suede Shoes' is too fast for it, 'Good Luck Charm' is too slow, but 'Don't be Cruel' and 'Hound Dog' are just right. I know when to spin on the kitchen lino with Fritz holding my hand; when to spin alone, and when to come back to Fritz's chest as he counts my steps to the rock 'n' roll dance: *one, two, three.* It's only been a day and our woods echo with *Tutti Frutti Maybe Baby Good Golly Miss Molly C'mon Everybody Johnny B. Goode Rock Around the Clock Boney Maronie Blue Suede Shoes* . . . until badgers tear at the frozen ground and the owls swoooooooop

and the men in the Wurlitzer jukebox cry out until we're all shook up.

Elvis is still *uh-uh*, but I've discovered Buddy Holly is *ha-ho.*

Gene Vincent is *aaahhhhh!*

Little Richard is ooooooooh!

It's a new language.

ba-

ba-

ba-ba

ha-ho

uh-uh

be-bop a –

lul-

la

awella

bama lama

whop-whop
dingaling
a whap bam

BOO!

There is one Patsy Cline single, 'I Fall to Pieces', and one Connie Francis, 'Stupid Cupid'.

I bother Fritz with questions.

'What's the United Nations?'

'What's a vacation?'

'What's a bellhop?'

'What's a Cadillac?'

'What's a Coup de Ville?'

'Who is "Be Bop a Lula"?'

'What's a congressman?'

'Is Tutti Frutti a girl or a boy?'

'What are "great balls of fire"?'

'What's "craahing", Fritz?'

When I wake in the dark, I feel the Wurlitzer hum beneath me. Now its glow guides me to the downstairs kitchen sink; rock 'n' roll air traffic control for that middle-of-the-night glass of water (because Fritz says don't drink the water from the bathroom tap). Some nights, thirsty or not, I bring my sleeping bag downstairs and curl up in the warmth of its neon stripes as ice scratches the inside of our windows.

It's morning but winter-dark in the kitchen, and I know the golden coins sit in a leather Mah-Jong cup on the jukebox top. We are not allowed to move that cup: if the coins are lost, we can't play the songs. I climb on the wooden settle to reach it.

I take one coin, jump down, push it into the slot and wait for the hollow dro-

o-

o-

o-

o-

p.

Clonk.

The Wurlitzer wakes with a whirr. I press ivory buttons: I can choose whatever I want.

L8.

The clicks get louder and the front dome brighter. One single from the silver cradle jerks out. There's a tremble, ticks ring, the stylus lifts and the needle drops and thumps; sounds crackle.

Elvis sings 'Heartbreak Hotel'.

It's such a strange echo, like Elvis really is singing alone in a hotel room and I'm listening through the door. I watch my cold breath in the light of the Wurlitzer and I press more buttons.

Elvis sings 'One Night!'

I think of my 'In the Ghetto' single from the Vicarage. I don't know where it is now, but I do know that Elvis will always make me want to rub myself across the carpet like our dogs do when they have worms.

The jukebox puts Elvis back in his silver cradle. I choose A3.

'*Be Bop a Lula*,' Gene Vincent croons, and the cats on our kitchen shelves yawn pink yawns and stretch their multiple toes.

'*Be Bop a Lula*' and my bare feet kick on the sticky lino. Dancing gets rid of the cold.

'*Be Bop a Lula*' and Gene Vincent screams, and just like Fritz taught me my toes and heels tap their rock 'n' roll dance.

I jerk my fingers out, crouched over like I'm wearing a Teddy boy jacket not Peacocks' pyjamas.

'Be Bop a Lula!'

I hear Fritz cough upstairs. He's off to London for meetings before Christmas Day. I get on with my odd jobs and clean up the cat shit in the living room to 'Don't be Cruel'.

'Good girl, Tiff.' Mum walks in and lights a match over the rolled-up newspapers in the fire. Elvis sings 'Don't' in the kitchen, and I sing along, as low and rumbling as I can possibly go, from the soles of my dirty feet, up.

'Don't'

'Don't'

'Don't'

'Don't . . .'

*

Elvis eats squirrels so I don't see why I shouldn't. The gamekeeper came and now there are whole animals and bits of animals on the outside table. Mum points at them and says, 'That is venison, those are woodcocks, he's a partridge, and you know pheasants and rabbits.' There are no squirrels. Mum won't go that far.

She's playing *Hunky Dory*. The meat smells and she calls it 'high'. This is a different high to the one the men have in our kitchen. Before he leaves Fritz drags out a gas heater that clicks and pops and whooooshes on, and living pheasants call out from the woods.

Mum and I pull and pluck and cut up different-coloured meats under the outside plastic awning because Mum is pre-preparing a game pie for the Boxing Day shoot. She says it's coals to Newcastle but that's what they asked for, and she doesn't understand shoots but she's getting paid. Boggle snatches at scraps.

Plucking makes a hollow sound. Mum chops off the heads and feet with a cleaver. *Thwoc!* She does the rabbit skinning, too. The sound a rabbit skin makes coming off is a big *schluuuuuurp.*

Our hands are bloody in the cold. I don't think about it.

Mum throws the livers to the dogs.

Fritz is still in London; Mum and I are on our own for the first time in a long time. Now she's done the game pie filling Mum doesn't have to cook for shoots, rock stars, wine bars, regiments or weddings over Christmas. She sips Heinz mushroom soup from a cup and I sip Heinz tomato. The cottage is quiet.

I do play songs on the Wurlitzer, though. I stand as close as I can to its glow and Mum says, 'do we *have* to have 'One Night' for the *nth* time, Tiffany?'

We sit together on the Chesterfield with towels beneath us because Boggle still gets his willy over it. Mum has *Black Narcissus* by Rumer Godden, and a Barbara Pym. I have *Charlie and the Chocolate Factory.* She also has books with wonky thin men on the front, all called *The Man Without Qualities*, and very old cookery books. We often take trips in the car to a second-hand bookshop in Llandrindod Wells where she buys *Mrs Beeton's Everyday Cookery*, *The Household Cookery Book: Practical and Elementary Methods* and very small copies of *Wuthering Heights* with gold edges. I'll sit on the floor of the shop and tower book piles around me. I am allowed one.

It's Christmas Eve and Fritz is coming home. In the garden Mum picks cold rosemary and sage. Deer have leaned over the fence and nibbled her brassicas.

'Who cares? They made us eat that at school, boiled to hell. I hated it.' She laughs and her breath is a cold cloud. I laugh, too. Boggle hops up to the fence around her vegetable garden and cocks his leg. 'Bloody dog,' she mutters, but she smiles.

Mum likes the no men, the no cooking, what she calls *the peace and quiet*, but only for a while. It's always, 'people, people, I must have people around me,' with Mum.

Frost crunches in the growing darkness but it's only three o' clock. Grey squirrels hiss. Bess sticks her nose in the mulch and snorts. I love the way Bess's body is brown but black at the paws and the muzzle. I call her to me, her tail wags and if I had a tail I might wag it, too. The phone rings and when Mum comes back out in her rabbit coat, she tells me Nanny is on her way. We usually visit her on Christmas Eve, and Nanny doesn't care for Primrose Cottage. She'll stand in my bedroom and tell Mum the black mould on my walls is dreadful, that I will get chilblains if I don't wear slippers, and this is a 'dialect cottage'.

'*Derelict*, Mother, the word is *derelict*, and we have a fire and Fritz bleaches the walls. We rent, it's not for ever.'

'You need gas heaters, Joan.'

'We're fine, Mother.'

'You live with *that man.*'

Nanny calls Fritz, *that man*. Mum says it's because he doesn't wear a suit and tie, and work in a bank.

When she does arrive, Nanny stands in the kitchen and sighs, the handles of heavy Marks & Spencer shopping bags digging into her palms: I know the packaged sausage rolls will go to the dogs.

'Poor little Tiffany Jane, she should be with her grandmother at Christmas.'

'You know you are welcome here, Mother.'

To Nanny I'm Oliver Twist; but I'm in a kitchen of beef

and cream, a shiny turkey, a pockmarked goose and the occasional king prawn. I grab Bess and run out into the dark garden without a coat because I don't feel the cold in this cottage any more (Mum says we have 'gone numb'). I hear Mum argue with my grandmother as Bess trots into the crunchy frost of shrivelled brown fern. The woods still have endless possibilities.

When Nanny has gone, Mum and I prepare Christmas vegetables in the kitchen.

'I do hope Fritz doesn't bring that gin-drinking pain in the arse back with him,' she says, 'because I am not going down to the village shop and buying his bloody Gordon's.' She sticks another orange up the turkey's bum.

Boxing Day Game Pie

Game pie was an odd choice for a shoot. I didn't like the whole thing at all, but beggars can't be choosers.

I use pheasant/rabbit/whatever the gamekeeper drops off, maybe venison, woodcock, partridge. These can be odd combinations. He did offer me a squirrel one day; I not-so politely refused it.

At one shoot they decided their very expensive claret was too cold and heated bottles in a microwave. They exploded. Awful. I thought, *Just leave the kitchen, Joan.*

I did it for Rockfield and called it 'chicken pie' until one band found shot in the so-called 'chicken pie'. I had to come clean and tell them the truth. Did not go down very well.

3 onions
1 or 2 desert spoons of redcurrant jelly
game meat (whatever the gamekeeper drops off)
thyme
1 bay leaf
red wine, half a bottle

Add game to wine/some water, salt, thyme and bay leaf in pot and boil up then simmer on lowest heat for 20-30 minutes (depending on age of meat). Strain, get rid of foreign objects. Once cooled pick off meat. Set aside.

Cut up 3 onions, put in game juice, reduce. In a small bowl mix a little flour with cold water, add 2 flat tablespoons flour and a little hot stock, mix until all lumps gone. Return to pan with onions and stock and stir. Add a swig of brandy (good preserver). Let it bubble, I don't burn it off. Add pepper, redcurrant jelly, one spoon first, taste ... taste ... another spoon? Make sure it really is reduced. Put back the meat. Make sure no shot remains. Cook for a while, add roast chicken last if doing for Rockfield.

Daisy in the village made my pastry. The bands would say, 'My nan made pastry like this, thanks, Joan.' Cut Daisy's pastry out bigger than the dish and then crimp the edges, brush whipped up egg on the top, cook for about 20 mins in 375/400F until it's golden brown.

(Any strong meat like venison, boil up separately with salt, 1 chopped onion, orange peel – large so I can get it out – *juniper* berries and red wine. Adding pepper at end and small coffee cup of port, reduce to get rid of the pure alcohol taste. To be honest this can be a pie or stew on its own.)

Boil up bones to make a game soup with lots of thyme and a bay leaf. Freeze that for a later date.

30.

'All Creatures of Our God and King', by St Francis of Assisi

Boxing Day and New Year's Eve, 1976

It's dawn. Fritz and I are beaters. I'm wearing the Davey Crockett hat I had for Christmas but I'm thinking of my brand-new bike at home. I follow Fritz and other hill families through frost-flattened bracken and tugs of bramble. There's Charlie, the farmer's daughter, and Darren Turley who thinks he's Elvis Presley and he just might be. Darren's not wearing his usual zip-up plastic boots with Cuban heels, today it's wellies. The whole hill is out.

'You going with your dad?' Charlie asks.

I don't know what to say so I nod. Fritz is Fritz.

They're hitting mounds of bracken and tree trunks with thick sticks, and I must, too. Thuds echo down the valley. I don't have gloves.

Fritz says we are corralling pheasants through the wood to where the guns are.

'Are they pheasants from the eggs in the chapel?'

'Of course.'

'And then the baby pheasants from the pens in the wood?'

'Where did you think they came from, Tiff?'

I think of watching the chicks' speckled bodies in the stone chapel as they peeeep, peeeep, peeeep.

I hear guns.

I stop hitting the fern and the trees. I remember Mum's game pie. I *do* think about it.

I throw my stick down.

But I must follow the crowd because Fritz says, *Keep up, you don't want to be shot, do you?*

We're close to the gunfire. People in caps and wax jackets stand in the clearing. The gamekeeper is at the rise of the hill. Pheasants thud to the ground around me. They bounce, and blood sprays. White and brown springer spaniels bounce, too, and grab them. Gold and black Labradors return to masters with limp birds in soft mouths.

'Fore!'

'Over!'

My ears ring. A man walks past with pheasants hooked between his fingers. They don't look like the dull oily ones Mum and I plucked, these are *all things bright and beautiful* with berry-red cheeks, a shimmer of green, and the rich chestnut of a red setter. I see bright blood in their beak holes.

The same man picks up a wood pigeon, he holds it up and tears its chest open. Wet grain pours out. The man winks at me, tells me it's the croup.

I throw up.

*

'Well, that was a disaster.' Fritz digs his crossed front teeth into a thick slice of game pie. Brown pastry crumbles onto his short beard. We're in the big shed with the beaters, the shooters, the gamekeeper, the farmer, the lords and the ladies, and maybe some missionary Fathers, Brothers and nuns out of holy uniform. They drink port or beer or hot cider, they eat up Mum's pie, her potato salad, her chicken and mushroom, and cream cod and pea vol-au-vents. I'm told to go outside because I smell of sick. I stand with the dogs.

In the yard they're laying the dead pheasants out in lines. They're taking pictures. Charlie's with them, her thick plait hidden under her work jacket. I don't see Darren Turley but there is a newly dead fox on the old concrete, one more for the gamekeeper's circle. I see a soft-grey huddle of croup-pulled wood pigeons.

Elvis ate squirrels. He must have shot squirrels.

'It's a better end than a snare, Tiff.' Fritz joins me in the yard, buttons his jacket up. 'And where do you think meat comes from?' He wipes the crumbs from his moustache. 'You were happily plucking pheasants with your mother yesterday.' This fact doesn't help. I have been wiping the memory from my hands since the first lush, shot pheasant dropped from the sky and bounced at my feet.

We don't go beating again.

I think Fritz is relieved. He says he only went because he thought I would like it.

I thought he'd like it, too.

New Year's Eve means Fritz is learning a new song from the jukebox, 'Running Bear' by Johnny Preston. I help by writing the words down with my neatest letters. Fritz doesn't love the song, but he says he'll need it tonight.

Fritz plays the Saracen's Head and Ye Olde Ferrie Inn by

the River Wye. He plays Saxty's Wine Bar in Hereford once a week. The pubs asked and Mum says it's good for him. Fritz plays the Crown, the Three Horseshoes, the Barrel, and legions and social clubs in the Forest of Dean.

When I write out the verses for 'Three Steps to Heaven' it's easy because Showaddywaddy sing it.

'Fritz, will you do "Under the Moon of Love"?'

'No.'

'Will you sing "Don't Give Up On Us"? I can never remember if David Soul is Starsky or Hutch.

'Absolutely not.'

'Will you sing "When a Child is Born" by Johnny Mathis?'

'No, Tiffany.'

'"Lost in France" by Bonnie Tyler?'

I enjoy winding him up. He tells me to write down 'Rock Around the Clock'.

Fritz dresses up for his gigs: black cowboy boots with white stitching, black cords tucked in, a black shirt and a rainbow guitar strap across his shoulder; if it's an acoustic set a Gibson Epiphone hangs from the strap. Fritz has a set list:

'Oh Boy!'
'Cut Across Shorty'
'Blue Suede Shoes'
'Wake Up Little Susie'
'That'll Be the Day'
'Return to Sender'
'Bye Bye Love'
'(Let Me Be Your) Teddy Bear'
'Six Days on the Road'
'Bony Moronie'
'Not Fade Away'
'Ob-La-De, Ob-La-Da'

'Twist and Shout'
'Trouble'

On 'Not Fade Away' Mum and I must clap the perfect beat: CLAP-CLAP. You must keep eye contact with Fritz at the important clapping and backing singer bits or he gets pissed off. CLAP-CLAP.

I have the beat.

Mum doesn't.

CLAP-CLAP.

The encore is 'One Night' then 'Hey Jude'. Fritz stands on a pub table, his cowboy boots stomping, spilling snakebite and black, lipstick-cigarette stubs bouncing in full tin ashtrays. If the crowd beg, and beg again, he might do the Four Pennies' 'Juliet'.

If the bar is loud and people aren't listening, Fritz will stand on tables *before* the encore. I'll watch the table wobble as he stamps, angry. Mum will have both hands on the edge as it sways. She's trying to steady it and him: one woman against a march.

The pub cries back, 'Hey Jude!'

I guard the red plush of Fritz's open guitar case. My eyes sting as he sings into a fog of Lambert & Butler, but I stay on the itchy pub carpet and count his golden strings, and 50p tips.

I am Fritz's roadie. My job is important. He pays me in Coke and animal-flavoured crisps.

'Chicken or smoky bacon?'

'Both.'

'No. Choose, Tiffany.'

Fritz says life is about hard choices.

If it's acoustic, I line up his plastic or paper squares that hold coiled golden strings: I must be ready if he breaks one.

I sort his tortoiseshell and brown plectrums. If it's electric I coil up the microphone and the leads by wrapping them across the dip of my thumb and under my elbow; up and over, up and over until they're a black lasso. When I stand on a stool on stage and say, 'onetwo, onetwo,' up into the mic, I always wipe the crisp-grease from my fingers first.

New Year's Eve at Bicknor Hill Social Club is packed. My teeth are sticky with Lilt and Fritz is the main act.

Mum sits by the door, car keys on the table. She's waiting to leave; she does not care for village halls and social clubs. I love these big venues because I can run around all night. Couples are doing perfect rock 'n' roll dances with blank, far-off stares. The men spin the women so fast they're candyfloss in the bowl at the Hereford May Fair. The room smells of lager and lime, sausages and sharp Daddies Sauce in white bread baps. It's so thick with smoke I can hardly see.

I've won a turkey in the raffle with the number 82. Mum said, 'NEVER trust a turkey at New Year,' but it's in the back of the car.

Elvis is king in the Forest of Dean, the men here have perfect Brylcreem quiffs in black or in white, depending on their age, and the women have Priscilla Presley beehives, in black or in white, too. Tonight, Fritz has a stage. He knows what's expected of him and he's played '(Let Me Be Your) Teddy Bear', 'Return to Sender', 'Blue Suede Shoes', and, although it's not Elvis, 'Running Bear', twice. He's sweating and he yells into the microphone, 'C'mon Everybody!'

People flood in. They are shoulder to shoulder. My lips are salty with sausages.

I push through the dancing bodies to get closer to the stage. It's like swimming through underwater legs at Ross pool, but

I must get to the front to check Fritz's guitar case, his leads, his strings, his plectrums. I *am* his roadie.

The spinning bodies get tighter. Fritz stops. They cheer.

'All right, my bab,' a man says to me as he holds his dancing partner.

They are shouting for 'Running Bear' again. Fritz was right.

In the loos I find a strange thing. I crouch down, chin on my knees, and stare at it as women with tan tights and beehives walk around me.

I think it is part of something dead that a cat brings in; like the nose-tip of a mouse attached to a gizzard. But there are long strands of black hair. There is blood, but not much. I want to poke it, but I haven't got a stick.

'Leave that, my bab,' a voice above me says, 'there's been a scrap.' Scraps are what Mum leaves out for the birds. Tan-tight legs huddle closer around me. 'Up you get, you don't want to touch that.'

Before a firm hand grips my underarm to pull me up, that's exactly what I do: I touch it.

'Now, what you do that for?' The no-nonsense hand has me up and at the sink in a second, my hand is rubbed hard with a small white bar of soap.

I think the thing was flesh: black human hair and a bit of scalp.

The woman keeps rubbing. 'You don't want to mess with that nasty thing, you want to go back and listen to your dad.'

She says 'dad' like '*daaaaaaaaaaaaaaad*', like it's the longest word in the world, but I'm not sure about it. Fritz is still Fritz.

I can't slip away because her face in the mirror tells me:

mess with me, my girl, and you'll be sorry. She dries my hands with a damp towel. Someone flushes the thing away and I smell Jeyes Fluid.

In the fogged-up bar, Fritz is on a table even though he has a stage because it's his crescendo, 'Hey Jude', before 'Auld Lang Syne'. I know this crowd don't like the Beatles as much as Elvis or whoever sang 'Tell Laura I Love Her', so I join in with the 'Hey Jude' as loud as I can.

When the fight starts, bodies rush forward, quick and messy. Fritz jumps back up on the stage. He tries to sing 'One Night' but chairs, cans and stools fly. Mum appears and pulls me to the exit. At the mic Fritz is saying, 'No fighting, man,' in an Elvis voice. I look back to see him take off his guitar, grab his microphone from the stand, and jump into the fighting throng, still singing 'One Night'.

OneOffEight, Fritz.

Mum and I are in the Audi. It's freezing after the heat of inside. When the doors of the social club crash open and the fighting swirls out into the car park, Mum says, 'Lock your door, Tiffany.'

I wipe condensation from the window, and watch. It's worse than a *Bash Street Kids* fight because there's no cloud of dust to hide the punches I see under the streetlight. The fight bulges with a mess of noise and fists and faces, then it shrinks, then stretches like the dough Mum kneads and pulls.

'Don't watch. Is your door locked?'

Bodies slam against the car and Mum shouts at them.

I look for Fritz. He's not there. I worry about his guitar, his plectrums and strings and the plush velvet inside his guitar case. I am his roadie and I have not done my job. I have failed.

Part 4

The Kings and I

1977–1979

Huey [Lewis] and I walked into Rockfield Studios main room and found everyone, including producer Mutt Lange and the engineers, totally clothesless. Huey had to catch a train to London and was a bit miffed at our childish antics, but the whole thing only took twenty minutes.

Alex Call, YouTube Channel

'It was a welcome change from eating takeout food while crowding around the console at Toronto Sound . . . We'd get up at the crack of noon, drag our butts to breakfast that someone else had prepared and take our sweet time before ambling to the control room and getting down to business. Pretty ideal.'

Geddy Lee, My Effin' Life

Set List

Unavailable, Clover
Sneakin' Suspicion, Dr Feelgood
A Farewell to Kings, Rush
Low, David Bowie
Rumours, Fleetwood Mac
Hemispheres, Rush
Stories of Adventure, Lee Fardon
Soldier, Iggy Pop
'Bright Eyes', Art Garfunkel
Quark, Strangeness and Charm, Hawkwind
Street-Legal, Bob Dylan
Back and Fourth, Lindisfarne
The Parkerilla, Graham Parker and the Rumour
New Morning, Bob Dylan
Taking Off, Neil Innes
Yachtless, Tyla Gang
'Suits Me, Suits You,' Tom Robinson Band
Reel to Reel Cacophony, Simple Minds
'Oh Bondage Up Yours!' X-Ray Spex

31.

'A Farewell to Kings'

Summer 1977

I'm avoiding the Rockfield kitchen. Mum is in a bad mood because she had such a good time last night; that's how it works for adults. There was a party at the Lodge, Charles Ward and Fritz played 'Bye Bye Love' on guitars and we danced and sang in Sandra's living room. I slept on Brigitte and Corrina's floor and stared at their posters of David Bowie and the Sex Pistols; Corrina asked if she could cut my hair. Now it's morning Dena is helping Mum in the Rockfield kitchen. Mum still says Dena is the calmest thing in her life, while Dena says 'Oh, Joan!' just like Sandra.

I'm in the Audi in the Quadrangle courtyard, finishing my book, *Fattypuffs and Thinifers*. What I really want to read is Alex Haley's *Roots* because we watched it at Easter and even Mum was silent. Charlie and I now wrap up feral kittens in a towel, and one by one, we lift them to the sky and name them.

They may be called Rush, but they are slow as they wander

about the courtyard. Rush live in Canada, where the fierce geese come from. There's a rumour that Rush have brought a thousand guitars with them. I open the car door. One of them is playing an acoustic guitar while someone follows him recording, cables drag. Birds tweet. They've been doing this since dawn, when I walked up here.

Mum says Rush are up all night tinking and bonking, though not *that* bonking, and when they didn't appear for their dinner, she started to leave out cold honeydew melon and Parma ham, and moussaka with instructions for warming. She says it must be *jet lag*. On Jubilee Day in early June, she left out coronation chicken vol-au-vents, cucumber sandwiches with no crusts, little red jellies and a shop-bought McVitie's Jamaica cake. She said as they're Canadian, they might know about the Queen, but I think Rush might be confused by the Jubilee, red jellies and the nodding horses of Rockfield. Maybe that's why they're walking about the courtyard right now, hitting blocks of wood.

The woodblock's hard knocks echo. Because of years of watching *Music Time* on the telly, I know if you take the rubber ball off the end of the stick to hit the block, it will make a *crack!* sound. This is the sort of percussion I play at the Primrose Cottage kitchen table with Fritz's friends, so I might ask Rush if I can bop or thonk something with the off-beat Fritz taught me. I can play tambourine, maracas, claves, rhythm sticks, bongos and castanets that sound like the magpies in the woods.

Rush only have that woodblock, though. *I have more.*

I leave my book and creep out of the car to the chalets. If I hide behind one of the wood pillars, I can watch the Canadian men record more birdsong and guitar, listen to the knock-knock of their woodblock, *and* wonder where Corrina is. Lisa, Amanda and Brigitte are out riding jumps with the horses. I tried jumping the jumps without a horse like I used to, but I'm nine now so I felt silly.

The tight door in the studio corridor has carved quarter-circle grooves into the parquet floor; that's years of it opening and closing. I step left into the games room because that's where Rush are playing their strange instruments. This sound isn't woodblocks or birdsong, it's vibrating plinks and plonks like *Space 1999* on the telly. The door sucks closed behind me, the room is big, and a *wwwweeeeeeooooooooooOOOOOHHH* spaceship noise calls from a far-off planet. It's coming from a keyboard that says, 'Minimoog'. One of Rush is pumping long pointy pedals that look like a giant's dirty toenails, and when the man plays his bass guitar, it sounds like an organ.

I lie down on the parquet floor, belly first, and I feel sound pour into me. I hear a church bell, a molten lava noise, wind chimes; it all swirls and it is *melancholy*: this is my new word. 'Waaaaaa, waaaa, waaaaa-waaaa-*waaaa*,' the strange organ-bass guitar says, and I am floating, in another galaxy. They stop. The rubber of my daps squeaks as I push myself across the floor.

Rush don't look up at me, but the man starts singing, high-pitched but strange, and my body jerks. I have never heard a voice like it.

Rush are at Rockfield for such a long time I discover they have more percussion instruments than a woodblock and they like to record outside in their shorts. I also learn new words:

Bass pedal synthesiser
Minimoog
Glockenspiel
Timpani

Xanadu
Boney M
Bar-*bra* Strei*sand*
Argentina
Honeydew
Jubilee
Vibra-slap
Bell tree triangle
Slingerland drums
Mull
Tyla Gang
Geddy Lee

*

I want to see Barbra Streisand and Kris Kristofferson in *A Star is Born.*

'She won't get in, Joan.'

'We won't have any peace until you take her, Fritz.'

I run upstairs, put Mum's bra over my head, around my flat chest and stuff it with hard white loo roll. When I'm downstairs, her old lipstick on my lips and cheeks, Mum laughs. 'You'll have to do better than that.' She picks up the Audi keys; she's off to cook for Rush, whether they appear for the meal or not.

'Joan, please don't make me do this alone,' Fritz says.

But Mum is gone.

I trip on the hem of Mum's kaftan in the red Roxy foyer and my loo-roll boob comes out. The girl at the kiosk doesn't look up: I could have come in wearing nappies.

Fritz pushes me into the auditorium towards the darkness

of the seats. 'Kia-Ora and a bag of Butterkist, right? Stay put, tuttle.'

When he comes back, I take the other loo-roll boob out of Mum's bra and hand it to him. 'What am I supposed to do with this?' he hisses, and stuffs it in his pockets.

Barbra's blue eyes and Kris Kristofferson's brown skin are beautiful. I suck my Kia-Ora carton dry. He is *John Norman Howard*. Barbra is *Esther*. She sings 'Evergreen' and he kisses her as they share a big mic and harmonise in a live room. *John Norman* has Jack Daniel's for breakfast like Lemmy did, but I think *John Norman* would smell sweeter.

Barbra and Kris Kristofferson take a bath together. Fritz squirms next to me and coughs. Sweet wrappers rustle and I hear snogging from the back row. I know what snogging is, *and* what Kris Kristofferson and Barbra are doing in that bath.

They build a house out of mud in a field, and when Kris Kristofferson who is *John Norman* drives his car too fast over the brow of a hill, that is that.

I cry so much Fritz must wait with me until the cinema empties.

'He's dead!' I keep saying in between sobs.

Fritz keeps saying, 'Yes'.

The girl comes in to sweep up the Butterkist popcorn packets, the plastic Kia-Ora cartons.

'He's *dead*!'

'It's acting, Tiff. Kris Kristofferson isn't really dead.'

'I kno-*ooooow*. It's *John Norman*!'

At home Mum says, 'Haven't we learned our lesson with these grown-up films, Fritz?'

In the film, *John Norman Howard* drives himself off that dusty road, so I asked Fritz about the musicians in his wooden chest of albums. Did they drive cars, too? Why was being a musician so dangerous? I couldn't stop thinking about these deaths. Not pheasant or wood pigeon or fox death, or even dog death: it was musician death. I wanted specifics.

Fritz told me, *Does it matter, Tiff? They are just dead.*

Which ones?

I hassled until he tick-tacked his fingers through his records: *dead, dead. But he's alive. She's dead.*

Otis Redding. Ritchie Valens. Buddy Holly. Patsy Cline. Eddie Cochran. Gram Parsons. Janis Joplin. Sam Cooke. Mama Cass. Gene Vincent. Billie Holiday. Tim Buckley. Jimi Hendrix. John Coltrane. Brian Jones. Jim Morrison.

I dragged Fritz to the front of the lit-up Wurlitzer and pointed at the title strips.

Fritz told me, 'Dead. Dead. Dead. Alive. Dead.'

He played me Kris Kristofferson's 'Me and Bobby McGee', but it didn't help; I just thought of Janis Joplin singing the same song.

Now when I stand at the Wurlitzer display or flick through Fritz's albums, I say: 'Dead. Dead. Dead.' They are as dead as the polecats and crows that hang from the gamekeeper's bailer twine.

A car crash.

A heart attack in the bath.

A swimming pool.

An aeroplane. A hotel room. A Joshua Tree.

'Drugs,' Mum says.

'Heroin,' Fritz corrects her.

Fore! Over!

I walk into the woods and stare up at the stinky circle of dangling foxes. I cry at the flies, but I'm fascinated. Mum drives to the bookshop in Llandrindod Wells to cheer me up. She buys me a second-hand paperback of *Watership Down.*

'It's a Puffin book and look, there's a sweet painting of a wild rabbit on the front.'

There's no heatwave this August. Charlie and I play *The Bionic Woman* in the woods, which means saying 'jadajada-jada' before we jump the gamekeeper's low electric fence; and 'beep-beep-beep' when we listen to squirrels with our bionic ears. On my own I watch whirlpools skim on the full River Wye, hold onto Bess and swim. Still wet, we run back up through the woods, past the youth hostel (but run, Tiff and Bess, run, in case of the weirdo men).

One morning, puffed from my run from the river, I take off my daps in the hall, refill Bess's water bowl at the kitchen tap, and Fritz is crying at the kitchen table, Boggle at his feet. Mum stands at the cooker and she raises her eyebrows but she purses her lips to a *shush.* Fritz walks to the jukebox, Boggle follows. I take a breath and wait for the mystery of what song will come.

The Wurlitzer machinery whirrs and clicks.

'Are You Lonesome Tonight?' Elvis croons.

Mum thickens her sauce with butter. Fritz sits back at the table, picks up his guitar and strums. For a moment I think Boggle is going to howl, but he doesn't. Bess laps her water then falls to the kitchen lino in a smiling pant. I look at my mother and she shakes her head. I'll ask her what the matter is later.

Elvis is dead. I lie on my bed and think of that as Fritz plays every Elvis song on our jukebox and Mum bangs pots, and cooks around the crying and the crooning. Mum likes Elvis, and loves the Wurlitzer, but she hates the fact it's in her kitchen and she must listen to other people's choices all day. I don't know why I'm not crying. I love Elvis but, somehow, I know the Elvis I've seen on the news today isn't my Elvis in *G.I. Blues* or *Jailhouse Rock*: my Elvis is different to the spangly-costume Elvis who is dead. Fritz is singing along to 'Marie's the Name' when Mum walks into my bedroom. She looks at the black-damp walls, sighs. 'I wish the bleach worked.'

She's not here for that, though. She takes off her apron. 'You're coming with me, Tiff. Give Fritz a break. Help me with the serving at the studio?'

I jump off the bed. I don't need to be asked twice. I can't remember who is at Rockfield now Rush have gone. Whoever it is, I know they're not dead, my mother is feeding them.

On the way to Monmouth, she opens the windows to the August early evening and plays Fleetwood Mac's *Rumours*. She starts on Side B, her favourite. This and David Bowie's *Low* are her summer tapes. She speeds down the A40 hill, we sing 'I Don't Want to Know' and I look back at Little Doward Woods. There's writing in those trees, two letters standing out in the different colours of larch and cedar: 'E.R', for Elizabeth Regina, the Queen. It will be there for ever, or until the trees are cut down.

On the main Rockfield road I hear familiar percussion from Fleetwood Mac: it's a cowbell. Mum and I put our heads out of the windows, and with Stevie Nicks we cry out to 'Gold Dust Woman.'

Later, she drives me between the studio and the Old Mill, where Black Sabbath are playing with guns in the early evening garden.

*

That Saturday Fritz is playing the Barrel in Ross-on-Wye. The Barrel has the stickiest, longest floor because they play skittles in here. I am dancing up and down it as Fritz sings 'Blue Suede Shoes'. I'm wearing my new Kicker boots, and I finally get it; the tap and the poke of the boot, the glide and the blank stare on my rock 'n' roll face because I'm lost to the steady beat and I'm not thinking at all. I'm not dancing, either; I'm flying. My rubber soles crack and suck on the gluey ground and there is only the song, and I am the song, and Elvis is letting me soar up and down this shitty sticky empty dance floor, with old men lining the bar and their smell of stale beer, old fags, old dogs and pickled eggs in cloudy jars. It is the best feeling in the world.

Until the music stops.

Fritz takes a break: he's still not quite ready for Elvis.

I hear something from the main bar. A different beat. It's a quick, deep pulse. I slip out of the long back room.

The song is coming from a short jukebox that isn't like our Wurlitzer at home. The sounds are a bit like the *Dr Who* theme, and the thud keeps going over and over, but there's also a woman's voice telling me something about love. She oooooohs. She moans, and I hear the words, 'I Feel Love'. She tells me it's good. The wang-wang thud repeats and I do feel it, but my feet don't kick out or move at all. I stand against the jukebox and the song pulses straight into me, through my trousers, into my hips, and on, and on, until I reach my arms up and I sway. The woman keeps singing 'I Feel Love' to the swirling *Dr Who* beat, and I close my eyes and I think *I do, I do.*

I laugh out loud. It's joy, and this woman is alive; she is alive for ever in this beat. I read her name on the jukebox display: *Donna Summer.* I beg Fritz for money to put the song on again.

Honeydew Melon and Parma Ham
Barbary Duck in Gooseberry Sauce

I did a lot of honeydew and ham for Rush that summer. If they didn't appear, I could simply leave it out. Because Rush worked through the night, I made food they could eat at any time: lasagne, moussaka, chilli con carne, steak sandwiches.

The duck, though, was my signature dish, served at 7.30 p.m.

2 Barbary duck (this is a special small breed, season it!)
tinned gooseberries, 2 or 3 small tins
1 cup Madeira
half a bottle white wine
salt and pepper
one or two proper spoons of single cream

Put all the ingredients in the bottom of a roasting pan, place the seasoned ducks on top, cook for about one hour. Baste. If the ducks get too brown cover with foil.

Remove ducks, place all ingredients from the pan into a liquidiser until smooth, put in a saucepan and simmer, reduce, if necessary, TASTE, season after tasting! There shouldn't be too much fat on a Barbary duck, spoon off if there is.

Add a little cream to smooth it, not too much. This is delicious. You can put ducks back in oven and heat gently. God, it was all about cream then. Halve the ducks with meat scissors.

We had our first family holiday late that summer. Do you remember? We went to Brittany on the ferry, and you walked into a plate-glass window.

32.

'Sign on the Window'

Summer 1978

Fritz saw the ad for the Bob Dylan gig in *NME*. 'Sod it, Joan. I'll drop the food off early, Dena and Sandra can put it out. Let's go.'

Mum says Fritz is impulsive, he says she's pot calling the kettle black.

'Rush will have to cope,' he told her. The Canadian band are back a year later. Graham Parker came in, too; he asked for Mum's trout.

The Audi judder-judders across the Severn Bridge because I have the top of my back window open. I watch the skin of the wide and ugly Severn River spin with whirlpools the Wye can only dream of. Horses get trapped down here, they drown in the mud, slick as worms. Fritz tells me tiny creatures called elvers live in that mud, too, and because he's over his grief he says 'ELVERS' like 'ELVIS' with a drawl and a curled lip, *uh-huh*. He tells me that's a pun. Fritz loves puns but I'm not sure about them.

In the brief sunlight the Severn turns silver. The clag of gold-top rests at the back of my throat because I ate too much Alpen from the catering-size box. I wind the window down further to breathe my sickness away.

'Tiffany, you're making that judder-judder noise worse,' Fritz says, and I wonder how he can hear when Motörhead made him deaf in one ear.

Fritz still can't believe I call Bob Dylan 'Val Doonican'.

'He is *not* Val Doonican. You know Bob Dylan because of The Band.'

'The names sound the same.'

'They do *not*.'

He slots a cassette in, hands me the case to read and tells me not to get car sick. He announces album titles and individual songs, 'This is *Blonde on Blonde*, Tiff. It starts with "Rainy Day Women #12 & 35".' I listen to people whooping over a tambourine as Bob Dylan sings about getting stoned. It sounds like Fritz's friends at our kitchen table. But it is true that these songs don't sound like "Delaney's Donkey" or "Paddy McGinty's Goat". Mum covers her ears when the harmonica starts.

I like 'Visions of Johanna' and 'Leopard-Skin Pill-Box Hat'. Fritz sings along but in a funny voice that forces the words up through a closed throat and a clenched jaw; it sounds like a cat getting rid of a furball.

We pass the Bristol turning.

'This album is *Desire*, Tiff. It has Emmylou on it.'

Fritz still worships Emmylou Harris. I love 'Hurricane' because it's a long story with a beginning, middle and end, which is what they teach us at school. The harmonies on 'One More Cup of Coffee' make my ears hurt.

'Try to remember, Tiff, think 'B' – *Blonde on Blonde*. BOB Dylan. We'll play *Blood on the Tracks* next. B. B. B. Bob Dylan. There's no Val Doonican in that.'

I watch the hard shoulder and try very hard not to think of Val Doonican in a lemon-coloured jumper.

Fritz shouts over the engine, about Joan Baez, 'Sad Eyed Lady of the Lowlands' and the Chelsea Hotel; about 'Sara', and Washington Square. Mum shouts back, 'Christ, that harmonica. And wind the window up, Tiffany!'

I ask Fritz if The Band will be there, and he says no.

It's raining in London although it's summer. Starlings flock in the sky and a queue trails out from Earl's Court down the street for miles. People in duffel coats and cagoules hold wet sleeping bags and brollies. There's a big poster of Bob Dylan on the side of the building. He's pulling his sunglasses down, as if he disapproves of us. I'm still fighting the picture of Val Doonican on a rocking chair on Christmas telly singing 'Windmills of Your Mind'.

Mum looks at the queue. 'Bloody hell, Fritz.' Queuing in the rain with others is not Mum's London. Mum's London is riding the Harrods lift wearing a Julie Christie-in-*Dr Zhivago* furry hat, with her first Pyrenean Mountain Dog, Cossack, sitting to attention at her side.

It's dark. I'm not sure how we got here but we're leaning against a back door of Earl's Court with a cluster of people who are damp like us; except, as Mum pointed out a little too loudly, these people are hippies.

'Breathe through your mouth,' she says; the rain is bringing the patchouli oil out in their jumpers. There's a light above Mum's head. In her rabbit coat in the wet summer dusk she looks like she's stepped out of the cover of *Ziggy Stardust and The Spiders from Mars.*

Mum tells us she *hasn't come up to London to lean against a bloody door at the back of Earl's bloody Court to listen to Bob bloody Dylan, she was at the Isle of Wight for God sakes and she saw Dylan, and The Band did their own set, and a bunch of public schoolboys offered her their tent, but she refused because, God, she's not camping for anyone, least of all Bob bloody Dylan.*

Fritz has his hands in the pockets of his blue velvet jacket. He sticks his good ear up against the door. 'Come and listen, Tiff.'

I nestle beneath him in my soggy dungarees. The wet hippies cluster too, but all I can hear is a tinny echo of a man's voice. I keep it secret that I love the smell of patchouli.

There must be at least ten of us leaning against the door. I press my ear and cheek in harder, I hear the roar of a crowd, still tinny. Mum lights a Sobranie. She's stopped muttering and her jaw is clenched.

That's when the door flings open.

Maybe it was the weight of us all. Maybe it was someone inside taking pity on us drowned rats, but we fall forward. The hippies squeal, struggle up and run into the vast space. It smells of concrete, sweet lager and smoke, and it's warm.

Mum comes to life. She's already standing over me. She takes off her rabbit coat, grabs my hand and pulls me up.

'Do not run,' she hisses.

We watch the hippies sprint and skip, their wet jumpers weighting them. They laugh, and I don't know why they're being so loud, but I do have the urge to skip with them. It looks fun.

Mum pulls me back. 'Walk slowly, child. Pretend we are already here. Pretend we are a family.'

I'm not sure how to do this. I can hear Bob Dylan loud now; he echoes. The hippies scatter into the wide space, and official-looking men appear from gaps and barriers, they run after the hippies and catch some across the bellies as if they're robbers. One screams out, 'Boooob!' before he falls.

'Blend,' Mum says. She diverts us into a stall filled with bright things. Posters and jackets and badges are on tables and shelves. She picks up a book and flicks through it. Fritz picks up a T-shirt. I think: PRETEND WE ARE A FAMILY.

'Choose something, Tiff,' she tells me, loud and bright, as the hippies scream beyond us. I choose a colour-in poster with strange creatures and swirls in plain black and white (I have to colour them in, you see). Fritz looks at it and says, 'Psychedelic, man,' and he sticks up the peace sign. The man behind the counter rolls the poster up into a cardboard tube. Fritz puts his Bob Dylan T-shirt on. Mum lights another Sobranie.

The line was: *we don't have our ticket stubs, we didn't know we had to keep them, we're a family.* Mum said, 'I'm terribly sorry, I simply did not know how concerts work.'

The man let us through the barrier. Fritz said, 'It's your mother's voice.' We walked into the auditorium; the crowd was huge. When people returned for their seats and we were in them, the line was, *Oh, I'm so sorry, we have the wrong seats.* Fritz hated it and took us to the front.

I'm too old and probably too heavy for this, but at least up on Fritz's shoulders I can see Bob Dylan. Fritz is right; there's no rocking chair or diamond-patterned jumper, no 'Memories Are Made of This'. Bob Dylan stands in the middle of so many musicians it's like a little orchestra, and although they are not The Band, they do look like friends rehearsing in a crowded living room. Three backing singers do their *oooooh-ooooh-oooooohs*. Bob even has a carpet. He is wearing a leather jacket, a waistcoat and white shoes. He's beautiful. He sings about being released and lights shining and Maggie's Farm.

'This is called "I Ain't Gonna Work On Maggie's Farm No More",' he says. 'I played this at the Newport Folk Festival, some time recently. This is the song that got me booed off the stage. This is it.'

Lit up in a bubble of light he looks like a sparkling gypsy from my favourite-ever telly programme, *Kizzy*.

We push through to the side, nearer the amps, and up on Fritz's shoulders my ears vibrate to bursting like they do in the Rockfield studio. It makes my insides hit against my ribs, and I know I will have the whine of Bob Dylan in my ears for days and I might love it. Beneath me Mum grabs hold of Fritz's arm because she hates crowds.

Bob Dylan sings 'One More Cup of Coffee', but my ears are past hurting. He sings 'Forever Young', and I think I will be.

When we drive past the motorway lights they go *schoom-schoom*. Mum's head hits against the passenger seat window but she doesn't wake up. Fritz plays a Bob Dylan album called *New Morning*. I like 'Went to See the Gypsy' and 'Sign on the Window', and I should like 'If Dogs Run Free' but the lady singing in it makes too many strange noises.

We cross back over the Severn Bridge and the moonlight doesn't make the river any less angry but it's not ugly any more. I think about the horses that get stuck in the mud below. I hug my cardboard tube, the poster rolled up inside. I'll spend the next weekends at the kitchen table colouring it in, and the creatures, psychedelic swirls, leaves and eyes on hands and stalks will thrill me, while my fingers will be stained with felt tip.

Sport's Day means egg and spoon in the playing field and jumping over a cane I've never seen the headmaster use. I've told everyone I went to London to see Bob Dylan but no one in my class knows who that is, so I told them it was Val Doonican.

At lunchtime the gym at Goodland Primary becomes our dining room: ropes are pulled back, climbing bars stand against the wall; the pommel horse rests. A big hatch opens and the steam of boiled mince wafts out. Dinner ladies shove aluminium pots and trays on the counter. The mince stink mixes with the rubbery smell of daps.

For a whole school year I've learned new words and phrases at Goodland Primary:

Hundreds and Thousands
Spotted dick
Jam roly poly or dead man's leg
Arctic roll
Proper father
FinishWhat'sInFrontOfYouOrYouWon'tGetYourPudding
Dollop
Dinner lady
Flan

When I ask Mum for dinner money she says, 'I'm not paying for you to eat that crap, Tiffany, and it's lunch not "dinner".'

Apart from the mince, I love school dinners. I'm giddy at pink custard; I swoon at thin Bisto drowning ice-cream scoops of mash. I'm bewitched by neat cubes of different-coloured vegetables that look and taste the same, and who cut them like that? I'm comforted by French beans so soft you can suck them through your teeth to a mush.

Beloved school dinners, but I can't have them, Mum said.

We sit at the packed-lunch table in a corner: me, Samantha, Tina, Denise, Joanne and Karen; I don't know why boys don't have packed lunches. Charlie from my hill has a proper school lunch but I can't spot her as the rest of the school scrapes and clangs cutlery in the big gym. Tina opens the lid of her powder-blue plastic box. I smell fishpaste sandwiches before I see them. I love their brown fish-and-margarine taste and white crustless tidiness. Tina sometimes gives me a quarter square. I offer to swap but she always says, 'No, thank you.' Denise bites into her small white square of sandwich and sharp vinegar hits me: it's Sandwich Spread.

I pull a lump of silver foil from my satchel. I can't remember what was on the Rockfield menu last night or what musician left this on his plate or didn't even start his dinner. Was it Rush or Lindisfarne, Neil Innes or Peter Hamill, Dave Edmunds or Nick Lowe, Dr Feelgood or the Tom Robinson Band? I press it and feel a thick bone. I think Lindisfarne are vegetarians so maybe not them. The packed-lunch table stares at the silver foil. It's always like this; we wait for the mystery of my lunch lumps to be revealed. I'd trade a million pork chops, duck confits, T-bones, cold sweet spare ribs and the sharp stab of a tiger prawn hair for one of Tina's fishpaste sandwiches, even Denise's white, sharp Sandwich Spread. I peel away the thin edges of my cold foil package.

'Urgh,' Denise says, 'that smells.' The other girls join in with 'urghs' but it's Denise who holds her nose.

The T-bone is rare. One side is missing but mushrooms in a cream and garlic sauce fill the gap. Mum's put a parsley garnish on the top. I want it to be Nick Lowe's steak because I still fancy him. I wonder if he bit into it? I push parsley and look for teeth marks. He probably cut into it with a knife and fork, but I don't have a choice because I don't have cutlery. I pick the bone up like a corn on the cob, the cold sauce drops, and I tear at it with my teeth.

'Urgh, germs,' Denise says, and she moves her chair away from me. I chew rare and cold Herefordshire beef and watch the dinner queue pressing up against the gym bars. It *is* pink custard today, over school cake with hundreds and thousands. They are bringing out the metal trays and jugs, thick pink slopping over the sides, creamy as Béarnaise. I let out a garlicky sigh. I will plead with the dinner ladies in pink gingham tabards and promise to hold their rough hands in the playground later.

After lunch it's races in the big field and we'll jump in sacks and carry eggs on spoons. Then we'll hang upside down off the monkey bars, our dresses falling over our heads, our knickers showing, and I'll wait for the rush of blood to my head. I'll be ten soon and I'm going to have a barbecue. I hope Polly and Tina will come up the hill to me and Charlie, and Darren Turley and his Elvis impression. But not bloody Denise.

This is my last day at Goodland Primary. I'm changing schools again and it's Denise's fault.

She said it in the playground on Friday. She isn't my best friend (that's Charlie) but our hands were up in the air because they were hooves. I was Champion the Wonder Horse and Denise was Black Beauty and she told me she couldn't play with me any more because I didn't have a proper father.

'What does that mean?' My hooves stayed up because I was protecting Rex the dog (Darren Turley) from a mountain lion (Polly).

Denise shrugged. 'My mum says I'm not allowed.'

I didn't understand it, so it didn't matter, and I played Champion the Wonder Horse with Polly instead because Polly's my other best friend and she's better at being Black Beauty than Denise anyway.

When Mum picked me up in the Audi, I asked her what did it mean?

She turned the engine off. 'Stay here, Tiffany.'

I watched her march down the school's main stone wall, straight to Denise's mum. I ducked down in the passenger seat, but Mum's voice is loud. 'You silly cow,' I heard. A crowd formed. The headmaster was rushing across the playground. I locked the doors from the inside, pushed down deeper and reached for the radio but the battery was off, so I sang Althea & Donna's 'Uptown Top Ranking' to myself.

Mum knocked on the window, her rabbit fur coat hackled, her face red. I pulled up her lock.

'*You*, Tiffany, are moving school.' She screeched out onto the road and flicked the V's at Denise's mum's car.

I looked out of the window and there was Polly, waving from the playground wall, her Black Beauty hand/hoof up.

Tiff's Packed School Lunch

I'm sorry but you know how terrible I am at convenience food. I thought the best thing for you was proper food. What's wrong with that?

I remember sending you in with a little red and white Bakelite lunch box and whatever was left over from the studio. That very conservative headmaster told me I shouldn't give you such extravagant food. I told him to get lost, and you always said you shared it, particularly with Polly. It was quite a big Bakelite box.

Half a Nick Lowe T-bone steak with mushroom sauce.

A chunk of Ian Gillan's poached Wye salmon, thin cucumber slices (peeled), lemon mayonnaise.

Graham Parker's chicken breast in a tarragon sauce.

A slice of Dr Feelgood's boeuf en croute.

Half a duck from Hawkwind.

Lovingly wrap in foil and place in Bakelite box.

33.

'Picture This'

Winter 1978, Parts 1 & 2

Part 1

She's Debbie Harry and Deborah Harry but she's not Blondie, that's the band. When she turns her back on the camera, I see a cave of dark hair beneath the blonde and it's magic.

We're all on the velvet Chesterfield watching *Top of the Pops*, Boggle's willy marks beneath us and Bess on my lap.

'How does she do that, Mum?'

'It's from a bottle, Tiff.'

I think of Mum's Marsala bottles in the kitchen.

The logs Fritz has taught me to chop burn in the open fire; I'm lost in the backstage world of 'Hanging on the Telephone' and the smoke of the sitting room. Debbie Harry, blonde but not blonde but not Blondie, is making her face up in a backstage mirror, looking like she's itching for a fight like the girls in the loos at the Barrel when Fritz plays in the skittle bar and they shout, 'SCRAP!'

In the video, when Debbie looks in the mirror, it's right at me.

Now she's pogo-ing on a stage made up of black and white stripes. She's beautiful but she's gurning like she couldn't give a shit. She frowns in a way Nanny tells me not to because I'll get lines, but I'm ten, I can frown all I want.

Fritz says, 'They're miming.'

Mum says, 'That's a video, Fritz.'

It's not all men on the telly now. When I watch *Top of The Pops*, *Revolver* and *The Old Grey Whistle Test* (if it doesn't make me fall asleep) I see them. Poly Styrene from X-Ray Spex with her metal teeth singing 'The Day the World Turned Day-Glo'. Kate Bush dancing with her hands and eyes to 'Wuthering Heights' (Legs & Co. dance to 'The Man with the Child in His Eyes'). Patti Smith sings 'Because the Night' with her big voice and a bowler hat on *The Old Grey Whistle Test*, and Fritz tells me it's a Bruce Springsteen song, *but we have* Horses, *Tiff*, and I know he means the album not the animals.

And Siouxsie Sioux. Now I dance in my bedroom like she does when she sings 'Hong Kong Garden' with her Banshees; arms slicing the air, legs kicking out.

'Can we go to Round Ear?' I ask Fritz.

Round Ear is a record shop in Monmouth and the best shop in the world, apart from Ferneyhough's Sweets. I can run between them with a paper bag of rosy apples and 'Rat Trap' by The Boomtown Rats.

Round Ear is painted black to bring out the bright posters and LP covers. John and Kate own it and they are in black, too, although they jangle with silver chains and studded belts. It was John and Kate who gave me Bess, after Boggle saw to their girl-dog in the Rockfield yard. On the back of Round Ear's door there's a poster for Queen's 'Fat Bottomed Girls', but that seems a lifetime ago, and the girls on racing bikes are skinny; their bums aren't fat.

'Hanging on the Telephone' is in a paper sleeve in the singles display behind the counter. The blue label says 'Chrysalis' with a drawing of a butterfly. John is so tall he hits his head on Round Ear's ceiling as he reaches for it.

'Can I have a bag, please?' I ask because the Round Ear bags have a cartoon cat on the front.

Fritz tick-tacks through albums in alphabetical order. He buys Bruce Springsteen's *Darkness on the Edge of Town*, and *Energy* by the Pointer Sisters. I stare at the black felt board of badges and take for ever to pick three. I'm not adventurous:

Blondie
X-Ray Spex
David Bowie as Aladdin Sane

On the way home we pass our turn to Primrose Cottage and Fritz goes on to Gwalia in Ross-on-Wye. It's long past Guy Fawkes Night, but he buys two scoops of fudge ice cream (I'm too old for cider lollies) and we eat them quickly in the car. We're delivering food to Rockfield later, and I'll play my new Blondie single to Brigitte and Corrina at the Lodge.

Part 2, Stories of Adventure

How to Cook with No Electricity

In short, don't. Keep a terrine in the freezer. It will defrost gradually. I use the Robert Carrier recipe with a few additions. If you have this, bread and butter, you can get by.

Mum put her foot down. Fritz was in Studio Two producing Lee Fardon & the Legionnaires, while she and I were snowed in at the top of our hill. Water froze in the pipes. The gas bottle ran empty. The electricity and phone line went out. We trudged to the cattle grid and the hill was solid with ice and snow; Mum couldn't drive the food to Rockfield. It soon spoilt in the fridge and chest freezer, and if we left it out in the cold the foxes ate it. We were stranded for two days before Mum walked to the gamekeeper with a spade and demanded he drive us and the dogs to Rockfield in his Land Rover. Mum's pots and pans, her Sabatier knife and what food she could salvage were in the truck's side-flapping back. Bess, Boggle, me and Mum shared the long front seat. We skidded on ice down the hill with no seat belts, and the pots clanged in the back.

We left food for the cats and a window open a crack.

I know I've grown because if I stand on the brown chair in the bedroom of our old Rockfield chalet, more than my head pokes out of the Velux window. I also know the roof window is called 'Velux'. Fritz told me.

Today the Quadrangle is compact with snow and the few horses that do stick their heads out of the tops of the stables are wearing coats. Corrina has a palomino called Caramel, and I watch its white breath. I don't know what band is in Studio One, but I mouth my sing-song prayer from the past, '*Sassafras, Brinsley Schwarz, Be-Bop Deluxe, Van der Graaf Generator, Queen.*'

There's a denim shirt and a few pairs of jeans on the bedroom floor; the clothes don't belong to us because we're not sleeping in here, we're staying with Fritz in the bungalow. I jump off the chair and leave the chalet before the occupant comes back.

Me and the Rockfield kids are riding bin liners down a snow-packed Little Ancre hill. We might wear the bin liners later, with one of Corrina's studded belts, but for now every bum-thudding bump ricochets through our bodies; every crash into the hawthorn hedge at the bottom of the hill is a potential dash to the hospital. Young Charles, Lisa, and Amanda bomb past me, and Charles Ward drives up the sharp hill. He shouts that he has a present for us. He's attached aluminium curtain tracks to the bottom of a wooden sledge. This means we can go faster. I let the others go first: I'm not brave enough. The sledge zips down the hill so fast I can't hear Brigitte and Corrina's screams. Their dad laughs and claps his hands at his daughters, then he goes back to his pickup, his strawberry-blond hair electric in the wind.

I do try his curtain-track sledge, and it's a piss-your-pants thrill ride, followed by a let's start the long climb back up Little Ancre hill and do it all over again.

It's Saturday night and I'm watching Corrina put eyeliner on with perfect Siouxsie Sioux shapes, while Brigitte curls her hair. Brigitte is sixteen and Corrina is fifteen now, but I am still ten. We're in their shared bedroom with their best friend Ceris, who laughs deep and loud. There are still posters of horses and David Bowie, but now PiL and not the Sex Pistols are on the wall.

I keep asking and they keep saying no.

'*Please* can I come?'

'Aw, girl, you're too young.'

'Mum will let me. I'll ask her!'

'The Rolls Hall won't let you in, Tiff.'

Brigitte puts on proper red lipstick. I smell jasmine-and-detergent Charlie perfume. Corrina's black hair is even shorter, and she wears all black too but no bin liners because we ripped them sledding. Ceris shows me how to put on foundation. The liquid smells of plasters and it dries too tight on my skin. I can't smile and I hate it, but I want to go with them, and I will go with them, so I don't grin but I do bear it and I don't say a thing.

In October I went with them to see *Grease* at Monmouth cinema. After the best film in the world, we ran into the Rockfield dining room like a gang, laughing and whoop-de-dooing about the T-Birds, the Pink Ladies. I said Kenickie, and Corrina and Brigitte said John Travolta, but we all said Rizzo. We sang, 'You're the One That I Want' and helped Mum, Dena and Sandra clear up. I reason that if I can go to the cinema with them, I can go to the Rolls Hall on a Saturday night, dance to 'You Make Me Feel (Mighty Real)' and 'Blame it on the Boogie'.

They wave at me from the back seat of the black Volvo, Sandra driving. I cry on the Lodge porch next to Charles Ward who claps his hands and rubs them together. Charles does this when he doesn't know what to say, which is now. The Volvo drives off and I chase it like a farm dog, but they're gone. It's too dark, so I run back up the track crying. Mum is in the Quadrangle kitchen, but I turn right towards Studio Two because Fritz is in there; the music business hasn't given him up yet.

It's the same black sofa that Motörhead sat in, and I don't know if it's leather or plastic, but if you're wearing a jumper you slide right off it when you slouch. The control room is lit but dim, and there's Fritz at the motherboard leaning over the penny sweet knobs, pushing some up, some down. I nestle close to the guitarist Jimmy who has black curls and very pretty dark eyes. He's wearing a stripy jumper and I wonder when he'll start to slide off the sofa. I hiccup a few sobs as I listen to the playback: Lee Fardon sings his *Stories of Adventure.* I love Lee's songs.

'I Mean it This Time'
'Fast at 17'
'Heatwave'
'Sleepwalking'
'I Don't Know How to Touch You'

I lean into Jimmy, whose name is Jimmy Dream, but I don't go to sleep like I do at the seated Dire Straits gigs Fritz takes us to in London. Maybe there's still a tang of Motörhead in this studio. Or the ghosts of songs and bacon sandwiches. I watch Fritz spin on his motherboard chair as my eardrums itch to the track 'Sleepwalking', and I am home again.

Winter Soups

I'd cook up a huge tureen of soup and leave it for them to help themselves to during the night.

Pumpkin Soup

I grew pumpkins in my garden so:

2 lb	*of pumpkin*	*2*	*pints of chicken stock (I made my own)*
2	*potatoes (medium), cooked*		*cream*
2	*large mild onions*		*salt and pepper*
4	*leeks*		

Peel and cut up pumpkin, potatoes, onion and white part of leeks.

Cook potatoes and pumpkins in salted water; strain but keep the veg water.

Sauté onions and leeks, add cooked pumpkin and potatoes, chicken stock.

Liquidise; if this is too thick, thin out with the veg water. Back into saucepan, salt and pepper, TASTE.

Before serving, yes you've guessed it, add some cream, about ½ cup.

(Substitute with any root vegetable mix)

34.

Bright Eyes and Boys

Summer 1979

Everyone and everything has myxomatosis.

'That's not strictly true, Tiff,' Fritz tells me. 'It's the rabbits.'

They shiver and scream from the hedgerows. When the cats drag them in, already dead, Fritz says it's best to snatch them back. He has dead rabbit fires that smoke down the valley.

I try to save the little ones. Charlie calls them 'kittens' but says they're best 'dispatched'. I clean the kittens' pus and blood eyes with our pump water, and push iceberg lettuce at their greasy faces. They die and Mum soaks my hands in a bowl of cloudy Dettol.

'If you still insist on saving the dying, darling, wear Marigolds.'

Hillbrook, my new school, has thirty-eight boys from all over the world who can't read and write properly, and six local girls who can. I am the seventh girl because my grandmother is paying. It is a *private* school, and I must wear a blazer with a white fox on it. Fritz says it's Bertie Wooster and *Goodbye, Mr. Chips*, without the world wars; he doesn't like taking Nanny's money. He tells Mum I need to go to the comprehensive and get real. Mum says, 'She's still primary school age, Fritz, give her a break.'

The boys at Hillbrook are boarders and they're called by their surnames or nicknames. We, the seven girls, get to keep our first names. Before lunch and supper, the headmaster says, *Benedictus, Benedicat per Jesum Christum Dominum Nostrum,* as we line up at tables in 'houses' named after mountains. Stuff like this happens at Hillbrook: talking in Latin, jam and toast for tea, cries of 'Oh, please, sir. We're begging you, sir!' and reading French books out loud beneath blossoming apple trees. If I'm punished, I must copy out Old Testament psalms in my exercise book.

Hillbrook has taught me new words:
Pyromaniac
Dyslexic
Boarding
Crush
Mercury, the element (we flick small balls of it in science class)
Manatee
Old Testament
Benedictus, Benedicat
Matron
British bulldogs
Dormitory
Master
Sick bay
Leg before wicket

Nature walks (just walking in the woods in a boiler suit)
Birthday table
Portacabin
Je m'appelle

Zelley is the prettiest boy in the school and he's standing at the edge of Hillbrook playing field singing 'Bright Eyes' by Art Garfunkel. In front of him Helen and Sophie, two of the younger first-name girls, are crying and grasping at each other's hands. This is because Zelley is holding a flat stone directly above a small shivering rabbit. We're wearing blue boiler suits over our uniforms because we've just come back from the daily nature walk, but the nature is right here.

'"Bright Eyes!"' Zelley sings. He found the rabbit because it was screaming in the high grass. It is greasy with the disease.

'Stop it, Zell,' I tell him.

He smiles at me. 'I am on your birthday table, aren't I, Tiff?'

This situation is my fault. I am eleven today and birthdays at Hillbrook mean you must choose ten people for your tea-time birthday table. It's tricky because a birthday table means a cake, sandwiches, plain crisps, Jammy Dodgers, Chocolate Fingers, Pink Wafers that make you cough pink dust, and the other tables scowling at you from plates of shepherd's pie, peas and carrots.

Zelley lifts the flat stone higher above the rabbit. Helen and Sophie wail.

'I am on your table, right?'

He is: I'm in love.

Sometimes after tea I take Zelley down to the school basement to play him a tape I've recorded on my cassette player. I don't tell him the songs are for him. He'll ask the titles as he lies back on a shelf with his blue eyes and dirty blond hair, in his corduroy grey shorts and his brown knees with grazes.

Tape for Zelley

'Rat Trap', the Boomtown Rats
'The Prettiest Star', David Bowie
'Heart of Glass', Blondie
'Is She Really Going Out with Him?', Joe Jackson
'Ever Fallen in Love', the Buzzcocks
'Accidents Will Happen' and 'Oliver's Army', Elvis Costello
'She', Gram Parsons
'Life on Mars?', David Bowie
'Cool for Cats', Squeeze
'Love Song', the Damned
'Lucky Number', Lene Lovich
'Hit Me with Your Rhythm Stick', Ian Dury and the Blockheads
'Waiting for an Alibi', Thin Lizzy
'You've Got to Hide Your Love Away', the Beatles
'Breakfast in America', Supertramp
'Magnolia', J. J. Cale
'Hold Back the Night', Graham Parker
~~'I Was Made for Dancin', Leif Garrett~~ (I record over it. Zelley can't know it's my favourite)

At the edge of the playing field the baby rabbit is panting in the long grass. 'Maybe I'll drop the stone anyway. It would be kinder,' Zelley says.

'Zell, don't.'

Sophie lets out a big sob and runs to the schoolhouse. 'I'm telling!' she cries. Helen runs after her.

Zelley sings the whole chorus of 'Bright Eyes'. He has a good voice. We both stare at the rabbit. 'It's going to die anyway,' he says, and he winks at me and drops the flat stone.

The baby rabbit is dead, and our muddy wellies are in the hall. The boys have school-issue socks with blue and yellow circles just below the knee; some boys wear garters. I put on my shoes because my socks are white and from Peacocks.

In the dining room my chocolate birthday cake tastes plastic, the ready salted crisps are soft and the seven Hillbrook girls (including me) are sobbing because the boys are singing 'Bright Eyes,' instead of 'Happy Birthday'. Everyone knows about Zelley and the rabbit. He's in detention in the library next door but he keeps running in to shout, 'Bright Eyes!' every time there's a lull. The teachers have lost control, even the *Benedictus, Benedicat* headmaster shakes his head.

I can't come back to Hillbrook next term: Fritz says in September I'm going to Monmouth Comprehensive like Brigitte and Corrina. I'll miss these boys with voices that waver from high to low, and their nice hair, and bad writing and bad reading, and pining for their mothers around the world.

*

Fritz has a 'Bring Your Records Session' at Mum's youth club: I'm sure I can play my *Parallel Lines* first because it was my birthday yesterday. We're in the side room of the village hall, which is Victorian Gothic like the Vicarage was, but fluorescent tubes hang on chains and the walls are white and cold.

Mum runs the youth club once a week. She says my old babysitters Mandy and Cheryl turned her into a proper volunteer with the local council. 'They gave me the roughest area, but I got the village hall free, and everyone is happy.'

The village isn't happy: they want to close the youth club. Mum tells the committee no kid has stolen anything from her or from the hall, and she's left the money out on purpose. She tells Fritz even if she must pull some kids apart in the loos and tell them *cling film does not a condom make*, they're not doing anyone any harm and they need a bloody outlet. Tonight, she's in the kitchen teaching anyone who wants to learn how to cook lasagne, shepherd's pie or chilli con carne. She brings down a cooked one first so they can taste it and smell it, she takes them through *budgets* and *storing food safely*. Some nights Fritz asks bands from Rockfield to play on the main stage, he teaches guitar, and we might have a disco. Mandy and Cheryl teach me Status Quo's 'Rockin' All Over the World' dance: it's hands at your waist, one shoulder down for two beats, then twist and the other shoulder down. It's not unlike the Brotherhood of Man 'Save Your Kisses for Me' dance.

My *Parallel Lines* by Blondie is on the pile by the youth-club record player but Fritz said I must wait my turn like everyone else.

'Me first.' Lee holds out a Status Quo album. I can't read the title and I wouldn't want to; I'm sulking.

'Me after,' says Dean. He has *Live and Dangerous* by Thin Lizzy: I perk up.

Lee and Dean are eighteen and seventeen. They have apprenticeships and a shared motorbike. When Fritz isn't watching they swig from two bottles of sweet GL cider that is as orange as the gamekeeper's bailer twine.

Clive has *Bat Out of Hell* by Meatloaf. Charlie has brought her *Grease* double album. She and I lie on our bellies and gaze at pictures of Rizzo and Kenickie. I love double albums because it's like opening a story book.

The village hall record player isn't great, but Fritz has

brought down his Philips speakers. I've made a bed for Bess next to her water bowl; Boggle is at home because he bites if he comes to the youth club. Lee gets his turn first and plays 'Again and Again' by Status Quo. The grown-up boys bite down on their fags, and they dance by hooking their thumbs in their jeans belts and jerking their shoulders side to side and back: it's the dance Mandy and Cheryl taught me. I watch their frothy hair shake. They wear pale jean jackets with no arms but lots of badges that you must pin or sew on, and I wonder who sewed on their Black Sabbath and Judas Priest badges so neatly.

Fritz sits by a speaker and untangles cables as Dean fills Bess's water bowl with orange GL. She laps it up.

Dean offers me a swig, 'I hear it was your birthday,' he winks.

I wipe the bottle first because Dean has a wispy moustache that Fritz calls bum fluff. The GL is warm, and thick as Lucozade. I like the sharp, sweet-sour bubbles. Dean picks up my black-and-white-striped *Parallel Lines* and gazes down at Debbie Harry. I don't like him doing that, so I snatch the album back. He laughs.

The moderated album playing is over because Fritz is giving Charlie a guitar lesson in the main hall where the younger kids are playing tag. In the record room the big boys are giving me the bumps to Blondie's 'One Way or Another'. It's too fast and I feel sick. The GL cider is sloshing around in me, and I wish I was having the bumps to 'Sunday Girl' because it's slower.

'Eight, nine, ten—'

The tall white ceiling of the gothic village hall comes closer as I rise, the dangling fluorescent tubes get brighter. I drop into the huddle of big boys and my stomach falls. I smell their fags and their All Spice, their wet denim, car grease and sweat, but I can't smell their boy-ness at all.

Dean and the others let me down hard on the wooden floor and my head spins and my stomach lurches. Bess is waddling around the room because she's drunk. That's what Lee says. He said she drank two whole bowls of GL. I look up and the ceiling is dropping down on me, like Zelley's stone dropped on that rabbit.

The big boys play 'Picture This' from my *Parallel Lines*; I hear it scratch. They are holding my album cover and getting *my* Debbie Harry dirty with their fingers; I want to shout, 'stop it!' but I'm too dizzy and they are stepping over me in their daps and their boots like I am not here. When the hissing break comes between songs, I hear my mother's laugh from the village-hall kitchen, and Fritz saying 'G ... G ... A' to Charlie. I close my eyes and will the room to stop spinning. When it does, I get up, I lift the stylus and say, 'Bugger off and leave my record alone,' to the boys.

I am now eleven: everything is going to change, not yet, but soon. I have been told. We are leaving Primrose Cottage. Mum is opening a restaurant. I feel like smashing my beloved *Parallel Lines* on the wooden floor.

The street is a hill in Ross-on-Wye, and it is dark apart from one light over the vet's door. I unbutton my cords, pull them and my knickers down, and I crouch by our car to pee. It flows down the road beyond the pool of light from the vet's; there is so much pee. I have been wanting to pee since my first sweet-orange taste of GL. I have been wanting to pee since the grown-up boys swung me up at the ceiling, I have been wanting to pee since Bess waddled out into the village road, a car came, hit her, and she flew up and into the youth-club wall.

She screamed high and loud like a myxomatosis rabbit in a hedgerow.

I have been wanting to pee since I held her in the back of Mum's car, and we all carried her in a pink blanket into the vet's; and the vet yawned because we had woken him up. I have been wanting to pee since I didn't tell him about the cider in Bess's water bowl. I have been wanting to pee since I realised she might die and it's all my fault.

My pee streams down the hill between road and pavement but the sharp pain in my side doesn't go.

Mum comes out and the bell at the top of the door rings into the night. We are surrounded by shops and houses, but everyone is asleep. I pull up my knickers.

'They're operating now, Tiff. Fritz will stay. There's nothing we can do here. Let's get you home.'

Mum starts to cry, and I do too.

Because of Bess we delay leaving Primrose Cottage for a whole summer: she takes that long to heal. I feed her morsels of chicken in a makeshift tent I make for her in the garden. The vet has taken her spleen, they have plastered her front leg, her face is stitched, but she does get better.

I never speak to those bloody boys again.

Treats for Bess

What dog can say no to proper butcher's sausages? But Bess was recovering, so …

I'd boil up a chicken.

Debone it. Boil the bones up separately for the next broth (no seasoning for dogs).

Add rice to the broth, cook it, and put the chicken meat (not skin) back in.

Serve.

35.

Soldier: David Bowie Dreamtime

Summer 1979

I'm in the front room of Rockfield Lodge wearing the hell out of my new red trousers that crackle when I walk. If anyone asks, I can dance to 'Knock on Wood' by Amii Stewart, but most importantly I have (unknown material) red trousers like him: David Bowie.

Mum told me he was wearing all red when she put out her hand in the Rockfield dining room and said, 'Hello David, I'm Joan.'

We are jumpy. *He's* here. There's an electricity in the air, more than when I run across the carpet wearing a nylon nightie. David Bowie has come to Rockfield. He's with Iggy Pop who runs about the place like Tigger: bouncy, bouncy.

Does that mean David Bowie is Christopher Robin?

In the Lodge's front room, Brigitte and Corrina stare down at my three new records: *Are 'Friends' Electric?*,

Tubeway Army; *Do it Yourself*, Ian Dury and the Blockheads; *Reproduction*, Human League. I stayed in London with Fritz's friend, Jeremy, and he let me choose them in the biggest record shop I had ever seen.

Next door in the sitting room the grown-ups play 'Girls Talk' by Dave Edmunds, but there's nothing on our turntable yet; we're stuck. I want to play Brigitte's *Aladdin Sane*, Corrina's golden-orange *Low*, her *Young Americans*, or my 'Boys Keep Swinging' single, but I can't. What if he's walking up the track right now and he hears? That would be *so* embarrassing. I would never ask David Bowie to sign my blue plastic autograph book.

No one is saying it out loud, but I think Sandra picked him up from Newport station in her black Volvo, Jason the black Labrador in the back seat. Maybe he arrived in a limo? I don't know. The adults won't tell us anything but there was a rush of sheet changing in the chalet. Sandra said, 'I don't care who he is, he still needs a clean pillowcase.' I asked her how long he was staying, and she said, 'Who knows, love, we didn't even know he was coming!'

Simple Minds are in Studio Two. They are allowed to run up to the Quadrangle and play with David Bowie but we're not. It's not fair. I heard Sandra tell Mum that David Bowie, Iggy Pop and Simple Minds already had a food fight, and the bread rolls and the Cheddar cheese were gone. Dena told me he asked for a glass of milk at dinner.

'Boys Keep Swinging', oh, glory be to the god on high, David Bowie is here!

I lean into the Lodge's patterned wallpaper, my thighs trembling with the effort of *not* sprinting out the door, up to the Quadrangle dining room where David Bowie might be at the table, sitting and smoking, so I can ask him, 'Would you like a cup of tea or a sandwich?' It must be worse for Brigitte and

Corrina because they have to fight the urge to run up and see him, *all the time*. At least I can go home. Out of temptation.

We don't know how long he'll be here for, *hush-hush*.

We play Tubeway Army as a distraction.

I press harder into the wall, trying to consider the question, 'Are "Friends" Electric?' but really, I'm dreaming of the short trip up the Rockfield track that I have walked hundreds of times. Rockfield is now a home with David Bowie in it. I'm not sure what to do with that.

We stand under the main light like Gary Numan does on the cover of the Tubeway Army sleeve. We cross our arms over our chests and sway to a creaking-door synthesiser.

I try to stay like this in case David Bowie walks in.

In my dream I'm a ghost but I'm wearing my crackly red trousers. I'm flying up the Rockfield track. Cleo the Great Dane and Lady the wolfhound are flying at my side: smoky whisps of big dogs. They are see-through but alive. I see their big dog hearts beating wildly, and all their arteries and veins and capillaries. I am so happy. The three of us float left into the Quadrangle and the horses neigh because horses can sense ghosts.

I know what chalet he is in because ghosts know everything. I waft through his closed front door, and it makes me shiver. The dogs bound up the pine stairs without touching the steps.

There he is on his bed and I'm glad he has his clothes on in my dream. I *am* only eleven.

We hover above him for such a long time. Then the dogs nudge him under the arms, and David Bowie smiles in his sleep. Cleo licks his face but there's no slobber, she's a dog-ghost. I wonder if my fingers will work so I can pull up his eyelids and see for myself, really and truly, which of his eyes I like best. But even if my ghost fingers did work, this would be very rude, and he wouldn't like it at all (it's bad enough we're spying on him). I bring my hover down to a sit at the edge of his bed and I tell him a bedtime story that I know off by heart.

'Once upon a time there were four brothers who were donkeys, Polydor, Parlophone, Polygon and Ned . . .'

When I wake up David Bowie has left Rockfield and for a moment I'm not quite sure if he was there at all.

But he was. Mum caved and let me into the Rockfield kitchen. 'Don't make a scene,' she said, and I walked out with his plate in my hand. I was serving David Bowie who was sitting at the table smoking, one knee up to his chest. He said, 'A little bit, please' and I didn't dare look him in the eyes, either one of them.

The David Bowie Buffet

He wasn't the kind of person you'd go up to and say, 'Ooh, you're David Bowie.' He would have had a nervous breakdown.

He was there to put something on a track or produce a track for Iggy Pop, I really don't remember. As much as I love his music, I didn't really take him in, I'm afraid. He'd come into the dining room but wouldn't stay at the table for long. He was quite beautiful. I know I should have talked to him more but quite honestly I had my own life to lead. I was getting ready to leave Rockfield, you see.

Iggy was a handful.

They had food fights with Simple Minds. The cheese went missing.

You've had my Saturday poached salmon recipe, Tiff. I've told you: he hardly ate. If you asked him, he'd say, 'A little bit, please.' Very polite. He drank milk. Always smoking.

If they didn't eat, I didn't take it personally. Well, not much.

one cold glass silver-top milk

pour and serve

Part 5

Where Do We Go from Here?

1979–1986

We raid the fridge in the quadrangle kitchen and, after scoffing chunky, cheesy, crusty sandwiches, washed down with tea, we are set to record the backing tracks.

Will Sergeant, Echoes

'Rockfield . . . the best days of our lives?'

Jim Kerr, Simple Minds

Set List

Days in Europa, The Skids
Empires and Dance, Simple Minds
The Black Album, The Damned
Kings of the Wild Frontier, Adam and the Ants
Kilimanjaro, The Teardrop Explodes
Crocodiles, Echo and the Bunnymen
Breaking Glass, Hazel O'Connor
Happy Birthday, Altered Images
Heaven Up Here, Echo and the Bunnymen
Gosh It's . . ., Bad Manners
The Sky's Gone Out, Bauhaus
'Ever So Lonely', Monsoon

Moules Marinière

I was thrilled to run a restaurant. I'd dreamt of it. Apart from an Egon Ronay listing, my greatest achievement was Forest of Dean bikers coming every Saturday in the summer. When they first appeared, they put their big black helmets next to couples who'd driven from Wiltshire or Penarth, but they soon preferred Fritz's cellar. They said, 'We hate garlic,' so I made those bikers fall in love with garlicky moules. I was very proud. 'Never thought we'd like those things,' they said. After a few months they demanded my garlic bread. They made me laugh in their leathers.

I never told the bikers how *much* garlic was in with the mussels. I loved converting them. Fritz said I was as evangelical as those missionaries on the hill. It was sad to say goodbye to Primrose Cottage.

30ish mussels
little bit of olive oil
4 shallots, cut in very thin slices
loads of fresh garlic, not crushed but cut into very small pieces
¾ bottle good white wine
small bunch fresh parsley

Wash moules and remove beards and scrape off any barnacles with a sharp small knife ... chuck any broken or open.

In a wide saucepan cook the shallots and garlic in olive oil, then add white wine, let that cook down a little bit, taste for salt and pepper.

Pour in mussels, lid on and then cook for 3 or 4 minutes or until open. DON'T OVERCOOK OR THEY WILL BE RUBBERY. And with a lid on the casserole, they will cook fast.

Sprinkle fresh parsley on the top.

Serve as soon as possible with fresh crusty bread or garlic bread.

36.

Halfway up the Stairs

1979–1980

Our things from Primrose are stored at Nanny's farm. We live above a restaurant now. Shellfish are back in a bath, spitting. Some days crab and lobster try to crawl up to the rim.

The restaurant is loud. If I put my ear to the floorboards of my new attic bedroom, I hear the hubbub three floors below. If I open my door, it's louder because nothing separates me from the diners (apart from a thin curtain across the ground-floor steps and the effort of climbing). When I find lost customers on my landing, Boggle growls.

Bess has recovered, but the staircase is difficult. She often pees in my bedroom. Boggle hates the restaurant and I do too.

At nights I watch the TV in Mum and Fritz's bedroom. I have discovered *Soap*, *Laverne & Shirley*, and *Roots: The Next Generations*. Like Supertramp, I have discovered America. I watch *Midnight Cowboy* and *Marathon Man*, and I want to live in New York City.

Monmouth Comprehensive has a sea of children who file into

lines in a playground below the A40. We squeeze into brown vinyl corridors at breaktimes. I underline THE SAXONS in red pen, I pour molten metal into moulds to make coat hooks, and I am joint top of the class for my chosen project, 'The Dog'.

I spend a lot of time in my bedroom. 'Get out of your pit,' Fritz says.

There are no woods, no bright moon at my window here: I hate that we left Primrose Cottage. Across the narrow cobbled street I can see into other houses and I feel trapped. This building is ancient. *Ye Olde England*, Fritz says, and I tell him we are in Wales.

Mum is in her kitchen all day, smiling. She loves her restaurant, and she cooks lunch *and* dinner. Dena and Corrina are with her, but not me. I am not allowed because I am an *utter nightmare*. My mother is happy, I am not, and it makes me angry.

I am permanently sweaty.

I hate blushing.

I hate sleeping. I love sleeping. I love Terry Hall.

I'm going through *a stage*.

Fritz has built a bar in the cellar. He plays The Band. Sometimes he sleeps behind it because he's too happy-drunk to walk the three – no, for him, four – flights to their bedroom opposite mine.

One for the barkeep!

Bands from Rockfield come here: Captain Sensible and The Skids visit Fritz, the bikers and the moules marinière in the cellar bar.

There *are* four good things about the restaurant, and if I open my attic sash window I can see three of them:

1. Round Ear, the record shop
2. The Savoy cinema

3. Mr Fernyhough's sweet shop
4. Rockfield. I can't see it, but I could walk the two miles if I tried

If I draw back the curtain at the bottom of the stairs, I can watch Mum in her kitchen because it's open plan. She'll be laughing and drinking white wine while the gas burners flash to orders of duck in gooseberry sauce. Corrina and Dena will be laughing too because they are the best sous-chefs Mum has ever had. 'We're in Egon Ronay!' Mum says. 'I'm over the moon!' Customers in the dining room around the corner chat and eat. Roadies knock on the big window to pick up orders because some bands at Rockfield demand the dishes they remember. When Sandra visits, she rolls up her sleeves to help with the washing-up because Sandra is still the kindest person I know.

This isn't Mum's restaurant: she has investors. Fritz says, 'Stop signing your name to the bills, Joan.' She has bought her kitchen on HP which isn't the sauce in a bottle.

My new words and phrases are:

Plat du jour
VAT
HP
Two Tone
Coventry
'A Message to You, Rudy'
Supplier
Adolescence
Rubella
Regatta de Blanc
Nits
Egon Ronay

A stage you're going through
First Form
SKA
Stretch mark
Scrap Scrap Scrap
Investor
B cup?

This week Mum is more pissed off with me than usual. I have brought two forbidden things into the restaurant: gerbils and nits. I got them both at Monmouth Comprehensive. One of the gerbils has escaped.

'Not now, Tiffany!' Mum says. 'What if it's pregnant?'

Mum and I smell of Vosene shampoo; Fritz is insisting on Prioderm.

The restaurant is closed tonight and I'm sitting on the floor outside the kitchen. There's a long shelf above me where people slide their breakfast trays to the till. We open for breakfast as well as lunch and dinner now. Mum is popular. Mum is tired. I'm sitting under the shelf eating a stale croissant. The cinema opposite is lit up in the dark, it's playing a film called *Scum*.

Mum and Fritz went to the gig without me. I had my chance.

'It's my one night off, Tiff. You're coming.'

'No.'

'Finbarr and Dena have backstage passes for us.'

I love those passes: I peel off the backs and slap them on my bedroom wall.

'You like Thin Lizzy, Tiff,' Fritz said.

He was right.

'Please yourself,' said Mum, and that made me storm upstairs, three flights, to wait for them to knock softly on my door, plead and coax me out like I try to coax the wandering (and hopefully barren) gerbil from underneath the restaurant floorboards.

But the glass door of the restaurant slammed. From my window I watched them disappear down the cobbled street. The bells of St Mary's rang out and I boiled over with *the stage I am going through*.

The thing is I could burn this restaurant down, like the Ruts sing in 'Babylon's Burning'. I could run down to Fritz's cellar bar and smash the upside-down bottles that hang against the wall, I could light a match to Smirnoff, Haig and Gordon's gin. I could turn on the gas in Mum's open-plan kitchen and spread cream and oil and bloody meat all over the walls. I could smash every plate and glass.

But I sulk under the breakfast counter, sob into a stale pastry and wait hours for Mum and Fritz to come back from the best Thin Lizzy gig they have ever seen.

'Phil Lynott was such a lovely man backstage, Tiff, very polite,' Mum says as she takes off her coat, 'and why do you have to leave croissant flakes all over the floor? You're eating too much, you know that, right?'

And I want to scream . . .

WHY ARE ROCK STARS ALWAYS POLITE, MUM?

ISN'T THERE FUCKING MORE THAN THIS.

MORE

THAN

THAT?

*

The stage I am going through means I wear my new Round Ear record-shop purchase to my grandmother's salmon luncheon in aid of St Michael's Church. It's a T-shirt that says **WE ARE ALL PROSTITUTES** in blood-red letters over a picture of Maggie Thatcher, who is smiling and giving the V's. Mum is catering the luncheon. 'Can't you put something over that, Tiff?' she says in the fishy car.

'No.'

Nanny doesn't say a word to me or look me in the eyes, but she does tie an apron around my middle.

The stage I am going through means I don't want anybody to see me, but I want everyone to notice me. The stage I am going through means I want to go to Rockfield on a Saturday morning for Brigitte to teach me to trot on her horse, but once I'm in the saddle I want to get off. The stage I am going through means I don't know how to tell Mum I need a bra, so I wear a blue cardigan over the strained middle button on my blue school shirt.

The stage I am going through means the cinema across the cobbles is my friend. I take in a white paper bag of Mr Ferneyhough's rosy apples. Fritz tells me, *Sit at the front, don't look at the dirty old men in macs at the back. If they sit next to you, move. If they move with you, come back to the restaurant.*

My Films

Rocky II (I see it every night for a week and twice on Saturday): *Adriaaaaaan!*

Alien (once with Fritz): Fritz can do an impression of the John Hurt T-shirt explosion. I go off eggs, but not Sigourney Weaver.

Tarka the Otter: I will never recover. It's tragic: Tarka is killed with a spade.
Life of Brian (three times with Fritz, we sit in the front row to laugh).
Mad Max: his family die, it's almost as tragic as *Tarka the Otter.*

From my room I stare down at lit-up film posters: *The Amityville Horror, Zombie*. Sex films are called *Six Swedish Girls in a Boarding School,* and *SEX, THE STORY*, which seems to be about gynaecologists. When I ask if I can go to a sex film, Fritz says, 'Absolutely not.' Mum tells him, 'If you say no, she'll *want* to.' I don't go but from my bedroom window I watch dirty old men in macs walk into the cinema: they are real.

Paul McCartney is singing 'Wonderful Christmastime' and Mum is in the local paper. She opens the page at the breakfast counter. 'Look at the picture of me! Awful.' Mum is the first *woman* in the county to secure a council mortgage. For £7,000 she's bought a cottage so derelict Fritz must borrow a mini digger and meet men in pubs to help him give it a roof, running water, floors, doors, windows, a septic tank and electricity. Mum says he needs something else but the cellar bar, and as things are going well for the first time in our lives (Mum is dramatic) we can stop renting. The cottage is called 'Greenway' and some weekends Fritz forces me to help with bashing down walls. 'It will do you good, Tiff.' He gives me a hammer and turns up 'Brass in Pocket' by the Pretenders on his portable radio.

Nanny says the cottage is more *dialect* than the last, and

what *that man* has brought us to because he doesn't wear a shirt and tie and work in a bank.

I lie in my bed at the attic top of the restaurant and listen to cars speed around the church in the dark; they play 'Nights in White Satin'. I buy the single 'Rapper's Delight' by the Sugarhill Gang from Round Ear.

The new decade slips in, 1980. I watch *The Rose* in the small cinema and Fritz tells me it's based on Janis Joplin's life: it has a *Tarka the Otter* ending. But there is always Rockfield, and every time I visit life is better. It always is.

It's late spring and Brigitte gives up teaching me to ride. 'You're not a natural, Tiff,' she laughs. At the Lodge's curtains I peek at the Teardrop Explodes, and then Echo and the Bunnymen in their black jumpers and long black coats. They look moody, and it suits me. I can hear their song, 'Happy Death Men', from across the track in Studio Two. There's Robert Plant walking about, too, but that's not unusual at Rockfield. When summer comes Brigitte takes Simple Minds pony trekking in the Forest of Dean and they complain about their bums hurting. Soon Dave Vanian is marching up and down the track in a Dracula cape, pointy black boots and black and white make-up. Dave Vanian is seen in graveyards around Monmouth. I think he must be writing songs. There's been talk of a vampire, but he's the lead singer of The Damned.

'He's coming back!' I cry from the curtain.

'I told you to stop that,' Sandra laughs. She'll be plunging vine leaves in boiling water for her dolmades soon.

Brigitte confesses she nearly killed Dave Vanian because she let him ride Myself, her Hanoverian. 'There I was at the gate; Dave dug in his heels and Myself shot off galloping across the field and that was that. Dave was gone, his cape flapping. I mean, what if I'd killed the lead singer of The Damned with my horse, Tiff?'

It's not long until I'm twelve. I look older so Mum says, 'please, Tiff, you must tell people, particularly men, that you're only eleven.' I buy 'Geno' by Dexys Midnight Runners from Round Ear.

The party is at the Old Mill where the bands rehearse; it must have those old-house acoustics. This is a party for The Damned, so I'm not sure why I'm in the cold, bright, parlour loo with a boy I've met called Christopher. He told me he's fourteen and he comes from Bristol, but I don't tell him I'm eleven and I live in an attic above a restaurant. I know he's very pretty, a bit like Leif Garrett. I didn't know he wanted to kiss me, but when he knocked on the door and asked if I was there, I pulled up my trousers and let him in.

The fluorescent light is too bright, the stone room is freezing, but his lips are warm, soft, and this first kiss might be the best thing that has ever happened. Although it's weird when he pokes his tongue in and his hand pushes into my chest.

I can taste him; it is smoke and lemons and something sweet. His eyes are green. In my head I sing the Leif Garrett song, 'I was Made for Dancin''. It's an old song, but I can't help it.

I've lost Christopher but up in one of the Old Mill's bedrooms people are crowded around a windowsill.

'Do you want some?' a woman asks, and she hands me a rolled-up £5 note and leads me to the white alcove where a man in black jeans and a studded belt is snorting a line of cocaine. I know what it is, I *am* almost twelve.

'Hold on,' I tell the woman and I hand the note back because that would be stealing. I push through the bodies and go downstairs to find my mother. The Damned are singing 'Wait for the Blackout' and I stand at the back of the big room and watch, lost to Dave Vanian and his Dracula cape.

I find Mum by the door.

'Are you having fun, Tiff?'

'Can I take some cocaine?' I shout.

She looks at me like she would look at a shoddy cut of meat. 'If you're stupid you can,' she says.

I run back upstairs to find the woman with the rolled-up £5 note.

'Hello. Sorry, my mum says I can't.'

The woman looks at me and her mouth opens but nothing comes out.

Later in the week I see Christopher with a group of boys at the bus stop outside WHSmith's in Monmouth. Maybe he doesn't live in Bristol? I haven't told anyone we kissed. I want to turn around and run but I'm going to Hereford to see my grandmother. When Christopher points at me and laughs, his friends laugh too. I blush so hard I think I might catch fire. My bus comes and, as the concertina doors open, Christopher shouts, 'Are you really eleven?'

How did he find out?

I pay the driver; my hands are sweaty. I run to the back.

'Are you?' he shouts into the bus. 'Only *eleven*?'

'Urgh, you're eleven!' the other boys echo. People stare.

I shrink down. The bus revs, the doors hiss to a close, and I think of *Carrie* and pouring pigs' blood over Christopher's head because I like Stephen King as well as *Swallows and Amazons*.

I am twelve now, anyway. It was my birthday two days ago. I take out my pencil case and scribble my blue Bic biro hard through Christopher's name. I write 'Joy Division' above it.

I never see him again.

Annabella Lwin from Bow Wow Wow is wearing a white pirate shirt and black hat on Mum and Fritz's TV. I sing 'C30C60C90Go!' with her. On Saturday I take my birthday money, catch the train from Newport to London on my own, walk down the King's Road, and at Sex at World's End I buy a burgundy, shiny pirate shirt with poppers at the wrist.

Mum is relieved about the shirt – 'It's certainly better than "We Are All Prostitutes", darling.'

37.

'To Cut a Long Story Short'

It's the school holidays and I go between the restaurant, Fritz's building site at the 'dialect' Greenway Cottage and the Lodge at Rockfield. There is *Taxi!* on Mum and Fritz's TV, and I buy *Crocodiles* by Echo and the Bunnymen at Round Ear. I write their name on my pencil case, but spell it, 'Bunneymen'.

Now it's August there's the Monmouth Show by the river, but I'm in Mum and Fritz's bedroom pressing the thick silver stop, rewind and play levers on their VHS machine. The chrome dazzle of David Bowie's 'Ashes to Ashes' video repeats. A synthesiser jangles and stabs. He's sinking in the water in a clown suit.

Major Tom is back. Maybe he's in space with Sigourney Weaver fighting the alien.

I press STOP

REWIND

PLAY

STOP

REWIND

PLAY

It's a stage we're all going through, this new David Bowie says to me.

When I walk up the Rockfield track the next day, Adam and the Ants are sitting on the top of the five-bar gate. Adam says, 'Hello', but I'm breathless and I can't get anything out. I have the album *Dirk Wears White Sox* and you must write the D backwards in AᗡAM. I scurry past them into the Lodge.

In the garden, Brigitte takes the photos while me, Corrina and Ceris with the gorgeous laugh pose for Polaroids. We're hoping that Adam and the Ants, but mainly AᗡAM, can hear us across the track. We've layered on white foundation, blended red lipstick on our cheeks. Corrina has crimped our hair (she has a brilliant V-shaped fringe that falls over her left eye). We want Adam and the Ants to come running round the corner, so we laugh harder, but we hear their playback; vocals whoop, a guitar sounds like a Clint Eastwood Spaghetti Western, and two sets of drums roar. We give up and go inside to play records.

I'm sure they are singing, 'DOGGYDOGGYDOGGYDOGGYDOGGYDOGGYDOGGYDOGGYDOG . . .'

Mum is busier than ever. She is booked up three weeks in advance at the restaurant. 'People drive from Cardiff, from Bristol, from London—' she stops because she's run out of cities. The fug of moussaka, of monkfish in tomato creeps up the stairs to my hot bedroom. Whenever I can I go to

Rockfield. The Teardrop Explodes are back on Little Ancre hill. They have a green army jeep they speed around in. I don't serve meals any more, but I like to watch Julian Cope: sometimes it looks like he's wearing a white sheet in the fields, other times it looks like he's playing giddy-up horsey in his army clothes along the Rockfield tracks. One day we're in the Lodge garden and we hear him crying out at the top of Little Ancre hill. We can see the far dot of him dancing on the ridge. He's singing, '"The Hills Are Alive"' from *The Sound of Music*. Brigitte says, 'is he wearing a Wee Willie Winkie nightshirt?'

We love Julian Cope.

At the cinema I watch Hazel O'Connor in *Breaking Glass* and I forget about Rocky Balboa and Tarka the Otter. Fritz still shouts, 'Get out of your pit, Tiff!' and I must go with him to our derelict-dialect cottage where I search for old coins under dirt thresholds with my metal detector while Fritz hammers in plasterboard. I find a thick brown coin from 1793.

The rain and school are back, the radio plays 'Dog Eat Dog' not *doggydoggydog* by Adam and the Ants, and I wonder why I didn't follow them into the studio at Rockfield. I don't like being a grown-up, and I can't figure out how to draw a white stripe across my nose without looking stupid.

Boggle disappears from the restaurant; he doesn't come back. Fritz puts adverts in local and faraway papers. He walks the streets of Monmouth through the night, drives to shelters deeper in Wales. He puts up a reward.

'Someone took him,' Fritz says because Boggle liked to make his own way from the restaurant to the River Monnow. After all, Boggle was the dog who could make his own way across London, changing red buses, to meet Fritz after work. We cry, including Mum.

One day, men push their way into the restaurant. Mid-lunch, people are told to leave. The men shut it down. Mum yells. Fritz shouts. I cry. Bess hides. Boggle is not there to snarl. The investors don't want the restaurant: they are closing it.

It happens fast.

'At least Fritz put the roof on the cottage last week,' Mum says, but she is still crying.

She's back cooking for Rockfield, and for weddings, funerals, regiments and drug companies to pay the debts. We don't mention the restaurant. Fritz can't sleep because he's sure Boggle is out there somewhere. At least we are surrounded by apple orchards, and our new home, Greenway Cottage, has chipboard floors upstairs and concrete ones downstairs. We have stud walls and, at last, plumbing and that roof. Fritz is working on central heating and flagstones. The stairs are short, so Bess loves it. I think she prefers being an only dog. Downstairs there is an open, smoky fire Fritz found behind other fireplaces; still the bedrooms are freezing. I have a fat chimney in mine; Fritz says it's not safe to light so I painted it black. In the mornings, I take out Mum's *Hunky Dory* and play 'Life on Mars?' on my bedroom record player that is a whole sideboard on legs. I get lost in the story and I'm still thinking about dancehalls and sailors when I walk the dark village lane to the bus stop to catch the bus back to Monmouth and school.

It's smoky in the sitting room because the fire doesn't draw properly yet, but Fritz and I are obsessed with *Dallas*. We can't wait to find out who shot J.R. so tonight we're filling in the blanks ourselves. Fritz plugs the mic into the VHS and speaks into it. Mum has gone to bed.

'Watch their lips on the screen, Tiff, and say something, anything. Press play and record. It's called overdub.'

J.R. is in hospital in a wheelchair looking angry. Fritz watches J.R.'s lips and gives him the line, 'Mah toe hurts!'

Our story is J.R. has been shot in the toe.

'Ahhhm gonna find out who shaaat me in mah toe!' I say into the mesh of the mic and I break down laughing. Fritz does, too. We laugh until I think we might die. Bess thumps her tail from the sofa. Fritz says, 'Right then, who's next?' He puts logs on the fire, and we do different voices for different characters into the woodsmoke. Cliff Barnes is French. He says, 'Ah deed naaat shoot JAY-ARRRRRrrrr.'

Sue Ellen Ewing is mainly noises, 'Ahbibly dibbly-doo, JAY-AR, ibbly dah doo. Ah am nat druuunk.'

Mum is at the hall door, shivering. 'Will you keep it down, you two, it's the middle of the bloody night.' She mutters something about peas in a pod.

Les is one of the men Fritz met in a pub and Les has finally finished Mum's new kitchen with wood he found in a skip. He told me, 'Folks don't know treasures nowadays, my bab.' Les is a winker, and when he winked at me with his blue eyes, I smiled. It's Sunday, and Mum is christening her skip-kitchen tops by cooking a sirloin beef joint. Fritz is her sous chef, I'm laying the table and we're playing *The River* by Bruce Springsteen very loud. We dance at the counters to 'The Ties that Bind'. Mum shouts over Bruce, 'Hot fat, hot fat, watch your backs!' I did argue for *Breaking Glass* by Hazel O'Connor but Mum said, 'Not a chance in hell, Tiff.' She suggested Stevie Wonder's *Hotter than July*.

I love this kitchen. Old red bricks on the chimney slant sharply. 'Hundreds of years ago that brickie was drunk,' Fritz will tell anyone who points it out when they're playing a guitar or a tambourine at the table, and he might talk about the damp proofing he's put in, or if they're lucky, the soakaway.

He's turning the record over in the 'music room', a tiny back room filled with his records, guitars and machines. His Philips amps are in the living room with the smoking fire, and Bruce is singing 'Hungry Heart'.

'Turn it down for the meal!' Mum says. I help her load the table with food.

When Fritz stands over her table, he always grins, fists on his hips, elbows out. 'Your mother's never happy without a million side dishes.' He's taken to calling her 'Tweetie Pie' while she calls him 'Meadow Mist'. Bess and I are perpetually embarrassed.

Fritz sharpens Mum's Sabatier knife over the well-rested roast.

'Of course, you're not having meat, are you, Tiffany?' Mum says with a bite.

I'm not; no meat is my new thing, but I'll have the gravy.

Fritz has put a small black wood burner in the wonky chimney and it's finally hot in here. Mum opens the top part of the front door, because the first room in her cottage is the kitchen. We can't see much from here; the driveway and a wide yew tree hanging over a pigscot. I suppose it's there to ward off bad spirits. I think of Oswald at the Vicarage telling me yew trees are in graveyards to suck at the blood and bones of the dead until their berries burst red.

I wonder if there are bodies buried out there.

Bess is waiting at my chair. Fritz says, 'Right then,' and starts carving.

*

I am always the first up in the mornings: even Bess sleeps on. This morning, instead of 'Life on Mars?', I turn on the radio. Dave Lee Travis is telling me something important in the dark as I find my school uniform.

It takes washing, brushing my teeth, feeding Bess and letting her out among the rubble piles and cement mixers of Fritz's work that never ends, to give me the courage. I make tea with honey for my parents. I walk up the curving staircase Fritz has put in, and it doesn't matter that the tea spills because we don't have carpets yet. I must put one mug down to open their door. They are both snoring.

'Fritz?' I whisper, 'Fritz?'

They don't wake. I creep to Mum's side, put both cups on her chest of drawers.

'Mum?' I have to shake her. 'Mum, wake up.'

'What is it?' she groans.

'Mum—'

'What?'

'Jack Lemmon's been shot.'

I know I have it wrong, but it's been building up since Dave Lee Travis said the words and I don't know how to get it out right.

Fritz stirs and reaches for his glasses because he needs them now. Their bedroom is still dark because it's December. I shiver but not because it's freezing in here.

'Fritz, I'm sorry, I mean John Lennon's been shot.'

On the bus to school, I try not to think of Fritz crying, or the sound of the television reports, or Mum saying, 'America is fucking crazy.' I don't know what Fritz will do today: the pointing or the painting, and if he will listen to *Rubber Soul*, or *Imagine* or even *Mind Games*, or his favourites, *Rock 'n'*

Roll Music and *Sergeant Pepper.* Maybe it will be no John Lennon or Beatles at all. I think about the day just a few months ago, when Fritz drove us to a living room in London to listen to *Double Fantasy,* because his friend had a test pressing.

Oxtail for Fritz

His favourite dish of mine to cheer him up

4 *oxtail pieces. Always get the middle section, as there is more flesh on it. Just think of a tail, it tapers into nothing ...*
2 *large onions*
fresh tomatoes
chopped up herbs: I use thyme, or 2 bouquets garnis
2 *bay leaves*
4 *garlic cloves (or, let's face it, about 6)*
a Spanish red

First brown oxtail, remove from casserole dish.

Chop up 2 large onions, cook in oil left over from oxtail, add a little more oil if necessary, cook don't burn, until they are translucent.

Add fresh tomatoes and then the herbs, bay leaves and garlic.

Then a bottle of good red. I used Spanish red, never use cheap wine in your cooking. I did this in the oven, but also works on the stove very slowly. Cook until oxtail almost falls off the bone. Salt and pepper.

It is actually best made a day before you want to eat it. Refrigerate overnight. Warm up next day very slowly. Good in times of crisis if you like oxtail. You never touched my oxtail, you were off meat but you ate the gravy.

38.

'Reward'

1981

I'm sitting at the Lodge kitchen table and Corrina is holding the cold piercing gun to my ear.

'I don't want it to go in,' I tell her.

'Don't be silly, girl, it won't hurt.'

The metal is cold on my lobe.

'Stay still.'

I watch Julian Cope as Corrina lines up the gun. She is studying beauty and hair at college and Julian Cope is kneeling on the Lodge's sitting-room carpet, pressing a thick VHS tape into Sandra's recorder. He's showing us the Teardrop Explodes on *Top of the Pops*. We wait. There's a black and white hissing fuzz on the television screen then the picture settles. There are trumpets. On the studio stage another Julian Cope is wearing an airman's sheepskin jacket and leather trousers, and he looks very happy as he swings his arm and jumps about. The song is called 'Reward'. I hold my breath because my ear is about to be shot through with a metal rod, but also because both Julian Cope on the TV and Julian Cope on the carpet are pretty.

He budges up to the telly as close as he can get to his song.

'Stay still now,' Corrina says, and Julian looks back, but the command isn't for him, it's for me. The piercing gun bolts, and I think of the knacker's yard. I smile because it doesn't hurt.

He's still watching his song, 'Reward', as I turn the new gold studs in my ears. They bleed, and Corrina tells me to wash my hands because I've touched the dogs, and the horses and God knows what else.

Corrina cleans the gun at the kitchen sink. Julian Cope has excellent teeth. I pour him an orange Quosh.

Echo and the Bunnymen are here again. The Teardrop Explodes *and* Echo and the Bunnymen ride in that jeep across the Rockfield kingdom now. Though the Teardrops are over at the Old Mill and it's their jeep, so some nights we hear Echo and the Bunnymen shout out as they walk from the studio, back up Little Ancre hill in the dark.

One dinnertime I'm spying on the lead singer of Monsoon as she practises her dance in the TV room. Her song, 'Ever so Lonely', plays. She knows I'm there and she smiles.

'It's my dance for *Top of the Pops*,' she says, and I don't think she's much older than me.

If I stay at the Lodge, I stuff my school uniform in my duffel bag for the next day. One night Corrina crimps my hair and I go to the Rolls Hall at last. I dance in a dress with shoulder pads to 'Sound of the Crowd' by the Human League. I sip vodka and neat orange cordial, Malibu and pineapple, which Fritz calls 'Malibu-de-bum-bum', and I sit down for the slow dances because I don't want to be touched by old men. The night is quieter than I imagined it would be, but I do watch the lines of people on the floor rowing an imaginary boat to 'Oops Up Side Your Head'. When Sandra picks us up, we all squeeze into the back of her black Volvo and talk about the night where nothing really happened at all.

One night in the Rockfield Quadrangle, something *does* happen. I'm standing under the outside stable light with a tall skinhead roadie from a Ska band. He is holding my hand. Under the light he rubs his shaved head on the neck of Brigitte's Hanoverian horse, Myself, and I can see the breath of the beautiful bay as its lips nuzzle his head stubble. He laughs. I like his laugh. Then the roadie (not the horse) leans down and kisses me. He must lean a long way because he is so tall. This is my second kiss. I don't think it's a kiss, though, it's a snog. It's interesting. Brigitte and Corrina find me and take me back to the Lodge.

By mid-morning my second kiss is gone and Mum stands, arms folded, in the Rockfield dining room. Brigitte and Corrina told her.

'Did you tell him you're thirteen?'

'No.'

'Did you even look at him?'

'He isn't a real skinhead, Mum, it's a Ska band.'

'He's in his twenties! He thought you were Corrina's age for Chrissakes, and when Fritz told him, he ran!' She gives me strict instructions for the future: 'You tell them your age, do you understand me?' She breathes, 'I trust you, Tiff, but it might scare them off.'

When Corrina cuts my hair into a Philip Oakey style (short one side, long on the other) for her hairdressing exams, Altered Images are in the studio with Steve Severin, and the lead singer, Clare, doesn't look much older than me. The Cure visited Altered Images last night and stayed over. There was a food fight.

Then one day she arrives: Siouxsie Sioux on the back of a motorbike roaring up the Rockfield track. I don't know who's driving but she's all in white, and she gets off at the Lodge to ask directions. When we open the door, she's an apparition, and her hair isn't spiked: it must be the helmet.

'Hello,' she says, 'which way is the studio?'

Brigitte grins. 'Follow the track up and turn left into the Quadrangle.'

We close the door, wait for the sound of the motorbike, and then we scream.

That night I close my eyes and I try to memorise the cupid-bow peaks of Siouxsie's lips. I would like all of the moments to stop with this one.

Bela Lugosi's Fed

You did get yourself in a state when Bauhaus were at Rockfield, Tiff. What was his name? Pete Murphy? Yes, very handsome.

I was moving away from rich sauces. It was the early 1980s and I rather enjoyed poaching small rods of peeled cucumber, but I hated the British interpretation of nouvelle cuisine. Ridiculous period. Nevertheless, I used juices and orange/lemon peel in sauces instead of cream. I discovered crème fraiche. People were beginning to turn against red meat, so it was chicken and fish.

I think Bauhaus were my very last band. I'm not sure. I was sad to leave Rockfield, but life goes on, doesn't it?

Orange Chicken

5 chicken breasts, cut in half to butterfly
cup of white wine
fresh orange juice
grated orange peel
Marsala wine
butter at end

Flour chicken, then lightly fry in mix of oil and butter, with salt and pepper.

Add a cup of white wine, also orange juice (freshly squeezed, but sieve it) and taste. Cook for about 10/15 mins in a frying pan.

Take out chicken and reduce wine and orange juice. Add grated (very thin) orange zest, not too much, taste. Finish it off with Marsala wine, not much, boil down.

At very end add a little butter to thicken, simmer, not too much or it will float to top. Put chicken back so juices seep in.

Serve with:
French beans
New potatoes

PLEASE DON'T
FEED THE
HORSES

39.

'The Night They Drove Old Dixie Down'

Christmas 1986

I have finished my A levels and I'm working as a nanny in Florida.

It's a strange place, but I've found a record store in Sarasota and three tapes: *Billie Holiday Sings the Blues*, *Aretha Live!* and Joni Mitchell's *Blue*. Straight out of school I have discovered nappies, mealtimes, night terrors and filling the hours with other people's children. I'm saving money for university, and I work with a Polish woman called Hanna, and a Floridian lady called Grace. I am constantly sweaty in the heat, but my brand-new scar that runs from hip to hip hurts less.

I have discovered American-sized packets of potato chips, sharks in the water and Audrey Hepburn. One morning I let her into this condominium while a thundershower fell. My instructions were to bring her up to the penthouse my employers were selling. Audrey Hepburn shook her raincoat in the lift and when she asked my name, I blushed and stammered, 'Er, Tiffany.'

'"Er Tiffany?"' she repeated, and I stared at our blurred reflections on the shiny lift door. Audrey Hepburn didn't buy the penthouse.

I have yet to see a manatee, but I have watched Roger Rees in a warehouse tell Floridian ladies of a certain age his *Christmas Carol.*

It's somewhere between Christmas and New Year, the grass is called 'elephant grass', the beach is white and I have time off because Mum and Fritz are visiting. I wish Bess could come, too. Mum only cooks for friends and Fritz now; Fritz only plays guitar at parties. We haven't gone back to Rockfield for four years. 'Life goes on,' Mum says. Their new life started by selling the stored things of Mum's past, because *the past is the past don't live in the past, Tiff,* and we needed to pay for the central-heating system. Mum's emerald hummingbirds in bell jars went first: they were covered by brown blankets, forgotten camel humps in an outbuilding at my grandparents' farm. Fritz sold the Wurlitzer. Now Mum and Fritz go to fields in Belgium and France before the sun rises to buy old things by torchlight. They drive home and dip the old things in vats of caustic soda the cats must stay away from. *Antiques.* Fritz is planning to bash through walls and paint and decorate his own shop. Mum says, 'I'm going to be a fucking shop girl, aren't I, Fritz?'

A condominium in Florida isn't for my parents, and the humidity isn't for Mum's hair, but they enjoyed a Caesar Salad. 'A revelation,' Mum told the waiter, hair frizzing. When women on checkouts ask her, 'and how are you today, Ma'am?' she stammers because she has no idea what to say.

'"Have a nice day?" What *do* they mean, Fritz?'

*

We are driving from Sarasota to somewhere called Clearwater because this morning Fritz found something in a local paper he couldn't quite believe.

'It's not really them.' He stood at the kitchen counter, staring at the advert.

I looked, too. 'No. It can't be.'

'Not in a cinema, in a *maaaaal*.' On this trip Fritz does his bad American accent, he says *mall*, *apartment*, *fanny pack*, and *hey maaaan* when we go shopping.

We kept staring at the newspaper.

Fritz smiled, 'Well, there's only one way to find out.'

In the rented car we are astounded by air conditioning. The highway is smooth.

'It must be a big cinema,' Fritz keeps saying, 'if it's really them.'

'These roads are bloody huge,' Mum says, loud. She has a Gladstone bag at her feet and American-sized codeine in her system. Her back went into spasm on the flight, she needs a hip replacement, and when she limps, she'll say 'it's the kitchen years!' Fritz is totally deaf in his left ear now, but otherwise he's 'ticketyboo'. I have that new scar across my belly, where a surgeon removed a thing he called 'a seven-pound benign cystic teratoma', but I called 'my cyster' to make Mum and Fritz laugh. Mum asked the specialist, 'Can she still have children?' and he smiled down at me and said, 'We'll have to see.'

I am the last of the line, then.

*

It isn't even in a mall, it's a parking lot squared by shops. A dry cleaners', a grocery store. The cinema has an awning but slotted-in letters do spell out 'THE BAND'. The letters aren't quite straight.

'Are you sure, Fritz?' Mum asks. We help her out of the car. 'Fuck,' she says at the pain, and people in big, pale shorts stare. It starts to thunder, then rain bursts in a way I don't think Mum has seen before. 'Dear Christ,' she says, but she can't run. She bursts out laughing and because Mum laughs, we do, too.

Inside, the cinema smells damp and we are soaked. The floor is old carpet. A man with long grey hair in a stringy ponytail is selling tie-dye T-shirts at a Formica table. Cheap chairs have been lined up in front of a small stage. We pay for three tickets.

'This can't be right,' Fritz looks like he's about to laugh out loud. His brown eyes bug.

'I have to sit down,' Mum says. 'Can you get me some good cold white wine, and a towel, Fritz?'

'This can't be The Band, Joan.'

'I don't know, please just get me a chair and a good glass of white.'

I hold her arm and we walk closer to the stage.

'No, not at the front, Tiff, not at the front.' Mum has a horror of 'the front'. I sit her at the end of the third row: there are only about ten. Fritz comes back with tie-dye T-shirts flipped over his shoulder, and three beers in plastic cups.

'What on earth?' Mum says at the frothy light beer; she laughs again, 'Oh well, when in Rome . . . Where the hell are we, Fritz?'

But he's too busy putting on his tie-dyed T-shirt, making the peace sign and saying, 'Hey, man,' as a Fritz-joke. He looks amazed and happy.

Mum calls the American beer 'piss water' but I drink mine. Fritz has reasoned that because I am British and eighteen, it's legal. The room doesn't fill up. The damp is clammy, Mum sucks in her breath sharply when she moves, and takes another codeine pill. 'I'm freezing in this air conditioning. Are you sure there's no wine? Champagne?'

Fritz is staring at the small stage. 'It can't be The Band,' he mutters again. He rubs his hands together. We wait. We wait for an hour.

The crowd, if it is a crowd, aren't worried. People mingle, chat. They know each other. They don't sit down yet.

Fritz turns to me. 'You know Robbie Robertson left, don't you, Tiff?' He looks back at the stage, eyes big. 'And earlier this year Richard Manuel killed himself.'

My skin puckers with the chill of damp.

'He killed himself in Florida, actually . . .' Fritz's voice tails off. He looks down at the stained carpet. 'After a gig.'

We don't say anything for a while.

'Who are The Band now, then?' I ask.

He counts on his fingers, 'Levon Helm, Rick Danko and Garth Hudson. Some new musicians maybe. I don't know.'

'What a strange day,' Mum says, giggling. The painkillers are kicking in.

When Rick Danko walks onto the stage, a bass strapped to him, Fritz stands up, and Mum claps.

Rick is wearing a patterned and colourful shirt. 'Hey, thanks for coming out,' he says.

Not every chair in this room is taken but people cheer and whoop. They're all standing, even Mum, with our help.

'Sorry for the wait, folks . . .'

Rick runs his big fingers up and down the bass and I can't believe what I'm seeing. Fritz is grinning. It's really *THE BAND* – or Rick, at least.

'So, Garth'll be out soon, and it looks like you got me for a while. Levon just got his pilot licence –' he points up at the low ceiling of the venue '– but he's caught in a Florida storm.'

I panic. The names Buddy Holly, Ritchie Valens, Patsy Cline reel in my head.

Rick starts to play, and the panic ebbs. Levon will be fine.

When Rick sings 'It Makes No Difference', alone with an acoustic guitar, my heart really does ache like all the songs tell us. It feels a bit like asthma, so it could be the damp room. Fritz and I look at each other: we are so close it would be easy to reach up and hug Rick. He is so beautiful. His voice cracks, though he's smiling. I watch his fingers on the neck of the guitar, and I think of the first time Fritz played The Band to me: I'm on the ratty Chesterfield with chickenpox in the Primrose Cottage sitting room; Mum is cooking at Rockfield, and Fritz doesn't know what to do with this child he's taken on. He's tick-tack-ticking through his record collection. He holds up the rainbow cover of *Stage Fright* and that is the delirium-chickenpox moment that Levon sings 'Strawberry Wine' and I giggle. It's the afternoon but 'Daniel and The Sacred Harp' is a bedtime story, and I fall asleep to 'The Rumor', lulled by each singer as they croon a line to me.

Stage Fright. Perhaps that's what Fritz had with me then.

'It Makes No Difference' is over and Rick is almost jogging side to side, grinning as we cheer. He changes back to his bass guitar and when Garth walks onto the Clearwater mall stage, the room erupts. His beard really is huge as he stands like a bear behind his keyboard. Rick and Garth play 'Stage Fright' and I laugh, maybe cry a little, too.

Levon does land the plane through the Florida storm, and when he walks on the stage, he doesn't say a word but sits behind the drums, lifts his chin across to his mic, hits a stick to the edge of his snare and he plays the opening *da-da, da-dum* of 'The Night They Drove Old Dixie Down'. Levon sings the song and Fritz is smiling, face up, eyes wide: he shakes his head and laughs, almost crying. Mum is clapping, chirruping her *dah-dah-dahs*. My breath leaves my body, and the room, no matter how small, hollers with joy.

Acknowledgements

This memoir has seen many forms over the past twenty years, I wrote part of this world as fiction in the novel *Diamond Star Halo*. I'd like to thank my parents, with love, for putting up with decades of me badgering, interviewing ('stop hassling, Tiffany!'). Thanks to Joan for allowing me to work through her recipes ('what do you mean, 'measurements?') and to distil her voice and life onto these pages, what an honour. This book is dedicated to the memory of Fritz Fryer: you gave me music; Mum gave me food. We were with you when you died, and you will always be with us. It is also dedicated to the beloved memories of Sandra Ward, Charles Ward, Otto Garms and Johnny Fean.

Without the assistance of the Royal Literary Fund, final drafting would have been impossible. Thank you for all you do for writers. Thank you to the Arts Council and the Society of Authors for their crucial awards and advice for other projects over the years. All roads lead somewhere. I can't thank you enough. Þakka þér fyrir, Kjartan Már Ómarsson and Reykjavík Bókmenntaborg UNESCO City of Literature, for a writing residency that brought it all together (when I should have been writing about Iceland).

Cathryn Summerhayes, star of agents, thank you for the resurrection, thanks also to Annabel White at Curtis Brown.

Rhiannon Smith, editorial director at Fleet, it's a dream working with you, your faith, care, creativity, guiding hand and attention have made this experience joyful. I now live to make you laugh. Thank you for everything. Grace Vincent, Katya Ellis, Lilly Cox, Zoe Carroll, Linda Silverman, and Abby Eckleben at Little Brown, what a team this book has, thank you for standing behind it so brilliantly, and giving it a life I couldn't imagine. Huge thanks to Amy Perkins for your early editorial work, and to our copyeditor Charley Chapman, and cartographer, Liane Payne.

I've had nothing but generosity in my research. To everyone I have contacted over the years, thank you. Particular thanks to Brian May for the use of your wonderful 3-D photograph of Freddie hugging Cleo, and for telling me about your time with Fritz recording 'April Lady'; it meant so much. Graham Parker, your emails were perfect, *Heat Treatment* forever! Jools Holland, thank you for your quote about Fritz and Squeeze, he certainly was 'a fine fellow'. Thank you, Geddy Lee, for your kindness, and Ron Eckel at CookeMcDermid. Thank you, Alex Call, for the 'Clover, Naked at Rockfield' clip from your YouTube channel, it made me giggle for about two years. Thank you to Phil Smart for allowing me to use the David Jackson quote from your Van der Graaf Generator website, and for sending me the Vicarage section of your *Van der Graaf Generator: The Book*. Abby Mosieri, Jason Griffiths, and Elizabeth Winter thank you for those *Bash Street Kids* memories (and your own rock star). Thank you to Caroline Corner for making the Vicarage come to life again.

Horslips, you know how much we treasure those memories. Barry, Jim, Charles, Eamon and Johnny, thank you from the clichéd bottom of my heart. Mark Cunningham, your fantastic Horslips biography, *Tall Tales*, was invaluable, your kindness, too. Ian Finlay, I'm honoured to be able to use your celebrated photography (and will you sign my original *October* LP?). Rockfield Studios: I am not a Ward, but beloved Rockfield, maker of legends, thank you for allowing me to be part of your kingdom for those short years, and for letting me back in. To Lisa Ward with love, thank you for your generosity, friendship, and laughter. The time you gave me at Rockfield in 2023 was perfect. A summer night: my head out of our old chalet roof window, swallows swooping across the quadrangle, the Charlatans walking the tracks, Brigitte's dog, Zac, barking, and the doof-dah-dah of drum playback as Amanda's horses nod from the stables. Don't tell Kingsley you also gave me the key to the studio, now that was some communing writing time. To Brigitte, with love, you let me ask the same questions again and again, thank you for looking after me as a kid and please let's dance by the fire soon. To the King of Rockfield, Kingsley Ward, and his queen, Anne, you've given generations of musicians a creative home, and the best days of their lives with your genius. Thank you for the chats around the duck pond (and yes, I do look just like my mother). Thank you, Dena Quinn for the brilliant answers, and Amanda Ward, Corrina Ward and Ceris Mainwaring-Smith. Thank you to all the Rockfield musicians, producers and engineers of that time, some with us, some not, and may the great gods of Rockfield bless the memory of Round Ear, the best record shop in Monmouth. Joan would particularly like to remember Sandra Ward, Kieran White, Jim Sullivan, and thank Jim Lockhart, Barry Devlin, John Anthony, Dena, Corrina and Brigitte for making her life 'a hell of a lot easier in the Rockfield kitchen'.

Who says 'yes' to 'would you read my book?' Sarah Salway, that's who. I will thank you forever, Sarah, for your perfect guiding voice. Thank you to Patrick Gale for your patient support and generations of beloved hounds, and thank you,

Aidan Hicks. Thank you also to Georgina Moore for all your guidance. Thank you also to Peter Florence, and to the wonderful writing group of: Lucinda Bowles, Marika Leino, Jo Minogue, Julia Roberts and Kate Wright; you kept me going. Davey Jones, my old school pal and celebrated 'Gilbert Rachet' Viz artist, you've brought *The Dirty Donkeys* to life, and I'm honoured. There's a Rockfield library it's been a pleasure to read: *Echoes* by Will Sergeant, *Head On/Repossessed* by Julian Cope, *My Effin' Life* by Geddy Lee, *Legends of Rockfield* by Jeff Collins (I remember Fritz talking to you from his bedroom in Portugal during his illness; he loved remembering his time for you, Jeff.) And *Horslips: Tall Tales, The Official Biography* by Mark Cunningham (and Fritz would have particularly loved this, Mark).

Some names and other details have been disguised to protect the privacy of the people concerned. A few months have been pulled together for narrative flow. Thank you to the living and dead who helped me with piecing it all back together.

I'm a lifetime grateful to Laurence McGovern for almost thirty years (*shh*) of living through these stories, and for a time under the same roof as Joan and Fritz. Have you recovered yet? To all the dogs: I'll see you in the HHG one day.

Credits

I would like to thank the authors of the following books:

Barefaced Lies and Boogie-Woogie Boasts, Jools Holland & Harriet Vyner

Echoes, Will Sergeant

Head On/Repossessed, Julian Cope

Horslips: Tall Tales, The Official Biography, Mark Cunningham

867-5309 Jenny The Song that Saved my Ass ... For a While, Alex Call

Legends of Rockfield, Jeff Collins

My Effin' Life, Geddy Lee

Queen in 3-D: A Photographic Biography, Brian May

Van Der Graaf Generator: The Book, A History of the Band Van der Graaf Generator 1967 to 1978, Phil Smart & Jim Christopulos

Grateful acknowledgement is made for the permission to reprint from the following material:

p.12 Smart, P. & Christopulos, J., *Van Der Graaf Generator: The Book, A History of the Band Van der Graaf Generator 1967 to 1978*, ('Phil and Jim', 2005) Thank you also to Phil Smart's website http://www.vandergraafgenerator.co.uk

p.36 May, Brian, *Queen in 3-D: A Photographic Biography* (London: The London Stereoscopic Company, 2017)

p.238 Holland, Jools, & Vyner, Harriet, *Barefaced Lies and Boogie-Woogie Boasts*, (London: Penguin, 2007)

p.296 Call, Alex, You Tube Channel, Clover keep on rolling naked, https://www.youtube.com/watch?v=JvTVbo-UFks

p.296 Lee, Geddy, *My Effin' Life* (London: Harper, 2023)

p.344 Sergeant, Will, *Echoes* (London: Constable, 2023)

Rockfield Studios logo designed by Sandra Pond, reproduced on pp. vi, 179 and 204 with kind permission from Sandra Pond, Lisa Ward and Rockfield Studios.

Citations

p.116 Ashton, Mark, 'Studio Choice', *International Musician & Recording World*, 1975

p.344 Kerr, Jim, https://www.simpleminds.com/2008/07/17/rockfield/

Photographs

p.12 The Vicarage
Family picture

p.17 Joan and Tiff
Family picture

p.28 Tiff and Elvis the bantam (with Abby Griffiths on the Vicarage gravel)
Family picture

p.33 Joan's Sabatier knife
Tiff Murray picture

p.36 Freddie hugs Cleo
Photographer: Brian May
May, Brian, *Queen in 3D: A Photographic Biography* (London: The London Stereoscopic Company, 2017)

p.61 Tiff with Ozzy's rock 'n' roll dog puppet (from Harrods)
Family picture

p.71 Tiff happy to have Horslips around
Photographer: Ian Finlay

p.73 Horslips try the rock god look in the apple orchards
Photographer: Ian Finlay

p.74 Boggle about to pounce
Photographer: Ian Finlay

p.76 Horslips playing at the Vicarage
Photographer: Ian Finlay

p.77 Barry Devlin in the Vicarage porch and his shamrock bass guitar
Photographer: Ian Finlay

p.81 Horslips, Fritz, Man Horrid, all impressed by Boggle
Photographer: Ian Finlay

p.82 Tiff and Nanny (the goat)
Family picture

p.90 Tiff doesn't like sand
Family picture

p.93 'Why are you always sulking?'
Family picture

p.116 Kingsley and Charles Ward in the control room, Rockfield Studios
Ward family pictures

p.118 Hawkwind in the Rockfield Quadrangle courtyard
Photographer: Michael Putland/Getty Images

p.308 Ozzy Osbourne, Tony Iommi, and Ozzy's gun at the Old Mill, Rockfield Studios
Mirrorpix/Getty Images

p.320 Fritz and the animals
Family picture

p.337 Bess recuperates on a blanket in the Primrose Cottage garden
Tiff Murray picture

p.372 Please Don't Feed the Horses, Rockfield stables sign
Tiff Murray picture

p.380 Van der Graaf Generator in the Vicarage living room, 1975
Armando Gallo/Getty Images